C-4866 CAREER EXAMINATION SERIES

This is your
PASSBOOK® for...

State Program Examiner III, IV

Test Preparation Study Guide
Questions & Answers

COPYRIGHT NOTICE

This book is SOLELY intended for, is sold ONLY to, and its use is RESTRICTED to individual, bona fide applicants or candidates who qualify by virtue of having seriously filed applications for appropriate license, certificate, professional and/or promotional advancement, higher school matriculation, scholarship, or other legitimate requirements of education and/or governmental authorities.

This book is NOT intended for use, class instruction, tutoring, training, duplication, copying, reprinting, excerption, or adaptation, etc., by:

1) Other publishers
2) Proprietors and/or Instructors of "Coaching" and/or Preparatory Courses
3) Personnel and/or Training Divisions of commercial, industrial, and governmental organizations
4) Schools, colleges, or universities and/or their departments and staffs, including teachers and other personnel
5) Testing Agencies or Bureaus
6) Study groups which seek by the purchase of a single volume to copy and/or duplicate and/or adapt this material for use by the group as a whole without having purchased individual volumes for each of the members of the group
7) Et al.

Such persons would be in violation of appropriate Federal and State statutes.

PROVISION OF LICENSING AGREEMENTS – Recognized educational, commercial, industrial, and governmental institutions and organizations, and others legitimately engaged in educational pursuits, including training, testing, and measurement activities, may address request for a licensing agreement to the copyright owners, who will determine whether, and under what conditions, including fees and charges, the materials in this book may be used them. In other words, a licensing facility exists for the legitimate use of the material in this book on other than an individual basis. However, it is asseverated and affirmed here that the material in this book CANNOT be used without the receipt of the express permission of such a licensing agreement from the Publishers. Inquiries re licensing should be addressed to the company, attention rights and permissions department.

All rights reserved, including the right of reproduction in whole or in part, in any form or by any means, electronic or mechanical, including photocopying, recording, or by any information storage and retrieval system, without permission in writing from the Publisher.

Copyright © 2024 by
National Learning Corporation

212 Michael Drive, Syosset, NY 11791
(516) 921-8888 • www.passbooks.com
E-mail: info@passbooks.com

PASSBOOK® SERIES

THE *PASSBOOK® SERIES* has been created to prepare applicants and candidates for the ultimate academic battlefield – the examination room.

At some time in our lives, each and every one of us may be required to take an examination – for validation, matriculation, admission, qualification, registration, certification, or licensure.

Based on the assumption that every applicant or candidate has met the basic formal educational standards, has taken the required number of courses, and read the necessary texts, the *PASSBOOK® SERIES* furnishes the one special preparation which may assure passing with confidence, instead of failing with insecurity. Examination questions – together with answers – are furnished as the basic vehicle for study so that the mysteries of the examination and its compounding difficulties may be eliminated or diminished by a sure method.

This book is meant to help you pass your examination provided that you qualify and are serious in your objective.

The entire field is reviewed through the huge store of content information which is succinctly presented through a provocative and challenging approach – the question-and-answer method.

A climate of success is established by furnishing the correct answers at the end of each test.

You soon learn to recognize types of questions, forms of questions, and patterns of questioning. You may even begin to anticipate expected outcomes.

You perceive that many questions are repeated or adapted so that you can gain acute insights, which may enable you to score many sure points.

You learn how to confront new questions, or types of questions, and to attack them confidently and work out the correct answers.

You note objectives and emphases, and recognize pitfalls and dangers, so that you may make positive educational adjustments.

Moreover, you are kept fully informed in relation to new concepts, methods, practices, and directions in the field.

You discover that you are actually taking the examination all the time: you are preparing for the examination by "taking" an examination, not by reading extraneous and/or supererogatory textbooks.

In short, this PASSBOOK®, used directedly, should be an important factor in helping you to pass your test.

STATE PROGRAM EXAMINER III, IV

DUTIES:

An employee in this class supervises a unit whose primary function is program evaluation and policy analysis of the Capital and Operating budget of a major budget unit. Responsibilities include overseeing the coordination and integration of studies and analyses of policies, programs and administrative process to evaluate their effectiveness in meeting programmatic and legislative intent. The incumbent develops the methodology needed to analyze a wide range of elements of program administration including legal and fiscal base, organizational structure, management practices, administrative procedures and the level and quality of services provided. The incumbent supervises and participates in the review of proposed legislation to determine financial and program impact, and is responsible for identifying and examining policy and program issues of various proposed fiscal resource allocations. This incumbent is responsible for supervising the collection and analysis of statistical data critical to the budget review process. Does related work as required.

SCOPE OF THE EXAMINATION:

The written test will cover knowledge, skills, and/or abilities in such areas as:

1. **Analyzing and evaluating information** - These questions test for the ability to analyze, interpret, and draw reasonable conclusions from information presented in text, data, images or symbols. This may involve identifying a significant problem or issue; focusing on relevant data and text; identifying trends, relationships, and significant features; assessing relevant alternatives; suggesting or evaluating possible conclusions; and applying logical principles to information provided.
2. **Working and interacting with others** - These questions test for knowledge of how to effectively approach work and maintain professional relationships with others in the workplace. Each question presents a situation and a number of possible approaches for handling it. Question topics may include working with supervisors and coworkers, interacting with members of the public, handling conflict, and managing workplace demands and priorities. The questions are not specific to any job title or place of work.
3. **Administrative supervision** - These questions test for knowledge of the principles and practices involved in directing the activities of a large subordinate staff, including subordinate supervisors. Questions relate to the personal interactions between an upper level supervisor and his/her subordinate supervisors in the accomplishment of objectives. These questions cover such areas as assigning work to and coordinating the activities of several units, establishing and guiding staff development programs, evaluating the performance of subordinate supervisors, and maintaining relationships with other organizational sections
4. **Preparing reports and official documents** - These questions test for the ability to prepare reports and other official documents for use within and among governmental agencies, in legal or regulatory settings, or for dissemination to the public. Some questions test for a knowledge of grammar, usage, punctuation, and sentence structure. Others test for the ability to present information clearly and accurately, to use the proper tone, and to organize paragraphs logically and comprehensibly.
5. **Understanding and applying administrative principles** – These questions test for knowledge of how to effectively manage and direct an organization or an organizational segment. These questions cover such areas as developing objectives, formulating policies, making decisions, forecasting and planning, developing personnel, organizing and coordinating work, communicating information, providing leadership, and delegating authority and responsibility.

HOW TO TAKE A TEST

I. YOU MUST PASS AN EXAMINATION

A. WHAT EVERY CANDIDATE SHOULD KNOW

Examination applicants often ask us for help in preparing for the written test. What can I study in advance? What kinds of questions will be asked? How will the test be given? How will the papers be graded?

As an applicant for a civil service examination, you may be wondering about some of these things. Our purpose here is to suggest effective methods of advance study and to describe civil service examinations.

Your chances for success on this examination can be increased if you know how to prepare. Those "pre-examination jitters" can be reduced if you know what to expect. You can even experience an adventure in good citizenship if you know why civil service exams are given.

B. WHY ARE CIVIL SERVICE EXAMINATIONS GIVEN?

Civil service examinations are important to you in two ways. As a citizen, you want public jobs filled by employees who know how to do their work. As a job seeker, you want a fair chance to compete for that job on an equal footing with other candidates. The best-known means of accomplishing this two-fold goal is the competitive examination.

Exams are widely publicized throughout the nation. They may be administered for jobs in federal, state, city, municipal, town or village governments or agencies.

Any citizen may apply, with some limitations, such as the age or residence of applicants. Your experience and education may be reviewed to see whether you meet the requirements for the particular examination. When these requirements exist, they are reasonable and applied consistently to all applicants. Thus, a competitive examination may cause you some uneasiness now, but it is your privilege and safeguard.

C. HOW ARE CIVIL SERVICE EXAMS DEVELOPED?

Examinations are carefully written by trained technicians who are specialists in the field known as "psychological measurement," in consultation with recognized authorities in the field of work that the test will cover. These experts recommend the subject matter areas or skills to be tested; only those knowledges or skills important to your success on the job are included. The most reliable books and source materials available are used as references. Together, the experts and technicians judge the difficulty level of the questions.

Test technicians know how to phrase questions so that the problem is clearly stated. Their ethics do not permit "trick" or "catch" questions. Questions may have been tried out on sample groups, or subjected to statistical analysis, to determine their usefulness.

Written tests are often used in combination with performance tests, ratings of training and experience, and oral interviews. All of these measures combine to form the best-known means of finding the right person for the right job.

II. HOW TO PASS THE WRITTEN TEST

A. NATURE OF THE EXAMINATION

To prepare intelligently for civil service examinations, you should know how they differ from school examinations you have taken. In school you were assigned certain definite pages to read or subjects to cover. The examination questions were quite detailed and usually emphasized memory. Civil service exams, on the other hand, try to discover your present ability to perform the duties of a position, plus your potentiality to learn these duties. In other words, a civil service exam attempts to predict how successful you will be. Questions cover such a broad area that they cannot be as minute and detailed as school exam questions.

In the public service similar kinds of work, or positions, are grouped together in one "class." This process is known as *position-classification*. All the positions in a class are paid according to the salary range for that class. One class title covers all of these positions, and they are all tested by the same examination.

B. FOUR BASIC STEPS

1) Study the announcement

How, then, can you know what subjects to study? Our best answer is: "Learn as much as possible about the class of positions for which you've applied." The exam will test the knowledge, skills and abilities needed to do the work.

Your most valuable source of information about the position you want is the official exam announcement. This announcement lists the training and experience qualifications. Check these standards and apply only if you come reasonably close to meeting them.

The brief description of the position in the examination announcement offers some clues to the subjects which will be tested. Think about the job itself. Review the duties in your mind. Can you perform them, or are there some in which you are rusty? Fill in the blank spots in your preparation.

Many jurisdictions preview the written test in the exam announcement by including a section called "Knowledge and Abilities Required," "Scope of the Examination," or some similar heading. Here you will find out specifically what fields will be tested.

2) Review your own background

Once you learn in general what the position is all about, and what you need to know to do the work, ask yourself which subjects you already know fairly well and which need improvement. You may wonder whether to concentrate on improving your strong areas or on building some background in your fields of weakness. When the announcement has specified "some knowledge" or "considerable knowledge," or has used adjectives like "beginning principles of..." or "advanced ... methods," you can get a clue as to the number and difficulty of questions to be asked in any given field. More questions, and hence broader coverage, would be included for those subjects which are more important in the work. Now weigh your strengths and weaknesses against the job requirements and prepare accordingly.

3) Determine the level of the position

Another way to tell how intensively you should prepare is to understand the level of the job for which you are applying. Is it the entering level? In other words, is this the position in which beginners in a field of work are hired? Or is it an intermediate or advanced level? Sometimes this is indicated by such words as "Junior" or "Senior" in the class title. Other jurisdictions use Roman numerals to designate the level – Clerk I, Clerk II, for example. The word "Supervisor" sometimes appears in the title. If the level is not indicated by the title, check the description of duties. Will you be working under very close supervision, or will you have responsibility for independent decisions in this work?

4) Choose appropriate study materials

Now that you know the subjects to be examined and the relative amount of each subject to be covered, you can choose suitable study materials. For beginning level jobs, or even advanced ones, if you have a pronounced weakness in some aspect of your training, read a modern, standard textbook in that field. Be sure it is up to date and has general coverage. Such books are normally available at your library, and the librarian will be glad to help you locate one. For entry-level positions, questions of appropriate difficulty are chosen – neither highly advanced questions, nor those too simple. Such questions require careful thought but not advanced training.

If the position for which you are applying is technical or advanced, you will read more advanced, specialized material. If you are already familiar with the basic principles of your field, elementary textbooks would waste your time. Concentrate on advanced textbooks and technical periodicals. Think through the concepts and review difficult problems in your field.

These are all general sources. You can get more ideas on your own initiative, following these leads. For example, training manuals and publications of the government agency which employs workers in your field can be useful, particularly for technical and professional positions. A letter or visit to the government department involved may result in more specific study suggestions, and certainly will provide you with a more definite idea of the exact nature of the position you are seeking.

III. KINDS OF TESTS

Tests are used for purposes other than measuring knowledge and ability to perform specified duties. For some positions, it is equally important to test ability to make adjustments to new situations or to profit from training. In others, basic mental abilities not dependent on information are essential. Questions which test these things may not appear as pertinent to the duties of the position as those which test for knowledge and information. Yet they are often highly important parts of a fair examination. For very general questions, it is almost impossible to help you direct your study efforts. What we can do is to point out some of the more common of these general abilities needed in public service positions and describe some typical questions.

1) General information

Broad, general information has been found useful for predicting job success in some kinds of work. This is tested in a variety of ways, from vocabulary lists to questions about current events. Basic background in some field of work, such as sociology or economics, may be sampled in a group of questions. Often these are principles which have become familiar to most persons through exposure rather than through formal training. It is difficult to advise you how to study for these questions; being alert to the world around you is our best suggestion.

2) Verbal ability

An example of an ability needed in many positions is verbal or language ability. Verbal ability is, in brief, the ability to use and understand words. Vocabulary and grammar tests are typical measures of this ability. Reading comprehension or paragraph interpretation questions are common in many kinds of civil service tests. You are given a paragraph of written material and asked to find its central meaning.

3) **Numerical ability**

Number skills can be tested by the familiar arithmetic problem, by checking paired lists of numbers to see which are alike and which are different, or by interpreting charts and graphs. In the latter test, a graph may be printed in the test booklet which you are asked to use as the basis for answering questions.

4) **Observation**

A popular test for law-enforcement positions is the observation test. A picture is shown to you for several minutes, then taken away. Questions about the picture test your ability to observe both details and larger elements.

5) **Following directions**

In many positions in the public service, the employee must be able to carry out written instructions dependably and accurately. You may be given a chart with several columns, each column listing a variety of information. The questions require you to carry out directions involving the information given in the chart.

6) **Skills and aptitudes**

Performance tests effectively measure some manual skills and aptitudes. When the skill is one in which you are trained, such as typing or shorthand, you can practice. These tests are often very much like those given in business school or high school courses. For many of the other skills and aptitudes, however, no short-time preparation can be made. Skills and abilities natural to you or that you have developed throughout your lifetime are being tested.

Many of the general questions just described provide all the data needed to answer the questions and ask you to use your reasoning ability to find the answers. Your best preparation for these tests, as well as for tests of facts and ideas, is to be at your physical and mental best. You, no doubt, have your own methods of getting into an exam-taking mood and keeping "in shape." The next section lists some ideas on this subject.

IV. KINDS OF QUESTIONS

Only rarely is the "essay" question, which you answer in narrative form, used in civil service tests. Civil service tests are usually of the short-answer type. Full instructions for answering these questions will be given to you at the examination. But in case this is your first experience with short-answer questions and separate answer sheets, here is what you need to know:

1) **Multiple-choice Questions**

Most popular of the short-answer questions is the "multiple choice" or "best answer" question. It can be used, for example, to test for factual knowledge, ability to solve problems or judgment in meeting situations found at work.

A multiple-choice question is normally one of three types—
- It can begin with an incomplete statement followed by several possible endings. You are to find the one ending which *best* completes the statement, although some of the others may not be entirely wrong.
- It can also be a complete statement in the form of a question which is answered by choosing one of the statements listed.

- It can be in the form of a problem – again you select the best answer.

Here is an example of a multiple-choice question with a discussion which should give you some clues as to the method for choosing the right answer:

When an employee has a complaint about his assignment, the action which will *best* help him overcome his difficulty is to
  A. discuss his difficulty with his coworkers
  B. take the problem to the head of the organization
  C. take the problem to the person who gave him the assignment
  D. say nothing to anyone about his complaint

In answering this question, you should study each of the choices to find which is best. Consider choice "A" – Certainly an employee may discuss his complaint with fellow employees, but no change or improvement can result, and the complaint remains unresolved. Choice "B" is a poor choice since the head of the organization probably does not know what assignment you have been given, and taking your problem to him is known as "going over the head" of the supervisor. The supervisor, or person who made the assignment, is the person who can clarify it or correct any injustice. Choice "C" is, therefore, correct. To say nothing, as in choice "D," is unwise. Supervisors have and interest in knowing the problems employees are facing, and the employee is seeking a solution to his problem.

2) True/False Questions

The "true/false" or "right/wrong" form of question is sometimes used. Here a complete statement is given. Your job is to decide whether the statement is right or wrong.

SAMPLE: A roaming cell-phone call to a nearby city costs less than a non-roaming call to a distant city.

This statement is wrong, or false, since roaming calls are more expensive.
This is not a complete list of all possible question forms, although most of the others are variations of these common types. You will always get complete directions for answering questions. Be sure you understand *how* to mark your answers – ask questions until you do.

V. RECORDING YOUR ANSWERS

Computer terminals are used more and more today for many different kinds of exams.
For an examination with very few applicants, you may be told to record your answers in the test booklet itself. Separate answer sheets are much more common. If this separate answer sheet is to be scored by machine – and this is often the case – it is highly important that you mark your answers correctly in order to get credit.
An electronic scoring machine is often used in civil service offices because of the speed with which papers can be scored. Machine-scored answer sheets must be marked with a pencil, which will be given to you. This pencil has a high graphite content which responds to the electronic scoring machine. As a matter of fact, stray dots may register as answers, so do not let your pencil rest on the answer sheet while you are pondering the correct answer. Also, if your pencil lead breaks or is otherwise defective, ask for another.

Since the answer sheet will be dropped in a slot in the scoring machine, be careful not to bend the corners or get the paper crumpled.

The answer sheet normally has five vertical columns of numbers, with 30 numbers to a column. These numbers correspond to the question numbers in your test booklet. After each number, going across the page are four or five pairs of dotted lines. These short dotted lines have small letters or numbers above them. The first two pairs may also have a "T" or "F" above the letters. This indicates that the first two pairs only are to be used if the questions are of the true-false type. If the questions are multiple choice, disregard the "T" and "F" and pay attention only to the small letters or numbers.

Answer your questions in the manner of the sample that follows:

32. The largest city in the United States is
    A. Washington, D.C.
    B. New York City
    C. Chicago
    D. Detroit
    E. San Francisco

1) Choose the answer you think is best. (New York City is the largest, so "B" is correct.)
2) Find the row of dotted lines numbered the same as the question you are answering. (Find row number 32)
3) Find the pair of dotted lines corresponding to the answer. (Find the pair of lines under the mark "B.")
4) Make a solid black mark between the dotted lines.

VI. BEFORE THE TEST

Common sense will help you find procedures to follow to get ready for an examination. Too many of us, however, overlook these sensible measures. Indeed, nervousness and fatigue have been found to be the most serious reasons why applicants fail to do their best on civil service tests. Here is a list of reminders:

- Begin your preparation early – Don't wait until the last minute to go scurrying around for books and materials or to find out what the position is all about.
- Prepare continuously – An hour a night for a week is better than an all-night cram session. This has been definitely established. What is more, a night a week for a month will return better dividends than crowding your study into a shorter period of time.
- Locate the place of the exam – You have been sent a notice telling you when and where to report for the examination. If the location is in a different town or otherwise unfamiliar to you, it would be well to inquire the best route and learn something about the building.
- Relax the night before the test – Allow your mind to rest. Do not study at all that night. Plan some mild recreation or diversion; then go to bed early and get a good night's sleep.
- Get up early enough to make a leisurely trip to the place for the test – This way unforeseen events, traffic snarls, unfamiliar buildings, etc. will not upset you.
- Dress comfortably – A written test is not a fashion show. You will be known by number and not by name, so wear something comfortable.

- Leave excess paraphernalia at home – Shopping bags and odd bundles will get in your way. You need bring only the items mentioned in the official notice you received; usually everything you need is provided. Do not bring reference books to the exam. They will only confuse those last minutes and be taken away from you when in the test room.
- Arrive somewhat ahead of time – If because of transportation schedules you must get there very early, bring a newspaper or magazine to take your mind off yourself while waiting.
- Locate the examination room – When you have found the proper room, you will be directed to the seat or part of the room where you will sit. Sometimes you are given a sheet of instructions to read while you are waiting. Do not fill out any forms until you are told to do so; just read them and be prepared.
- Relax and prepare to listen to the instructions
- If you have any physical problem that may keep you from doing your best, be sure to tell the test administrator. If you are sick or in poor health, you really cannot do your best on the exam. You can come back and take the test some other time.

VII. AT THE TEST

The day of the test is here and you have the test booklet in your hand. The temptation to get going is very strong. Caution! There is more to success than knowing the right answers. You must know how to identify your papers and understand variations in the type of short-answer question used in this particular examination. Follow these suggestions for maximum results from your efforts:

1) Cooperate with the monitor

The test administrator has a duty to create a situation in which you can be as much at ease as possible. He will give instructions, tell you when to begin, check to see that you are marking your answer sheet correctly, and so on. He is not there to guard you, although he will see that your competitors do not take unfair advantage. He wants to help you do your best.

2) Listen to all instructions

Don't jump the gun! Wait until you understand all directions. In most civil service tests you get more time than you need to answer the questions. So don't be in a hurry. Read each word of instructions until you clearly understand the meaning. Study the examples, listen to all announcements and follow directions. Ask questions if you do not understand what to do.

3) Identify your papers

Civil service exams are usually identified by number only. You will be assigned a number; you must not put your name on your test papers. Be sure to copy your number correctly. Since more than one exam may be given, copy your exact examination title.

4) Plan your time

Unless you are told that a test is a "speed" or "rate of work" test, speed itself is usually not important. Time enough to answer all the questions will be provided, but this does not mean that you have all day. An overall time limit has been set. Divide the total time (in minutes) by the number of questions to determine the approximate time you have for each question.

5) Do not linger over difficult questions

If you come across a difficult question, mark it with a paper clip (useful to have along) and come back to it when you have been through the booklet. One caution if you do this – be sure to skip a number on your answer sheet as well. Check often to be sure that you have not lost your place and that you are marking in the row numbered the same as the question you are answering.

6) Read the questions

Be sure you know what the question asks! Many capable people are unsuccessful because they failed to *read* the questions correctly.

7) Answer all questions

Unless you have been instructed that a penalty will be deducted for incorrect answers, it is better to guess than to omit a question.

8) Speed tests

It is often better NOT to guess on speed tests. It has been found that on timed tests people are tempted to spend the last few seconds before time is called in marking answers at random – without even reading them – in the hope of picking up a few extra points. To discourage this practice, the instructions may warn you that your score will be "corrected" for guessing. That is, a penalty will be applied. The incorrect answers will be deducted from the correct ones, or some other penalty formula will be used.

9) Review your answers

If you finish before time is called, go back to the questions you guessed or omitted to give them further thought. Review other answers if you have time.

10) Return your test materials

If you are ready to leave before others have finished or time is called, take ALL your materials to the monitor and leave quietly. Never take any test material with you. The monitor can discover whose papers are not complete, and taking a test booklet may be grounds for disqualification.

VIII. EXAMINATION TECHNIQUES

1) Read the general instructions carefully. These are usually printed on the first page of the exam booklet. As a rule, these instructions refer to the timing of the examination; the fact that you should not start work until the signal and must stop work at a signal, etc. If there are any *special* instructions, such as a choice of questions to be answered, make sure that you note this instruction carefully.

2) When you are ready to start work on the examination, that is as soon as the signal has been given, read the instructions to each question booklet, underline any key words or phrases, such as *least, best, outline, describe* and the like. In this way you will tend to answer as requested rather than discover on reviewing your paper that you *listed without describing*, that you selected the *worst* choice rather than the *best* choice, etc.

3) If the examination is of the objective or multiple-choice type – that is, each question will also give a series of possible answers: A, B, C or D, and you are called upon to select the best answer and write the letter next to that answer on your answer paper – it is advisable to start answering each question in turn. There may be anywhere from 50 to 100 such questions in the three or four hours allotted and you can see how much time would be taken if you read through all the questions before beginning to answer any. Furthermore, if you come across a question or group of questions which you know would be difficult to answer, it would undoubtedly affect your handling of all the other questions.

4) If the examination is of the essay type and contains but a few questions, it is a moot point as to whether you should read all the questions before starting to answer any one. Of course, if you are given a choice – say five out of seven and the like – then it is essential to read all the questions so you can eliminate the two that are most difficult. If, however, you are asked to answer all the questions, there may be danger in trying to answer the easiest one first because you may find that you will spend too much time on it. The best technique is to answer the first question, then proceed to the second, etc.

5) Time your answers. Before the exam begins, write down the time it started, then add the time allowed for the examination and write down the time it must be completed, then divide the time available somewhat as follows:
    - If 3-1/2 hours are allowed, that would be 210 minutes. If you have 80 objective-type questions, that would be an average of 2-1/2 minutes per question. Allow yourself no more than 2 minutes per question, or a total of 160 minutes, which will permit about 50 minutes to review.
    - If for the time allotment of 210 minutes there are 7 essay questions to answer, that would average about 30 minutes a question. Give yourself only 25 minutes per question so that you have about 35 minutes to review.

6) The most important instruction is to *read each question* and make sure you know what is wanted. The second most important instruction is to *time yourself properly* so that you answer every question. The third most important instruction is to *answer every question*. Guess if you have to but include something for each question. Remember that you will receive no credit for a blank and will probably receive some credit if you write something in answer to an essay question. If you guess a letter – say "B" for a multiple-choice question – you may have guessed right. If you leave a blank as an answer to a multiple-choice question, the examiners may respect your feelings but it will not add a point to your score. Some exams may penalize you for wrong answers, so in such cases *only*, you may not want to guess unless you have some basis for your answer.

7) Suggestions
    a. Objective-type questions
        1. Examine the question booklet for proper sequence of pages and questions
        2. Read all instructions carefully
        3. Skip any question which seems too difficult; return to it after all other questions have been answered
        4. Apportion your time properly; do not spend too much time on any single question or group of questions

5. Note and underline key words – *all, most, fewest, least, best, worst, same, opposite,* etc.
6. Pay particular attention to negatives
7. Note unusual option, e.g., unduly long, short, complex, different or similar in content to the body of the question
8. Observe the use of "hedging" words – *probably, may, most likely,* etc.
9. Make sure that your answer is put next to the same number as the question
10. Do not second-guess unless you have good reason to believe the second answer is definitely more correct
11. Cross out original answer if you decide another answer is more accurate; do not erase until you are ready to hand your paper in
12. Answer all questions; guess unless instructed otherwise
13. Leave time for review

   b. Essay questions
      1. Read each question carefully
      2. Determine exactly what is wanted. Underline key words or phrases.
      3. Decide on outline or paragraph answer
      4. Include many different points and elements unless asked to develop any one or two points or elements
      5. Show impartiality by giving pros and cons unless directed to select one side only
      6. Make and write down any assumptions you find necessary to answer the questions
      7. Watch your English, grammar, punctuation and choice of words
      8. Time your answers; don't crowd material

8) Answering the essay question

Most essay questions can be answered by framing the specific response around several key words or ideas. Here are a few such key words or ideas:

M's: manpower, materials, methods, money, management
P's: purpose, program, policy, plan, procedure, practice, problems, pitfalls, personnel, public relations

   a. Six basic steps in handling problems:
      1. Preliminary plan and background development
      2. Collect information, data and facts
      3. Analyze and interpret information, data and facts
      4. Analyze and develop solutions as well as make recommendations
      5. Prepare report and sell recommendations
      6. Install recommendations and follow up effectiveness

   b. Pitfalls to avoid
      1. *Taking things for granted* – A statement of the situation does not necessarily imply that each of the elements is necessarily true; for example, a complaint may be invalid and biased so that all that can be taken for granted is that a complaint has been registered

2. *Considering only one side of a situation* – Wherever possible, indicate several alternatives and then point out the reasons you selected the best one
3. *Failing to indicate follow up* – Whenever your answer indicates action on your part, make certain that you will take proper follow-up action to see how successful your recommendations, procedures or actions turn out to be
4. *Taking too long in answering any single question* – Remember to time your answers properly

IX. AFTER THE TEST

Scoring procedures differ in detail among civil service jurisdictions although the general principles are the same. Whether the papers are hand-scored or graded by machine we have described, they are nearly always graded by number. That is, the person who marks the paper knows only the number – never the name – of the applicant. Not until all the papers have been graded will they be matched with names. If other tests, such as training and experience or oral interview ratings have been given, scores will be combined. Different parts of the examination usually have different weights. For example, the written test might count 60 percent of the final grade, and a rating of training and experience 40 percent. In many jurisdictions, veterans will have a certain number of points added to their grades.

After the final grade has been determined, the names are placed in grade order and an eligible list is established. There are various methods for resolving ties between those who get the same final grade – probably the most common is to place first the name of the person whose application was received first. Job offers are made from the eligible list in the order the names appear on it. You will be notified of your grade and your rank as soon as all these computations have been made. This will be done as rapidly as possible.

People who are found to meet the requirements in the announcement are called "eligibles." Their names are put on a list of eligible candidates. An eligible's chances of getting a job depend on how high he stands on this list and how fast agencies are filling jobs from the list.

When a job is to be filled from a list of eligibles, the agency asks for the names of people on the list of eligibles for that job. When the civil service commission receives this request, it sends to the agency the names of the three people highest on this list. Or, if the job to be filled has specialized requirements, the office sends the agency the names of the top three persons who meet these requirements from the general list.

The appointing officer makes a choice from among the three people whose names were sent to him. If the selected person accepts the appointment, the names of the others are put back on the list to be considered for future openings.

That is the rule in hiring from all kinds of eligible lists, whether they are for typist, carpenter, chemist, or something else. For every vacancy, the appointing officer has his choice of any one of the top three eligibles on the list. This explains why the person whose name is on top of the list sometimes does not get an appointment when some of the persons lower on the list do. If the appointing officer chooses the second or third eligible, the No. 1 eligible does not get a job at once, but stays on the list until he is appointed or the list is terminated.

X. HOW TO PASS THE INTERVIEW TEST

The examination for which you applied requires an oral interview test. You have already taken the written test and you are now being called for the interview test – the final part of the formal examination.

You may think that it is not possible to prepare for an interview test and that there are no procedures to follow during an interview. Our purpose is to point out some things you can do in advance that will help you and some good rules to follow and pitfalls to avoid while you are being interviewed.

What is an interview supposed to test?

The written examination is designed to test the technical knowledge and competence of the candidate; the oral is designed to evaluate intangible qualities, not readily measured otherwise, and to establish a list showing the relative fitness of each candidate – as measured against his competitors – for the position sought. Scoring is not on the basis of "right" and "wrong," but on a sliding scale of values ranging from "not passable" to "outstanding." As a matter of fact, it is possible to achieve a relatively low score without a single "incorrect" answer because of evident weakness in the qualities being measured.

Occasionally, an examination may consist entirely of an oral test – either an individual or a group oral. In such cases, information is sought concerning the technical knowledges and abilities of the candidate, since there has been no written examination for this purpose. More commonly, however, an oral test is used to supplement a written examination.

Who conducts interviews?

The composition of oral boards varies among different jurisdictions. In nearly all, a representative of the personnel department serves as chairman. One of the members of the board may be a representative of the department in which the candidate would work. In some cases, "outside experts" are used, and, frequently, a businessman or some other representative of the general public is asked to serve. Labor and management or other special groups may be represented. The aim is to secure the services of experts in the appropriate field.

However the board is composed, it is a good idea (and not at all improper or unethical) to ascertain in advance of the interview who the members are and what groups they represent. When you are introduced to them, you will have some idea of their backgrounds and interests, and at least you will not stutter and stammer over their names.

What should be done before the interview?

While knowledge about the board members is useful and takes some of the surprise element out of the interview, there is other preparation which is more substantive. It *is* possible to prepare for an oral interview – in several ways:

1) Keep a copy of your application and review it carefully before the interview

This may be the only document before the oral board, and the starting point of the interview. Know what education and experience you have listed there, and the sequence and dates of all of it. Sometimes the board will ask you to review the highlights of your experience for them; you should not have to hem and haw doing it.

2) Study the class specification and the examination announcement

Usually, the oral board has one or both of these to guide them. The qualities, characteristics or knowledges required by the position sought are stated in these documents. They offer valuable clues as to the nature of the oral interview. For example, if the job involves supervisory responsibilities, the announcement will usually indicate that knowledge of modern supervisory methods and the qualifications of the candidate as a supervisor will be tested. If so, you can expect such questions, frequently in the form of a hypothetical situation which you are expected to solve. NEVER go into an oral without knowledge of the duties and responsibilities of the job you seek.

3) Think through each qualification required

Try to visualize the kind of questions you would ask if you were a board member. How well could you answer them? Try especially to appraise your own knowledge and background in each area, *measured against the job sought*, and identify any areas in which you are weak. Be critical and realistic – do not flatter yourself.

4) Do some general reading in areas in which you feel you may be weak

For example, if the job involves supervision and your past experience has NOT, some general reading in supervisory methods and practices, particularly in the field of human relations, might be useful. Do NOT study agency procedures or detailed manuals. The oral board will be testing your understanding and capacity, not your memory.

5) Get a good night's sleep and watch your general health and mental attitude

You will want a clear head at the interview. Take care of a cold or any other minor ailment, and of course, no hangovers.

What should be done on the day of the interview?

Now comes the day of the interview itself. Give yourself plenty of time to get there. Plan to arrive somewhat ahead of the scheduled time, particularly if your appointment is in the fore part of the day. If a previous candidate fails to appear, the board might be ready for you a bit early. By early afternoon an oral board is almost invariably behind schedule if there are many candidates, and you may have to wait. Take along a book or magazine to read, or your application to review, but leave any extraneous material in the waiting room when you go in for your interview. In any event, relax and compose yourself.

The matter of dress is important. The board is forming impressions about you – from your experience, your manners, your attitude, and your appearance. Give your personal appearance careful attention. Dress your best, but not your flashiest. Choose conservative, appropriate clothing, and be sure it is immaculate. This is a business interview, and your appearance should indicate that you regard it as such. Besides, being well groomed and properly dressed will help boost your confidence.

Sooner or later, someone will call your name and escort you into the interview room. *This is it.* From here on you are on your own. It is too late for any more preparation. But remember, you asked for this opportunity to prove your fitness, and you are here because your request was granted.

What happens when you go in?

The usual sequence of events will be as follows: The clerk (who is often the board stenographer) will introduce you to the chairman of the oral board, who will introduce you to the other members of the board. Acknowledge the introductions before you sit down. Do not be surprised if you find a microphone facing you or a stenotypist sitting by. Oral interviews are usually recorded in the event of an appeal or other review.

Usually the chairman of the board will open the interview by reviewing the highlights of your education and work experience from your application – primarily for the benefit of the other members of the board, as well as to get the material into the record. Do not interrupt or comment unless there is an error or significant misinterpretation; if that is the case, do not hesitate. But do not quibble about insignificant matters. Also, he will usually ask you some question about your education, experience or your present job – partly to get you to start talking and to establish the interviewing "rapport." He may start the actual questioning, or turn it over to one of the other members. Frequently, each member undertakes the questioning on a particular area, one in which he is perhaps most competent, so you can expect each member to participate in the examination. Because time is limited, you may also expect some rather abrupt switches in the direction the questioning takes, so do not be upset by it. Normally, a board member will not pursue a single line of questioning unless he discovers a particular strength or weakness.

After each member has participated, the chairman will usually ask whether any member has any further questions, then will ask you if you have anything you wish to add. Unless you are expecting this question, it may floor you. Worse, it may start you off on an extended, extemporaneous speech. The board is not usually seeking more information. The question is principally to offer you a last opportunity to present further qualifications or to indicate that you have nothing to add. So, if you feel that a significant qualification or characteristic has been overlooked, it is proper to point it out in a sentence or so. Do not compliment the board on the thoroughness of their examination – they have been sketchy, and you know it. If you wish, merely say, "No thank you, I have nothing further to add." This is a point where you can "talk yourself out" of a good impression or fail to present an important bit of information. Remember, *you close the interview yourself*.

The chairman will then say, "That is all, Mr. _____, thank you." Do not be startled; the interview is over, and quicker than you think. Thank him, gather your belongings and take your leave. Save your sigh of relief for the other side of the door.

How to put your best foot forward

Throughout this entire process, you may feel that the board individually and collectively is trying to pierce your defenses, seek out your hidden weaknesses and embarrass and confuse you. Actually, this is not true. They are obliged to make an appraisal of your qualifications for the job you are seeking, and they want to see you in your best light. Remember, they must interview all candidates and a non-cooperative candidate may become a failure in spite of their best efforts to bring out his qualifications. Here are 15 suggestions that will help you:

1) Be natural – Keep your attitude confident, not cocky

If you are not confident that you can do the job, do not expect the board to be. Do not apologize for your weaknesses, try to bring out your strong points. The board is interested in a positive, not negative, presentation. Cockiness will antagonize any board member and make him wonder if you are covering up a weakness by a false show of strength.

2) Get comfortable, but don't lounge or sprawl

Sit erectly but not stiffly. A careless posture may lead the board to conclude that you are careless in other things, or at least that you are not impressed by the importance of the occasion. Either conclusion is natural, even if incorrect. Do not fuss with your clothing, a pencil or an ashtray. Your hands may occasionally be useful to emphasize a point; do not let them become a point of distraction.

3) Do not wisecrack or make small talk

This is a serious situation, and your attitude should show that you consider it as such. Further, the time of the board is limited – they do not want to waste it, and neither should you.

4) Do not exaggerate your experience or abilities

In the first place, from information in the application or other interviews and sources, the board may know more about you than you think. Secondly, you probably will not get away with it. An experienced board is rather adept at spotting such a situation, so do not take the chance.

5) If you know a board member, do not make a point of it, yet do not hide it

Certainly you are not fooling him, and probably not the other members of the board. Do not try to take advantage of your acquaintanceship – it will probably do you little good.

6) Do not dominate the interview

Let the board do that. They will give you the clues – do not assume that you have to do all the talking. Realize that the board has a number of questions to ask you, and do not try to take up all the interview time by showing off your extensive knowledge of the answer to the first one.

7) Be attentive

You only have 20 minutes or so, and you should keep your attention at its sharpest throughout. When a member is addressing a problem or question to you, give him your undivided attention. Address your reply principally to him, but do not exclude the other board members.

8) Do not interrupt

A board member may be stating a problem for you to analyze. He will ask you a question when the time comes. Let him state the problem, and wait for the question.

9) Make sure you understand the question

Do not try to answer until you are sure what the question is. If it is not clear, restate it in your own words or ask the board member to clarify it for you. However, do not haggle about minor elements.

10) Reply promptly but not hastily

A common entry on oral board rating sheets is "candidate responded readily," or "candidate hesitated in replies." Respond as promptly and quickly as you can, but do not jump to a hasty, ill-considered answer.

11) Do not be peremptory in your answers

A brief answer is proper – but do not fire your answer back. That is a losing game from your point of view. The board member can probably ask questions much faster than you can answer them.

12) Do not try to create the answer you think the board member wants

He is interested in what kind of mind you have and how it works – not in playing games. Furthermore, he can usually spot this practice and will actually grade you down on it.

13) Do not switch sides in your reply merely to agree with a board member

Frequently, a member will take a contrary position merely to draw you out and to see if you are willing and able to defend your point of view. Do not start a debate, yet do not surrender a good position. If a position is worth taking, it is worth defending.

14) Do not be afraid to admit an error in judgment if you are shown to be wrong

The board knows that you are forced to reply without any opportunity for careful consideration. Your answer may be demonstrably wrong. If so, admit it and get on with the interview.

15) Do not dwell at length on your present job

The opening question may relate to your present assignment. Answer the question but do not go into an extended discussion. You are being examined for a *new* job, not your present one. As a matter of fact, try to phrase ALL your answers in terms of the job for which you are being examined.

Basis of Rating

Probably you will forget most of these "do's" and "don'ts" when you walk into the oral interview room. Even remembering them all will not ensure you a passing grade. Perhaps you did not have the qualifications in the first place. But remembering them will help you to put your best foot forward, without treading on the toes of the board members.

Rumor and popular opinion to the contrary notwithstanding, an oral board wants you to make the best appearance possible. They know you are under pressure – but they also want to see how you respond to it as a guide to what your reaction would be under the pressures of the job you seek. They will be influenced by the degree of poise you display, the personal traits you show and the manner in which you respond.

ABOUT THIS BOOK

This book contains tests divided into Examination Sections. Go through each test, answering every question in the margin. We have also attached a sample answer sheet at the back of the book that can be removed and used. At the end of each test look at the answer key and check your answers. On the ones you got wrong, look at the right answer choice and learn. Do not fill in the answers first. Do not memorize the questions and answers, but understand the answer and principles involved. On your test, the questions will likely be different from the samples. Questions are changed and new ones added. If you understand these past questions you should have success with any changes that arise. Tests may consist of several types of questions. We have additional books on each subject should more study be advisable or necessary for you. Finally, the more you study, the better prepared you will be. This book is intended to be the last thing you study before you walk into the examination room. Prior study of relevant texts is also recommended. NLC publishes some of these in our Fundamental Series. Knowledge and good sense are important factors in passing your exam. Good luck also helps. So now study this Passbook, absorb the material contained within and take that knowledge into the examination. Then do your best to pass that exam.

EXAMINATION SECTION

LOGICAL REASONING
EVALUATING CONCLUSIONS IN LIGHT OF KNOWN FACTS
EXAMINATION SECTION
TEST 1

COMMENTARY

This section is designed to provide practice questions in evaluating conclusions when you are given specific data to work with.

We suggest you do the questions three at a time, consulting the answer key and then the solution section for any questions you may have missed. It's a good idea to try the questions again a week before the exam.

In the validity of conclusion type of question, you are first given a reading passage which describes a particular situation. The passage may be on any topic, as it is not your knowledge of the topic that is being tested, but your reasoning abilities. The passage is likely to detail several proposed courses of action and factors affecting these proposals. The reading passage is followed by a conclusion based on the facts in the passage, or a description of a decision taken regarding the situation. The conclusion is followed by a number of statements which have a possible connection to the conclusion. For each statement, you are to determine whether:

- A. The statement proves the conclusion.
- B. The statement supports the conclusion but does not prove it.
- C. The statement disproves the conclusion.
- D. The statement weakens the conclusion but does not disprove it.
- E. The statement has no relevance to the conclusion.

Remember that the conclusion after the passage is to be accepted as the outcome of what actually happened, and that you are being asked to evaluate the impact each statement would have had on the conclusion.

Questions 1-8.

DIRECTIONS: Questions 1 through 8 are based on the following paragraph.

In May of 2018, Mr. Bryan inherited a clothing store on Main Street in a small New England town. The store has specialized in selling quality men's and women's clothing since 1920. Business has been stable throughout the years, neither increasing nor decreasing. He has an opportunity to buy two adjacent stores which would enable him to add a wider range and style of clothing. In order to do this, he would have to borrow a substantial amount of money. He also risks losing the goodwill of his present clientele.

CONCLUSION: On November 7, 2018, Mr. Bryan tells the owner of the two adjacent stores that he has decided not to purchase them. He feels that it would be best to simply maintain his present marketing position, as there would not be enough new business to support an expansion.

A. The statement proves the conclusion.
B. The statement supports the conclusion but does not prove it.
C. The statement disproves the conclusion.
D. The statement weakens the conclusion.
E. The statement is irrelevant to the conclusion.

1. A large new branch of the county's community college holds its first classes in September.   1.____

2. The town's largest factory shuts down with no indication that it will reopen.   2.____

3. The United States Census showed that the number of children per household dropped from 2.4 to 2.1 since the last census.   3.____

4. Mr. Bryan's brother tells him of a new clothing boutique specializing in casual women's clothing which is opening soon.   4.____

5. Mr. Bryan's sister buys her baby several items for Christmas at Mr. Bryan's store.   5.____

6. Mrs. McIntyre, the President of the Town Council, brings Mr. Bryan a home-baked pumpkin pie in honor of his store's 100th anniversary. They discuss the changes that have taken place in the town, and she comments on how his store has maintained the same look and feel over the years.   6.____

7. In October, Mr. Bryan's aunt lends him $50,000.   7.____

8. The Town Council has just announced that the town is eligible for funding from a federal project designed to encourage the location of new businesses in the central districts of cities and towns.   8.____

Questions 9-18.

DIRECTIONS: Questions 9 through 18 are based on the following paragraph.

A proposal was put before the legislative body of a country to require air bags in all automobiles manufactured for domestic use in that country after 2019. The air bag, made of nylon or plastic, is designed to inflate automatically within a car at the impact of a collision, thus protecting front-seat occupants from being thrown forward. There has been much support of the measure from consumer groups, the insurance industry, key legislators, and the general public. The country's automobile manufacturers, who contend the new crash equipment would add up to $1,000 to car prices and provide no more protection than existing seat belts, are against the proposed legislation

CONCLUSION: On April 21, 2014, the legislation requiring air bags in all automobiles manufactured for domestic use in that country after 2019.

A. The statement proves the conclusion.
B. The statement supports the conclusion but does not prove it.
C. The statement disproves the conclusion.
D. The statement weakens the conclusion.
E. The statement is irrelevant to the conclusion.

9. A study has shown that 59% of car occupants do not use seat belts. 9.____

10. The country's Department of Transportation has estimated that the crash protection equipment would save up to 5,900 lives each year. 10.____

11. On April 27, 2013, Augusta Raneoni was named head of an advisory committee to gather and analyze data on the costs, benefits, and feasibility of the proposed legislation on air bags in automobiles. 11.____

12. Consumer groups and the insurance industry accuse the legislature of rejecting passage of the regulation for political reasons. 12.____

13. A study by the Committee on Imports and Exports projected that the sales of imported cars would rise dramatically in 2019 because imported cars do not have to include air bags, and can be sold more cheaply. 13.____

14. Research has shown that air bags, if produced on a large scale, would cost about $200 apiece, and would provide more reliable protection than any other type of seat belt. 14.____

15. Auto sales in 2011 increased 3% over the previous year. 15.____

16. A Department of Transportation report in July of 2020 credits a drop in automobile deaths of 4,100 to the use of air bags. 16.____

17. In June of 2014, the lobbyist of the largest insurance company receives a bonus for her work on the passage of the air bag legislation. 17.____

18. In 2020, the stock in crash protection equipment has risen three-fold over the previous year. 18.____

Questions 19-25.

DIRECTIONS: Questions 19 through 25 are based on the following paragraph.

On a national television talk show, Joan Rivera, a famous comedienne, has recently insulted the physical appearances of a famous actress and the dead wife of an ex-President. There has been a flurry of controversy over her comments, and much discussion of the incident has appeared in the press. Most of the comments have been negative. It appears that this tie she might have gone too far. There have been cancellations of two of her five scheduled performances in the two weeks since the show was televised, and Joan's been receiving a lot of negative mail. Because of the controversy, she has an interview with a national news magazine at the end of the week, and her press agent is strongly urging her to apologize publicly. She feels strongly that her comments were no worse than any other she has ever made, and that the whole incident will *blow over* soon. She respects her press agent's judgment, however, as his assessment of public sentiment tends to be very accurate.

CONCLUSION: Joan does not apologize publicly, and during the interview she challenges the actress to a weight-losing contest. For every pound the actress loses, Joan says she will donate $1 to the Cellulite Prevention League.

A. The statement proves the conclusion.
B. The statement supports the conclusion but does not prove it.
C. The statement disproves the conclusion.
D. The statement weakens the conclusion.
E. The statement is irrelevant to the conclusion.

19. Joan's mother, who she is very fond of, is very upset with Joan's comments. 19._____

20. Six months after the interview, Joan's income has doubled. 20._____

21. Joan's agent is pleased with the way Joan handles the interview. 21._____

22. Joan's sister has been appointed Treasurer of the Cellulite Prevention League 22._____
In her report, she states that Joan's $12 contribution is the only amount that has been donated to the League in its first six months.

23. The magazine receives many letters commending Joan for the courage it 23._____
took for her to apologize publicly in the interview.

24. Immediately after the interview appears, another one of Joan's performances 24._____
is cancelled.

25. Due to a printers' strike, the article was not published until the following week. 25._____

Questions 26-30.

DIRECTIONS: Questions 25 through 30 are based on the following paragraph.

The law-making body of Country X must decide what to do about the issue of recording television shows for home use. There is currently no law against recording shows directly from the TV as long as the DVDs are not used for commercial purposes. The increasing popularity of pay TV and satellite systems, combined with the increasing number of homes that own recording equipment, has caused a great deal of concern in some segments of the entertainment industry. Companies that own the rights to films, popular television shows, and sporting events feel that their copyright privileges are being violated, and they are seeking compensation or the banning of TV recording. Legislation has been introduced to make it illegal to record television programs for home use. Separate proposed legislation is also pending that would continue to allow recording of TV shows for home use, but would place a tax of 10% on each DVD that is purchased for home use. The income from that tax would then be proportionately distributed as royalties to those owning the rights to programs being aired. A weighted point system coupled with the averaging of several national viewing rating systems would be used to determine the royalties. There is a great deal of lobbying being done for both bills, as the manufacturers of DVDs and recording equipment are against the passage of the bills.

CONCLUSION: The legislature of Country X rejects both bills by a wide margin.

- A. The statement proves the conclusion.
- B. The statement supports the conclusion but does not prove it.
- C. The statement disproves the conclusion.
- D. The statement weakens the conclusion.
- E. The statement is irrelevant to the conclusion.

26. Country X's Department of Taxation hires 500 new employees to handle the increased paperwork created by the new tax on DVDs.

26.____

27. A study conducted by the country's most prestigious accounting firm shows that the cost of implementing the proposed new DVD tax would be greater than the income expected from it.

27.____

28. It is estimated that 80% of all those working in the entertainment industry, excluding performers, own DVD recorders.

28.____

29. The head of Country X's law enforcement agency states that legislation banning the home recording of TV shows would be unenforceable.

29.____

30. Financial experts predict that unless a tax is placed on DVDs, several large companies in the entertainment industry will have to file for bankruptcy.

30.____

Questions 31-38.

DIRECTIONS: Questions 31 through 38 are variations on the type of question you just had. It is important that you read the question very carefully to determine exactly what is required.

31. In this question, select the choice that is MOST relevant to the conclusion.
    I. The Buffalo Bills football team is in second place in its division.
    II. The New England Patriots are in first place in the same division.
    III. There are two games left to play in the season, and the Bills will not play the Patriots again.
    IV. The New England Patriots won ten games and lost four games, and the Buffalo Bills have won eight games and lost six games.
    CONCLUSION: The Buffalo Bills win their division.
    A. The conclusion is proved by sentences I-IV.
    B. The conclusion is disproved by sentences I-IV.
    C. The facts are not sufficient to prove or disprove the conclusion.

31.____

32. In this question, select the choice that is MOST relevant to the conclusion.   32.____
    I. On the planet of Zeinon there are only two different eye colors and only two different hair colors.
    II. Half of those beings with purple hair have golden eyes.
    III. There are more inhabitants with purple hair than there are inhabitants with silver hair.
    IV. One-third of those with silver hair have green eyes.
    CONCLUSION: There are more golden-eyed beings on Zeinon than green-eyed ones.
    A. The conclusion is proved by sentences I-IV.
    B. The conclusion is disproved by sentences I-IV.
    C. The facts are not sufficient to prove or disprove the conclusion.

33. In this question, select the choice that is MOST relevant to the conclusion.   33.____
    John and Kevin are leaving Amaranth to go to school in Bethany. They've decided to rent a small truck to move their possessions. Joe's Truck Rental charges $100 plus 30¢ a mile. National Movers charges $50 more but gives free mileage for the first 100 miles. After the first 100 miles, they charge 25¢ a mile.
    CONCLUSION: John and Kevin rent their truck from National Movers because it is cheaper.
    A. The conclusion is proved by the facts in the above paragraph.
    B. The conclusion is disproved by the facts in the above paragraph.
    C. The facts are not sufficient to prove or disprove the conclusion.

34. For this question, select the choice that supports the information given in the passage.   34.____
    Municipalities in Country X are divided into villages, towns, and cities. A village has a population of 5,000 or less. The population of a town ranges from 5,001 to 15,000. In order to be incorporated as a city, the municipality must have a population over 15,000. If, after a village becomes a town, or a town becomes a city, the population drops below the minimum required (for example, the population of a city goes below 15,000), and stays below the minimum for more than ten years, it loses its current status, and drops to the next category. As soon as a municipality rises in population to the next category (village to town, for example), however, it is immediately reclassified to the next category.
    In the 2000 census, Plainfield had a population of 12,000. Between 2000 and 2010, Plainfield grew 10%, and between 2010 and 2020 Plainfield grew another 20%. The population of Springdale doubled from 2000 to 2010, and increased 25% from 2010 to 2020. The city of Smallville's population, 20,283, has not changed significantly in recent years. Granton had a population of 25,000 people in 1990, and has decreased 25% in each ten year period since then. Ellenville had a population of 4,283 in 1990, and grew 5% in each ten year period since 1990.

In 2020,
- A. Plainfield, Smallville, and Granton are cities.
- B. Smallville is a city, Granton is a town, and Ellenville is a village.
- C. Springdale, Granton, and Ellenville are towns.
- D. Plainfield and Smallville are cities, and Ellenville is a town.

35. For this question, select the choice that is MOST relevant to the conclusion.
    A study was done for a major food-distributing firm to determine if there is any difference in the kind of caffeine containing products used by people of different ages. A sample of one thousand people between the ages of twenty and fifty were drawn from selected areas in the country. They were divided equally into three groups.
    Those individuals who were 20-29 were designated Group A, those 30-39 were Group B, and those 40-50 were placed in Group C.
    It was found that on the average, Group A drank 1.8 cups of coffee, Group B 3.1, and Group C 2.5 cups of coffee daily. Group A drank 2.1 cups of tea, Group B drank 1.2, and Group C drank 2.6 cups of tea daily. Group A drank 3 1.8 ounces glasses of cola, Group B drank 1.9, and Group C drank 1.5 glasses of cola daily.
    CONCLUSION: According to the study, the average person in the 20-29 age group drinks less tea daily than the average person in the 40-50 age group, but drinks more coffee daily than the average person in the 30-39 age group drinks cola.
    - A. The conclusion is proved by the facts in the above paragraph.
    - B. The conclusion is disproved by the facts in the above paragraph.
    - C. The facts are not sufficient to prove or disprove the conclusion.

36. For this question, select the choice that is MOST relevant to the conclusion
    I. Mary is taller than Jane but shorter than Dale.
    II. Fred is taller than Mary but shorter than Steven.
    III. Dale is shorter than Steven but taller than Elizabeth.
    IV. Elizabeth is taller than Mary but not as tall as Fred.
    CONCLUSION: Dale is taller than Fred.
    - A. The conclusion is proved by sentences I-IV.
    - B. The conclusion is disproved by sentences I-IV.
    - C. The facts are not sufficient to prove or disprove the conclusion.

37. For this question, select the choice that is MOST relevant to the conclusion.
    I. Main Street is between Spring Street and Glenn Blvd.
    II. Hawley Avenue is one block south of Spring Street and three blocks north of Main Street.
    III. Glenn Street is five blocks south of Elm and four blocks south of Main.
    IV. All the streets mentioned are parallel to one another.
    CONCLUSION: Elm Street is between Hawley Avenue and Glenn Blvd.
    - A. The conclusion is proved by the facts in sentences I-IV.
    - B. The conclusion is disproved by the facts in sentences I-IV.
    - C. The facts are not sufficient to prove or disprove the conclusion.

38. For this question, select the choice that is MOST relevant to the conclusion.	38.____
   I. Train A leaves the town of Hampshire every day at 5:50 A.M. and arrives in New London at 6:42 A.M.
   II. Train A leaves New London at 7:00 A.M. and arrives in Kellogsville at 8:42 A.M.
   III. Train B leaves Kellogsville at 8:00 A.M. and arrives in Hampshire at 10:45 A.M.
   IV. Due to the need for repairs, there is just one railroad track between New London and Hampshire.
   CONCLUSION: It is impossible for Train A and Train B to follow these schedules without colliding.
   A. The conclusion is proved by the facts in sentences I-IV.
   B. The conclusion is disproved by the facts in sentences I-IV.
   C. The facts are not sufficient to prove or disprove the conclusion.

KEY (CORRECT ANSWERS)

1.	D	11.	C	21.	D	31.	C
2.	B	12.	C	22.	A	32.	A
3.	E	13.	D	23.	C	33.	C
4.	B	14.	B	24.	B	34.	B
5.	C	15.	E	25.	E	35.	B
6.	A	16.	B	26.	C	36.	C
7.	D	17.	A	27.	B	37.	A
8.	B	18.	B	28.	E	38.	B
9.	B	19.	D	29.	B		
10.	B	20.	E	30.	D		

SOLUTIONS TO QUESTIONS

1. The answer is D. This statement weakens the conclusion, but does not disprove it. If a new branch of the community college opened in September, it could possibly bring in new business for Mr. Bryant. Since it states in the conclusion that Mr. Bryant felt there would not be enough new business to support the additional stores, this would tend to disprove the conclusion. Choice C would not be correct because it's possible that he felt that the students would not have enough additional money to support his new venture, or would not be interested in his clothing styles. It's also possible that the majority of the students already live in the area, so that they wouldn't really be a new customer population. This type of question is tricky, and can initially be very confusing, so don't feel badly if you missed it. Most people need to practice with a few of these types of questions before they feel comfortable recognizing exactly what they're being asked to do.

2. The answer is B. It supports the conclusion because the closing of the factory would probably take money and customers out of the town, causing Mr. Bryant to lose some of his present business. It doesn't prove the conclusion, however, because we don't know how large the factory was. It's possible that only a small percentage of the population was employed there, or that they found other jobs.

3. The answer is E. The fact that the number of children per household dropped slightly nationwide in the decade is irrelevant. Statistics showing a drop nationwide doesn't mean that there was a drop in the number of children per household in Mr. Bryant's hometown. This is a tricky question, as choice B, supporting the conclusion but not proving it, may seem reasonable. If the number of children per household declined nationwide, then it may not seem unreasonable to feel that this would support Mr. Bryant's decision not to expand his business. However, we're preparing you for promotional exams, not "real life." One of the difficult things about taking exams is that sometimes you're forced to make a choice between two statements that both seem like they could be the possible answer. What you need to do in that case is choose the best choice. Becoming annoyed or frustrated with the question won't really help much. If there's a review of the exam, you can certainly appeal the question. There have been many cases where, after an appeal, two possible choices have been allowed as correct answers. We've included this question, however, to help you see what to do should you get a question like this. It's most important not to get rattled, and to select the BEST choice. In this case, the connection between the statistical information and Mr. Bryant's decision is pretty remote. If the question had said that the number of children in Mr. Bryant's town had decreased, then choice B would have been a more reasonable choice. It could also help in this situation to visualize the situation. Picture Mr. Bryant in his armchair reading that, nationwide, the average number of children per household has declined slightly. How likely would this be to influence his decision, especially since he sells men's and women's clothing? It would take a while for this decline in population to show up, and we're not even sure if it applies to Mr. Bryant's hometown. Don't feel badly if you missed this; it was tricky. The more of these you do, the more comfortable you'll feel.

4. The answer is B. If a new clothing boutique specializing in casual women's clothing were to open soon, this would lend support to Mr. Bryant's decision not to expand, but would not prove that he had actually made the decision to expand. A new women's clothing boutique would most likely be in competition with his existing business, thus making any possible expansion a riskier venture. We can't be sure from this, however, that he didn't go ahead and expand his business despite the increased competition. Choice A, proves the conclusion, would only be the answer if we could be absolutely sure from the statement that Mr. Bryant had actually not expanded his business.

5. The answer is C. This statement disproves the conclusion. In order for his sister to buy several items for her baby at Mr. Bryant's store, he would have to have changed his business to include children's clothing.

6. The answer is A. It definitely proves the conclusion. The passage states that Mr. Bryan's store had been in business since 1920. A pie baked in honor of his store's 100th anniversary would have to be presented sometime in 2020. The conclusion states that he made his decision not to expand on November 7, 2018. If, more than a year later Mrs. MacIntyre comments that his store has maintained the same look and feel over the years, it could not have been expanded, or otherwise significantly changed.

7. The answer is D. If Mr. Bryant's aunt lent him $50,000 in October, this would tend to weaken the conclusion, which took place in November. Because it was stated that Mr. Bryant would need to borrow money in order to expand his business, it would be logical to assume that if he borrowed money he had decided to expand his business, weakening the conclusion. The reason C, disproves the conclusion, is not the correct answer is because we can't be sure Mr. Bryant didn't borrow the money for another reason.

8. The answer is B. If Mr. Bryant's town is eligible for federal funds to encourage the location of new businesses in the central district, this would tend to support his decision not to expand his business. Funds to encourage new business would increase the likelihood of there being additional competition for Mr. Bryant's store to contend with. Since we can't say for sure that there would be direct competition from a new business, however, choice A would be incorrect. Note that this is also a tricky question. You might have thought that the new funds weakened the conclusion because it would mean that Mr. Bryant could easily get the money he needed. Mr. Bryant is expanding his present business, not creating a new business. Therefore, he is not eligible for the funding.

9. The answer is B. This is a very tricky question. It's stated that 59% of car occupants don't use seat belts. The legislature is considering the use of air bags because of safety issues. The advantage of air bags over seat belts is that they inflate upon impact, and don't require car occupants to do anything with them ahead of time. Since the population has strongly resisted using seat belts, the air bags could become even more important in saving lives. Since saving lives is the purpose of the proposed legislation, the information that a small percentage of people use seat belts could be helpful to the passage of the legislation. We can't be sure that this is reason enough for the legislature to vote for the legislation, however, so choice A in incorrect.

10. The answer is B, as the information that 5,900 lives could be saved would tend to support the conclusion. Saving that many lives through the use of air bags could be a very persuasive reason to vote for the legislation. Since we don't know for sure that it's enough of a compelling reason for the legislature to vote for the legislation, however, choice A could not be the answer.

11. The answer is C, disproves the conclusion. If the legislation had been passed as stated in the conclusion, there would be no reason to appoint someone head of an advisory committee six days later to analyze the "feasibility of the proposed legislation." The key word here is "proposed." If it has been proposed, it means it hasn't been passed. This contradicts the conclusion and, therefore, disproves it.

12. The answer is C, disproves the conclusion. If the legislation had passed, there would be no reason for supporters of the legislation to accuse the legislature of rejecting the legislation for political reasons. This question may have seemed so obvious that you might have thought there was a trick to it. Exams usually have a few obvious questions, which will trip you up if you begin reading too much into them.

13. The answer is D, as this would tend to disprove the conclusion. A projected dramatic rise in imported cars could be very harmful to the country's economy and could be a very good reason for some legislators to vote against the proposed legislation. It would be assuming too much to choose C, however, because we don't know if they actually did vote against it.

14. The answer is B. This information would tend to support the passage of the legislation. The estimate of the cost of the air bags is $800 less than the cost estimated by opponents, and it's stated that the protection would be more reliable than any other type of seat belt. Both of these would be good arguments in favor of passing the legislation. Since we don't know for sure, however, how persuasive they actually were, choice A would not be the correct choice.

15. The answer is E, as this is irrelevant information. It really doesn't matter whether auto sales in 2001 have increased slightly over the previous year. If the air bag legislation were to go into effect in 2004, that might make the information somehow more relevant. But the air bag legislation would not take effect until 2009, so the information is irrelevant, since it tells us nothing about the state of the auto industry then.

16. The answer is B, supports the conclusion. This is a tricky question. While at first it might seem to prove the conclusion, we can't be sure that the air bag legislation is responsible for the drop in automobile deaths. It's possible air bags came into popular use without the legislation, or with different legislation. There's no way we can be sure that it was the proposed legislation mandating the use of air bags that was responsible.

17. The answer is A. If, in June of 2009, the lobbyist received a bonus "for her work on the air bag legislation," we can be sure that the legislation passed. This proves the conclusion.

18. The answer is B. This is another tricky question. A three-fold stock increase would strongly suggest that the legislation had been passed, but it's possible that factors other than the air bag legislation caused the increase. Note that the stock is in "crash protection

equipment." Nowhere in the statement does it say air bags. Seat belts, motorcycle helmets, and collapsible bumpers are all crash protection equipment and could have contributed to the increase. This is just another reminder to read carefully because the questions are often designed to mislead you.

19. The answer is D. This would tend to weaken the conclusion because Joan is very fond of her mother and she would not want to upset her unnecessarily. It does not prove it, however, because if Joan strongly feels she is right, she probably wouldn't let her mother's opinion sway her. Choice E would also not be correct, because we cannot assume that Joan's mother's opinion is of so little importance to her as to be considered irrelevant.

20. The answer is E. The statement is irrelevant. We are told that Joan's income has doubled but we are not old why. The phrase "six months after the interview" can be misleading in that it leads us to assume that the increase and the interview are related. Her income could have doubled because she regained her popularity but it could also have come from stocks or some other business venture. Because we are not given any reason for her income doubling, it would be impossible to say whether or not this statement proves or disproves the conclusion. Choice E is the best choice of the five possible choices. One of the problems with promotional exams is that sometimes you need to select a choice you're not crazy about. In this case, "not having enough information to made a determination" would be the best choice. However, that's not an option, so you're forced to work with what you've got. On these exams it's sometimes like voting for President; you have to pick the "lesser of the two evils" or the least awful choice. In this case, the information is more irrelevant to the conclusion than it is anything else.

21. The answer is D, weakens the conclusion. We've been told that Joan's agent feels that she should apologize. If he is pleased with her interview, then it would tend to weaken the conclusion but not disprove it. We can't be sure that he hasn't had a change of heart, or that there weren't other parts of the interview he liked so much that they outweighed her unwillingness to apologize.

22. The answer is A. The conclusion states that Joan will donate $1 to the Cellulite Prevention League for every pound the actress loses. Joan's sister's financial report on the League's activities directly supports and proves the conclusion.

23. The answer is C, disproves the conclusion. If the magazine receives many letters commending Joan for her courage in apologizing, this directly contradicts the conclusion, which states that Joan didn't apologize.

24. The answer is B. It was stated in the passage that two of Joan's performances were cancelled after the controversy first occurred. The cancellation of another performance immediately after her interview was published would tend to support the conclusion that she refused to apologize. Because we can't be sure, however, that her performance wasn't cancelled for another reason, choice A would be incorrect.

25. The answer is E, as this information is irrelevant. Postponing the article an extra week does not affect Joan's decision or the public's reaction to it.

13 (#1)

26. The answer is C. If 500 new employees are hired to handle the "increased paperwork created by the new tax on DVDs," this would directly contradict the conclusion, which states that the legislature defeated both bills. (They should all be this easy.)

27. The answer is B. The results of the study would support the conclusion. If implementing the legislation was going to be so costly, it is likely that the legislature would vote against it. Choice A is not the answer, however, because we can't be sure that the legislature didn't pass it anyway.

28. The answer is E. It's irrelevant to the conclusion that 80% of all those working in the entertainment industry own DVD recorders. Sometimes if you're not sure about these, it can help a lot to try and visualize the situation. Why would someone voting on this legislation care about this fact? It doesn't seem to be the kind of information that would make any difference or impact upon the conclusion.

29. The answer is B. The head of the law enforcement agency's statement that the legislation would be unenforceable would support the conclusion. It's possible that many legislators would question why they should bother to pass legislation that would be impossible to enforce. Choice A would be incorrect, however, because we can't be sure that the legislation wasn't passed in spite of his statement.

30. The answer is D. This would tend to weaken the conclusion because the prospect of several large companies going bankrupt would seem to be a good argument in favor of the legislation. The possible loss of jobs and businesses would be a good reason for some people to vote for the legislation. We can't be sure, however, that this would be a competing enough reason to ensure passage of the legislation so choice C is incorrect.

This concludes our section on the "Validity of Conclusion" type of questions. We hope these weren't too horrible for you. It's important to keep in mind exactly what you've been given and exactly what they want you to do with it. It's also necessary to remember that you may have to choose between two possible answers. In that case, you must choose the one that seems the best. Sometimes you may think there is no good answer. You will probably be right, but you can't let that upset you. Just choose the one you dislike the least.

We want to repeat that it is unlikely that this exact format will appear on the exam. The skills required to answer these questions, however, are the same as those you'll need for the exam so we suggest that you review this section before taking the actual exam.

31. The answer is C. This next set of questions requires you to "switch gears" slightly, and get used to different formats. In this type of question, you have to decide whether the conclusion is proved by the facts give, disproved by the facts given, or neither because note enough information has been provided. Fortunately, unlike the previous questions, you don't have to decide whether particular facts support or don't support the conclusion. This type of question is more straight forward, but the reasoning behind it is the same. We are told that the Bills have won two games less than the Patriots, and that the Patriots are in first place and the Bills are in second place. We are also told that there are two games left to play, and that they won't play each other again. The conclusion states that the Bills won the division. Is there anything in the four statements that would prove this? We have

no idea what the outcome of the last two games of the season was. The Bills and Patriots could have ended up tied at the end of the season, or the Bills could have lost both or one of their last games while the Patriots did the same. There might even be another team tied for first or second place with the Bills or Patriots. Since we don't know for sure, Choice A is incorrect. Choice B is trickier. It might seem at first glance that the best the Bills could do would be to tie the Patriots if the Patriots lost their last two games and the Bills won their last two games. But it would be too much to assume that there is no procedure for a tiebreaker that wouldn't give the Bills the division championship. Since we don't know what the rules are in the event of a tie (for example, what if a tie was decided on the results of what happened when the two teams had played each other, or on the best record in the division, or on most points scored?), we can't say for sure that it would be impossible for the Bills to win their division. For this reason, choice C is the answer, as we don't have enough information to prove or disprove the conclusion. This question looked more difficult than it actually was. It's important to disregard any factors outside of the actual question, and to focus only on what you've been given. In this case, as on all of these types of questions, what you know or don't know about a subject is actually irrelevant. It's best to concentrate only on the actual facts given.

32. The answer is A. The conclusion is proved by the facts given.

    In this type of problem, it is usually best to pull as many facts as possible from the sentences and then put them into a simpler form. The phrasing and the order of exam questions are designed to be confusing so you need to restate things as clearly as possible by eliminating the extras.

    Sentence I tells us that there are only two possible colors for eyes and two for hair. Looking at the other sentences we learn that eyes are either green or gold and that hair is either silver or purple. If half the beings with purple hair have golden eyes, then the other half must have green eyes since it is the only other eye color. Likewise, if one-third of those with silver hair have green eyes, the other two-thirds must have golden eyes.

    This information makes it clear that there are more golden-eyed beings on Zeinon than green-eyed ones. It doesn't matter that we don't know exactly how many are actually living on the planet. The number of those with gold eyes (1/2 plus 2/3) will always be greater than the number of those with green eyes (1/2 plus 1/3), no matter what the actual figures might be. Sentence III is totally irrelevant because even if there were more silver-haired inhabitants it would not affect the conclusion.

33. The answer is C. The conclusion is neither proved nor disproved by the facts because we don't know how many miles Bethany is from Amoranth.

    With this type of question, if you're not sure how to approach it, you can always substitute in a range of "real numbers" to see what the result would be. If they were 200 miles apart, Joe's Truck Rental would be cheaper because they would charge a total of $160 while National Movers would charge $175.

    Joe's - $100 plus .30 x 200 (or $60) = $160
    National - $150 plus .25 x 100 (or $25) = $175

    If the towns were 600 miles apart, however, National Movers would be cheaper. The cost of renting from National would be $275 compared to the $280 charged by Joe's Trucking.

    Joe's - $100 plus .30 x 600 (or $180) = $280
    National - $150 plus .25 x 500 (or $125) = $275

34. The answer is B. We've varied the format once more, but the reasoning is similar. This is a tedious question that is more like a math question, but we wanted to give you some practice with this type, just in case. You won't be able to do this question if you've forgotten how to do percents. Many exams require this knowledge, so if you feel you need a review we suggest you read Booklets 1, 2 or 3 in this series.

The only way to attack this problem is to go through each choice until you find the one that is correct. Choice A states that Plainfield, Smallville, and Granton are cities. Let's begin with Plainfield. The passage states that in 1990 Plainfield had a population of 12,000, and that it grew 10% between 1990 and 2000, and another 20% between 2000 and 2010. Ten percent of 12,000 is 1200 (12,000 x .10 = 1200). Therefore, the population grew from 12,000 in 1990 to 12,000 + 1200 between 1990 and 2000. At the time of the 2000 Census, Plainfield's population was 13,200. It then grew another 20% between 2000 and 2010, so, 13,200 x .20 = 2640. 13,200 plus the additional increase of 2640 would make the population of Plainfield 15,840. This would qualify it as a city, since its population is over 15,000. Since a change upward in the population of a municipality is re-classified immediately, Plainfield would have become a city right away. So far, statement A is true. The passage states that Smallville's population has not changed significantly in the last twenty years. Since Smallville's population was 20,283, Smallville would still be a city. Granton had a population of 25,000 (what a coincidence that so any of these places have such nice, even numbers) in 1980. The population has decreased 25% in each ten year period since that time. So from 1980 to 1990, the population decreased 25%. 25,000 x .25 = 6,250. 25,000 minus 6,250 = 18,750. So the population of Granton in 1990 would have been 18,750. (Or, you could have saved a step and multiplied 25,000 by .75 to get 18,750.) The population from 1990 to 2000 decreased an additional 25%. So: 18,750 x .25 = 4,687.50. 18,750 minus 4,687.50 = 14,062.50. Or: 18,750 x .75 = 14,062.50. (Don't let the fact that a half of a person is involved confuse you; these are exam questions, not real life.) From 2000 to 2010 the population decreased an additional 25%. This would mean that Granton's population was below 15,000 for more than ten years, so it's status as a city would have changed to that of a town, which would make choice A incorrect.

Choice B states that Smallville is a city and Granton is a town, which we know to be true from the information above. Choice B is correct so far. We next need to determine if Ellenville is a village. Ellenville had a population of 4,283 in 1980, and increased 5% in each ten year period since 1980. 4,283 x .05 = 214.15. 4,283 plus 214.15 = 4,497.15, so Ellenville's population from 1980 to 1990 increased to 4,497.15. (Or: 4,283 x 1.05 – 4,497.15.) From 1990 to 2000 Ellenville's population increased another 5%: 4,497.15 x .05 = 224.86. 4,497.15 plus 224.86 = 4,772.01 (or: 4,497.15 x 1.05 = 4,722.01.) From 2000 to 2010, Ellenville's population increased another 5%: 4,722.01 x .05 = 236.10. 4,722.01 plus 236.10 = 4,958.11. (Or: 4,722.01 x 1.05 = 4,958.11.).

Ellenville's population is still under 5,000 in 2010, so it would continue to be classified as a village. Since all three statements in choice B are true, choice B must be the answer. However, we'll go through the other choices. Choice C states that Springdale is a town. The passage tells us that the population of Springdale doubled from 1990 to 2000, and increased 25% from 2000 to 2010. It doesn't give us any actual population figures, however, so it's impossible to know what the population of Springdale is, making choice C incorrect. Choice C also states that Granton is a town, which is true, and that Ellenville is a town, which is false (from choice B we know it's a village). Choice D states that Plainfield and Smallville are cities, which is information we already know is true, and that Ellenville is a town. Since Ellenville is a village, choice D is also incorrect.

This was a lot of work for just one question and we doubt you'll get one like this on this section of the exam, but we included it just in case. On an exam, you can always put a check mark next to a question like this and come back to it later, if you feel you're pressed for time and cold spend your time more productively on other, less time-consuming problems.

35. The answer is B. This question requires very careful reading. It's best to break the conclusion down into smaller parts in order to solve the problem. The first half of the conclusion states that the average person in the 20-29 age group (Group A) drinks less tea daily than the average person in the 40-50 age group (Group C). The average person in Group A drinks 2.1 cups of tea daily, while the average person in Group C drinks 2.6 cups of tea daily. Since 2.1 is less than 2.6, the conclusion is correct so far. The second half of the conclusion states that the average person in Group A drinks more coffee daily than the average person in the 30-39 age group (Group B) drinks cola. The average person in Group A drinks 1.8 cups of coffee daily, while the average person in Group B drinks 1.9 glasses of cola. This disproves the conclusion, which states that the average person in Group A drinks more coffee daily than the average person in Group B drinks cola.

36. The answer is C. The easiest way to approach a problem that deals with the relationship between a number of different people or things is to set up a diagram. This type of problem is usually too confusing to do in your head. For this particular problem, the "diagram" could be a line, one end of which would be labeled tall and the other end labeled short. Then, taking one sentence at a time, place the people on the line to see where they fall in relation to one another.

The diagram of the first sentence would look like this:

Tall _____ Dale _____ Mary _____ Jane _____ Short
(left)   (right)

Mary is taller than Jane but shorter than Dale, so she would fall somewhere between the two of them. We have placed tall on the left and labeled it left just to make the explanation easier. You could just as easily have reversed the position.

The second sentence places Fred somewhere to the left of Mary because he is taller than she is. Steven would be to the left of Fred for the same reason. At this point we don't know whether Steven and Fred are taller or shorter than Dale. The new diagram would look like this:

Tall _____ Dale _____ Mary _____ Jane _____ Short
(left)   (right)
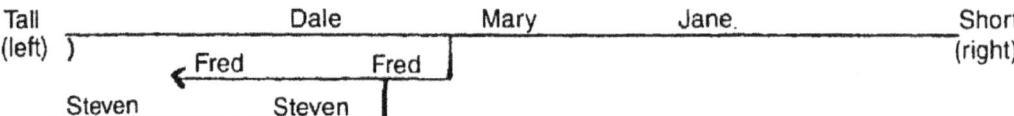

The third sentence introduces Elizabeth, presenting a new problem. Elizabeth can be anywhere to the right of Dale. Don't make the mistake of assuming she falls between Dale and Mary. At this point we don't know where she fits in relation to Mary, Jane, or even Fred.

We do get information about Steven, however. He is taller than Dale so he would be to the left of Dale. Since he is also taller than Fred (see sentence II), we know that Steven is the tallest person thus far. The diagram would now look like this:

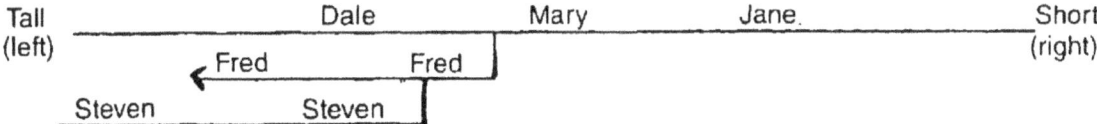

Fred's height is somewhere between Steven and Mary, Elizabeth's anywhere between Dale and the end of the line.

The fourth sentence tells us where Elizabeth stands, in relation to Fred and the others in the problem. The fact that she is taller than Mary means she is also taller than Jane. The final diagram would look like this:

Tall   Steven   Dale   Elizabeth   Mary   Jane   Short
(left)   Fred   (right)

We still don't know whether Dale or Fred is taller, however. Therefore, the conclusion that Dale is taller than Fred can't be proved. It also can't be disproved because we don't know for sure that he isn't. The answer has to be choice C, as the conclusion can't be proved or disproved.

37. The answer is A. This is another problem that is easiest for most people if they make a diagram. Sentence I states that Main Street is between Spring Street and Glenn Blvd. At this point we don't know if they are next to each other or if they are separated by a number of streets. Therefore, you should leave space between streets as you plot your first diagram.

    The order of the streets could go either:

         Spring St.   or   Glenn Blvd.
         Main St.   Main St.
         Glenn Blvd.   Spring St.

    Sentence II states that Hawley Street is one block south of Spring Street and 3 blocks north of Main Street. Because most people think in terms of north as above and south as below and because it was stated that Hawley is one block south of Spring Street and three blocks north of Main Street, the next diagram could look like this:

<u>Spring</u>
<u>Hawley</u>

―――

<u>Main</u>
<u>Glenn</u>

The third sentence states that Glenn Street is five blocks south of Elm and four blocks south of Main. It could look like this:

<u>Spring</u>
<u>Hawley</u>

<u>Elm</u>
<u>Main</u>

―――

―――

<u>Glenn</u>

The conclusion states that Elm Street is between Hawley Avenue and Glenn Blvd. From the above diagram, we can see that this is the case.

38. The answer is B. For most people, the best way to do this problem is to draw a diagram, plotting the course of both trains. Sentence I states that Train A leaves Hampshire at 5:50 A.M. and reaches New London at 6:42. Your first diagram might look like this:

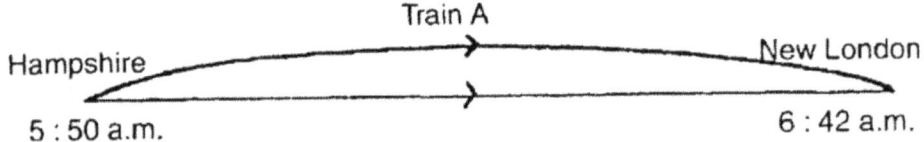

Sentence II states that the train leaves New London at 7:00 a.m. and arrives in Kellogsville at 8:42 a.m. The diagram might now look like this:

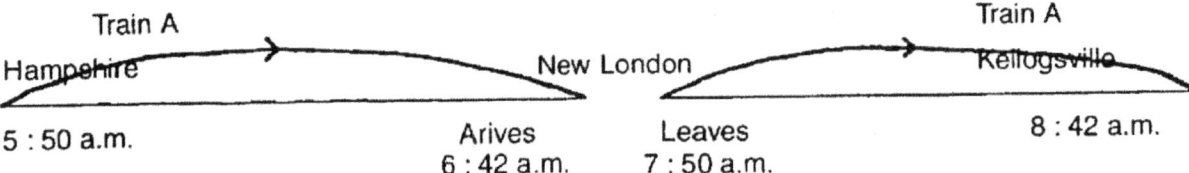

Sentence III gives us the rest of the information that must be included in the diagram. It introduces Train B, which moves in the opposite direction, leaving Kellogsville at 8:00 a.m. and arriving at Hampshire at 10:42 a.m. The final diagram might look like this:

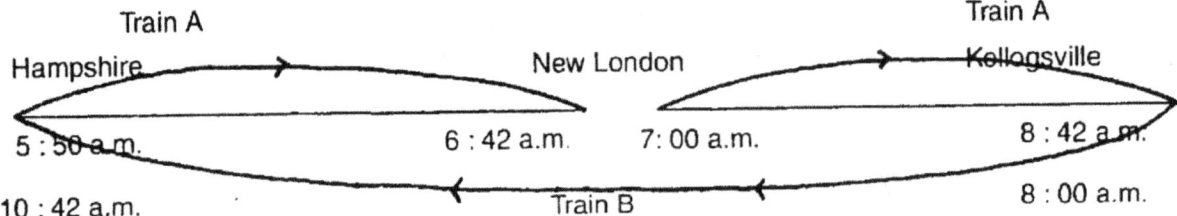

19 (#1)

As you can see from the diagram, the routes of the two trains will overlap somewhere between Kellogsville and New London. If you read sentence IV quickly and assumed that that was the section with only one track, you probably would have assumed that there would have had to be a collision. Sentence IV states, however, that there is only one railroad track between New London and Hampshire. That is the only section, then, where the two trains could collide. By the time Train B gets to that section, however, Train A will have passed it. The two trains will pass each other somewhere between New London and Kellogsville, not New London and Hampshire.

EVALUATING CONCLUSIONS IN LIGHT OF KNOWN FACTS

EXAMINATION SECTION

TEST 1

DIRECTIONS: Each question or incomplete statement is followed by several suggested answers or completions. Select the one that BEST answers the question or completes the statement. *PRINT THE LETTER OF THE CORRECT ANSWER IN THE SPACE AT THE RIGHT.*

Questions 1-9.

DIRECTIONS: In Questions 1 through 9, you will read a set of facts and a conclusion drawn from them. The conclusion may be valid or invalid, based on the facts—it's your task to determine the validity of the conclusion.

For each question, select the letter before the statement that BEST expresses the relationship between the given facts and the conclusion that has been drawn from them. Your choices are:
- A. The facts prove the conclusion;
- B. The facts disprove the conclusion; or
- C. The facts neither prove nor disprove the conclusion.

1. FACTS: If the supervisor retires, James, the assistant supervisor, will not be transferred to another department. James will be promoted to supervisor if he is not transferred. The supervisor retired.

    CONCLUSION: James will be promoted to supervisor.
    - A. The facts prove the conclusion.
    - B. The facts disprove the conclusion.
    - C. The facts neither prove nor disprove the conclusion.

    1.____

2. FACTS: In the town of Luray, every player on the softball team works at Luray National Bank. In addition, every player on the Luray softball team wear glasses.

    CONCLUSIONS: At least some of the people who work at Luray National Bank wear glasses.
    - A. The facts prove the conclusion.
    - B. The facts disprove the conclusion.
    - C. The facts neither prove nor disprove the conclusion.

    2.____

3. FACTS: The only time Henry and June go out to dinner is on an evening when they have childbirth classes. Their childbirth classes meet on Tuesdays and Thursdays.

    3.____

CONCLUSION: Henry and June never go out to dinner on Friday or Saturday.
  A. The facts prove the conclusion.
  B. The facts disprove the conclusion.
  C. The facts neither prove nor disprove the conclusion.

4. FACTS: Every player on the field hockey team has at least one bruise. Everyone on the field hockey team also has scarred knees.

   CONCLUSION: Most people with both bruises and scarred knees are field hockey players.
   A. The facts prove the conclusion.
   B. The facts disprove the conclusion.
   C. The facts neither prove nor disprove the conclusion.

4.____

5. FACTS: In the chess tournament, Lance will win his match against Jane if Jane wins her match against Mathias. If Lance wins his match against Jane, Christine will not win her match against Jane.

   CONCLUSION: Christine will not win her match against Jane if Jane wins her match against Mathias.
   A. The facts prove the conclusion.
   B. The facts disprove the conclusion.
   C. The facts neither prove nor disprove the conclusion.

5.____

6. FACTS: No green lights on the machine are indicators for the belt drive status. Not all of the lights on the machine's upper panel are green. Some lights on the machine's lower panel are green.

   CONCLUSION: The green lights on the machine's lower panel may be indicators for the belt drive status.
   A. The facts prove the conclusion.
   B. The facts disprove the conclusion.
   C. The facts neither prove nor disprove the conclusion.

6.____

7. FACTS: At a small, one-room country school, there are eight students: Amy, Ben, Carla, Dan, Elliot, Francine, Greg, and Hannah. Each student is in either the 6th, 7th, or 8th grade. Either two or three students are in each grade. Amy, Dan, and Francine are all in different grades. Ben and Elliot are both in the 7th grade. Hannah and Carl are in the same grade.

   CONCLUSION: Exactly three students are in the 7th grade.
   A. The facts prove the conclusion.
   B. The facts disprove the conclusion.
   C. The facts neither prove nor disprove the conclusion.

7.____

8. FACTS: Two married couples are having lunch together. Two of the four people are German and two are Russian, but in each couple the nationality of the spouse is not necessarily the same as the other's. One person in the group is a teacher, the other a lawyer, one an engineer, and the other a writer. The teacher is a Russian man. The writer is Russian, and her husband is an engineer. One of the people, Mr. Stern, is German.

   CONCLUSION: Mr. Stern's wife is a writer.
   A. The facts prove the conclusion.
   B. The facts disprove the conclusion.
   C. The facts neither prove nor disprove the conclusion.

8._____

9. FACTS: The flume ride at the county fair is open only to children who are at least 36 inches tall. Lisa is 30 inches tall. John is shorter than Henry, but more than 10 inches taller than Lisa.

   CONCLUSION: Lisa is the only one who can't ride the flume ride.
   A. The facts prove the conclusion.
   B. The facts disprove the conclusion.
   C. The facts neither prove nor disprove the conclusion.

9._____

Questions 10-17.

DIRECTIONS: Questions 10 through 17 are based on the following reading passage. It is not your knowledge of the particular topic that is being tested, but your ability to reason based on what you have read. The passage is likely to detail several proposed courses of action and factors affecting these proposals. The reading passage is followed by a conclusion or outcome based on the facts in the passage, or a description of a decision taken regarding the situation. The conclusion is followed by a number of statements that have a possible connection to the conclusion. For each statement, you are to determine whether:
   A. The statement proves the conclusion.
   B. The statement supports the conclusion but does not prove it.
   C. The statement disproves the conclusion.
   D. The statement weakens the conclusion but does not disprove it.
   E. The statement has no relevance to the conclusion.

   Remember that the conclusion after the passage is to be accepted as the outcome of what actually happened, and that you are being asked to evaluate the impact each statement would have had on the conclusion.

PASSAGE:

The Grand Army of Foreign Wars, a national veteran's organization, is struggling to maintain its National Home, where the widowed spouses and orphans of deceased members are housed together in a small village-like community. The Home is open to spouses and children who are bereaved for any reason, regardless of whether the member's death was related to military service, but a new global conflict has led to a dramatic surge in the number of members' deaths: many veterans who re-enlisted for the conflict have been killed in action.

The Grand Army of Foreign Wars is considering several options for handling the increased number of applications for housing at the National Home, which has been traditionally supported by membership due. At its national convention, it will choose only one of the following:

The first idea is a one-time $50 tax on all members, above and beyond the dues they pay already. Since the organization has more than a million member, this tax should be sufficient for the construction and maintenance of new housing for applicants on the existing grounds of the National Home. The idea is opposed, however, by some older members who live on fixed incomes. These members object in principle to the taxation of Grand Army members. The Grand Army has never imposed a tax on its members.

The second idea is to launch a national fundraising drive the public relations campaign that will attract donations for the National Home. Several national celebrities are members of the organization, and other celebrities could be attracted to the cause. Many Grand Army members are wary of this approach, however: in the past, the net receipts of some fundraising efforts have been relatively insignificant, given the costs of staging them.

A third approach, suggested by many of the younger members, is to have new applicants share some of the costs of construction and maintenance. The spouses and children would pay an up-front "enrollment" fee, based on a sliding scale proportionate to their income and assets, and then a monthly fee adjusted similarly to contribute to maintenance costs. Many older members are strongly opposed to this idea, as it is in direct contradiction to the principles on which the organization was founded more than a century ago.

The fourth option is simply to maintain the status quo, focus the organization's efforts on supporting the families who already live at the National Home, and wait to accept new applicants based on attrition.

CONCLUSION: At its annual national convention, the Grand Army of Foreign Wars votes to impose a one-time tax of $10 on each member for the purpose of expanding and supporting the National Home to welcome a larger number of applicants. The tax is considered to be the solution most likely to produce the funds needed to accommodate the growing number of applicants.

10. Actuarial studies have shown that because the Grand Army's membership consists mostly of older veterans from earlier wars, the organization's membership will suffer a precipitous decline in numbers in about five years.
    A. The statement proves the conclusion.
    B. The statement supports the conclusion but does not prove it.
    C. The statement disproves the conclusion.
    D. The statement weakens the conclusion but does not disprove it.
    E. The statement has no relevance to the conclusion.

10.____

11. After passage of the funding measure, a splinter group of older members appeals for the "sliding scale" provision to be applied to the tax, so that some members may be allowed to contribute less based on their income.
    A. The statement proves the conclusion.
    B. The statement supports the conclusion but does not prove it.
    C. The statement disproves the conclusion.
    D. The statement weakens the conclusion but does not disprove it.
    E. The statement has no relevance to the conclusion.

11.____

5 (#1)

12. The original charter of the Grand Army of Foreign Wars specifically states that the organization will not levy taxes or duties on its members beyond its modest annual dues. It takes a super-majority of attending delegates at the national convention to make alterations to the charter.
    A. The statement proves the conclusion.
    B. The statement supports the conclusion but does not prove it.
    C. The statement disproves the conclusion.
    D. The statement weakens the conclusion but does not disprove it.
    E. The statement has no relevance to the conclusion.

12.____

13. Six months before Grand Army of Foreign Wars' national convention, the Internal Revenue Service rules that because it is an organization that engages in political lobbying, the Grand Army must no longer enjoy its own federal tax-exempt status.
    A. The statement proves the conclusion.
    B. The statement supports the conclusion but does not prove it.
    C. The statement disproves the conclusion.
    D. The statement weakens the conclusion but does not disprove it.
    E. The statement has no relevance to the conclusion.

13.____

14. Two months before the national convention, Dirk Rockwell, arguably the country's most famous film actor, announces in a nationally televised interview that he has been saddened to learn of the plight of the National Home, and that he is going to make it his own personal crusade to see that it is able to house and support a greater number of widowed spouses and orphans in the future.
    A. The statement proves the conclusion.
    B. The statement supports the conclusion but does not prove it.
    C. The statement disproves the conclusion.
    D. The statement weakens the conclusion but does not disprove it.
    E. The statement has no relevance to the conclusion.

14.____

15. The Grand Army's final estimate is that the cost of expanding the National Home to accommodate the increased number of applicants will be about $61 million.
    A. The statement proves the conclusion.
    B. The statement supports the conclusion but does not prove it.
    C. The statement disproves the conclusion.
    D. The statement weakens the conclusion but does not disprove it.
    E. The statement has no relevance to the conclusion.

15.____

16. Just before the national convention, the Federal Department of Veterans Affairs announces steep cuts in the benefits package that is currently offered to the widowed spouses and orphans of veterans.
    A. The statement proves the conclusion.
    B. The statement supports the conclusion but does not prove it.
    C. The statement disproves the conclusion.
    D. The statement weakens the conclusion but does not disprove it.
    E. The statement has no relevance to the conclusion.

16.____

17. After the national convention, the Grand Army of Foreign Wars begins charging a modest "start-up" fee to all families who apply for residence at the national home.
    A. The statement proves the conclusion.
    B. The statement supports the conclusion but does not prove it.
    C. The statement disproves the conclusion.
    D. The statement weakens the conclusion but does not disprove it.
    E. The statement has no relevance to the conclusion.

17.____

Questions 18-25.

DIRECTIONS: Questions 18 through 25 each provide four factual statements and a conclusion based on these statements. After reading the entire question, you will decide whether:
    A. The conclusion is proved by statements I-IV;
    B. The conclusion is disproved by statements I-IV.
    C. The facts are not sufficient to prove or disprove the conclusion.

18. FACTUAL STATEMENTS:
    I. In the Field Day high jump competition, Martha jumped higher than Frank.
    II. Carl jumped higher than Ignacio.
    III. Ignacio jumped higher than Frank.
    IV. Dan jumped higher than Carl.

    CONCLUSION: Frank finished last in the high jump competition.
    A. The conclusion is proved by statements I-IV;
    B. The conclusion is disproved by statements I-IV.
    C. The facts are not sufficient to prove or disprove the conclusion.

18.____

19. FACTUAL STATEMENTS:
    I. The door to the hammer mill chamber is locked if light 6 is red.
    II. The door to the hammer mill chamber is locked only when the mill is operating.
    III. If the mill is not operating, light 6 is blue.
    IV. Light 6 is blue.

    CONCLUSION: The door to the hammer mill chamber is locked.
    A. The conclusion is proved by statements I-IV;
    B. The conclusion is disproved by statements I-IV.
    C. The facts are not sufficient to prove or disprove the conclusion.

19.____

20. FACTUAL STATEMENTS:
    I. Ziegfried, the lion tamer at the circus, has demanded ten additional minutes of performance time during each show.
    II. If Ziegfried is allowed his ten additional minutes per show, he will attempt to teach Kimba the tiger to shoot a basketball.
    III. If Kimba learns how to shoot a basketball, then Ziegfried was not given his ten additional minutes.
    IV. Ziegfried was given his ten additional minutes.

20.____

7 (#1)

CONCLUSION: Despite Ziegfried's efforts, Kimba did not learn how to shoot a basketball.
   A. The conclusion is proved by statements I-IV;
   B. The conclusion is disproved by statements I-IV.
   C. The facts are not sufficient to prove or disprove the conclusion.

21. FACTUAL STATEMENTS:
   I. If Stan goes to counseling, Sara won't divorce him.
   II. If Sara divorces Stan, she'll move back to Texas.
   III. If Sara doesn't divorce Stan, Irene will be disappointed.
   IV. Stan goes to counseling.

   CONCLUSION: Irene will be disappointed.
   A. The conclusion is proved by statements I-IV;
   B. The conclusion is disproved by statements I-IV.
   C. The facts are not sufficient to prove or disprove the conclusion.

21.____

22. FACTUAL STATEMENTS:
   I. If Delia is promoted to district manager, Claudia will have to be promoted to team leader.
   II. Delia will be promoted to district manager unless she misses her fourth-quarter sales quota.
   III. If Claudia is promoted to team leader, Thomas will be promoted to assistant team leader.
   IV. Delia meets her fourth-quarter sales quota.

   CONCLUSION: Thomas is promoted to assistant team leader.
   A. The conclusion is proved by statements I-IV;
   B. The conclusion is disproved by statements I-IV.
   C. The facts are not sufficient to prove or disprove the conclusion.

22.____

23. FACTUAL STATEMENTS:
   I. Clone D is identical to Clone B.
   II. Clone B is not identical to Clone A.
   III. Clone D is not identical to Clone C.
   IV. Clone E is not identical to the clones that are identical to Clone B.

   CONCLUSION: Clone E is identical to Clone D.
   A. The conclusion is proved by statements I-IV;
   B. The conclusion is disproved by statements I-IV.
   C. The facts are not sufficient to prove or disprove the conclusion.

23.____

24. FACTUAL STATEMENTS:
   I. In the Stafford Tower, each floor is occupied by a single business.
   II. Big G Staffing is on a floor between CyberGraphics and MainEvent.
   III. Gasco is on the floor directly below CyberGraphics and three floors above Treehorn Audio.
   IV. MainEvent is five floors below EZ Tax and four floors below Treehorn Audio.

24.____

8 (#1)

CONCLUSION: EZ Tax is on a floor between Gasco and MainEvent.
 A. The conclusion is proved by statements I-IV;
 B. The conclusion is disproved by statements I-IV.
 C. The facts are not sufficient to prove or disprove the conclusion.

25. FACTUAL STATEMENTS: 25.____
 I. Only county roads lead to Nicodemus.
 II. All the roads from Hill City to Graham County are federal highways.
 III. Some of the roads from Plainville lead to Nicodemus.
 IV. Some of the roads running from Hill City lead to Strong City.

CONCLUSION: Some of the roads from Plainville are county roads.
 A. The conclusion is proved by statements I-IV;
 B. The conclusion is disproved by statements I-IV.
 C. The facts are not sufficient to prove or disprove the conclusion.

KEY (CORRECT ANSWERS)

1.	A		11.	A
2.	A		12.	D
3.	A		13.	E
4.	C		14.	D
5.	A		15.	B
6.	B		16.	B
7.	A		17.	C
8.	A		18.	A
9.	A		19.	B
10.	E		20.	A

21.	A
22.	A
23.	B
24.	A
25.	A

SOLUTIONS TO PROBLEMS

1. **CORRECT ANSWER: A**
   Given Statement 3, we deduce that James will not be transferred to another department. By Statement 2, we can conclude that James will be promoted.

2. **CORRECT ANSWER: A**
   Since every player on the softball team wears glasses, these individuals compose some of the people who work at the bank. Although not every person who works at the bank plays softball, those bank employees who do play softball wear glasses.

3. **CORRECT ANSWER: A**
   If Henry and June go out to dinner, we conclude that it must be on Tuesday or Thursday, which are the only two days when they have childbirth classes. This implies that if it is not Tuesday or Thursday, then this couple does not go out to dinner.

4. **CORRECT ANSWER: C**
   We can only conclude that if a person plays on the field hockey team, then he or she has both bruises and scarred knees. But there are probably a great number of people who have both bruises and scarred knees but do not play on the field hockey team. The given conclusion can neither be proven or disproven.

5. **CORRECT ANSWER: A**
   From statement 1, if Jane beats Mathias, then Lance will beat Jane. Using statement 2, we can then conclude that Christine will not win her match against Jane.

6. **CORRECT ANSWER: B**
   Statement 1 tells us that no green light can be an indicator of the belt drive status. Thus, the given conclusion must be false.

7. **CORRECT ANSWER: A**
   We already know that Ben and Elliot are in the 7th grade. Even though Hannah and Carl are in the same grade, it cannot be the 7th grade because we would then have at least four students in this 7th grade. This would contradict the third statement, which states that either two or three students are in each grade. Since Amy, Dan, and Francine are in different grade, exactly one of them must be in the 7th grade. Thus, Ben, Elliot, and exactly one of Amy, Dan, and Francine are the three students in the 7th grade.

8. **CORRECT ANSWER: A**
   One man is a teacher, who is Russian. We know that the writer is female and is Russian. Since her husband is an engineer, he cannot be the Russian teacher. Thus, her husband is of German descent, namely Mr. Stern. This means that Mr. Stern's wife is the writer. Note that one couple consists of a male Russian teacher and a female German lawyer. The other couple consists of a male German engineer and a female Russian writer.

10 (#1)

9. CORRECT ANSWER: A
Since John is more than 10 inches taller than Lisa, his height is at least 46 inches. Also, John is shorter than Henry, so Henry's height must be greater than 46 inches. Thus, Lisa is the only one whose height is less than 36 inches. Therefore, she is the only one who is not allowed on the flume ride.

18. CORRECT ANSWER: A
Dan jumped higher than Carl, who jumped higher than Ignacio, who jumped higher than Frank. Since Martha jumped higher than Frank, every person jumped higher than Frank. Thus, Frank finished last.

19. CORRECT ANSWER: B
If the light is red, then the door is locked. If the door is locked, then the mill is operating. Reversing the logical sequence of these statements, if the mill is not operating, then the door is not locked, which means that the light is blue. Thus, the given conclusion is disproved.

20. CORRECT ANSWER: A
Using the contrapositive of statement III, Ziegfried was given his ten additional minutes, then Kimba did not learn how to shoot a basketball. Since statement IV is factual, the conclusion is proved.

21. CORRECT ANSWER: A
From Statements IV and I, we conclude that Sara doesn't divorce Stan. Then statement III reveals that Irene will be disappointed. Thus, the conclusion is proved.

22. CORRECT ANSWER: A
Statement II can be rewritten as "Delia is promoted to district manager or she misses her sales quota." Furthermore, this statement is equivalent to "If Delia makes her sales quota, then she is promoted to district manager." From statement I, we conclude that Claudia is promoted to team leader. Finally, by statement III, Thomas is promoted to assistant team leader.

23. CORRECT ANSWER: B
By statement IV, Clone E is not identical to any clones identical to Clone B. Statement I tells us that Clones B and D are identical. Therefore, Clone E cannot be identical to Clone D. The conclusion is disproved.

24. CORRECT ANSWER: A
Based on all four statements, CyberGraphics is somewhere below MainEvent. Gasco is one floor below CyberGraphics. EZ Tax is two floors below Gasco. Treehorn Audio is one floor below EZ Tax. MainEvent is four floors below Treehorn Audio. Thus, EZ Tax is two floors below Gasco and five floors above MainEvent. The conclusion is proved.

25. CORRECT ANSWER: A
From statement III, we know that some of the roads from Plainville lead to Nicodemus. But statement I tells us that only county roads lead to Nicodemus. Therefore, some of the roads from Plainville must be county roads. The conclusion is proved.

TEST 2

DIRECTIONS: Each question or incomplete statement is followed by several suggested answers or completions. Select the one that BEST answers the question or completes the statement. *PRINT THE LETTER OF THE CORRECT ANSWER IN THE SPACE AT THE RIGHT.*

Questions 1-9.

DIRECTIONS: In Questions 1 through 9, you will read a set of facts and a conclusion drawn from them. The conclusion may be valid or invalid, based on the facts—it's your task to determine the validity of the conclusion.

For each question, select the letter before the statement that BEST expresses the relationship between the given facts and the conclusion that has been drawn from them. Your choices are:
    A. The facts prove the conclusion;
    B. The facts disprove the conclusion; or
    C. The facts neither prove nor disprove the conclusion.

1. FACTS: Some employees in the testing department are statisticians. Most of the statisticians who work in the testing department are projection specialists. Tom Wilks works in the testing department.

   CONCLUSION: Tom Wilks is a statistician.
   A. The facts prove the conclusion.
   B. The facts disprove the conclusion.
   C. The facts neither prove nor disprove the conclusion.

2. FACTS: Ten coins are split among Hank, Lawrence, and Gail. If Lawrence gives his coins to Hank, then Hank will have more coins than Gail. If Gail gives her coins to Lawrence, then Lawrence will have more coins than Hank.

   CONCLUSION: Hank has six coins.
   A. The facts prove the conclusion.
   B. The facts disprove the conclusion.
   C. The facts neither prove nor disprove the conclusion.

3. FACTS: Nobody loves everybody. Janet loves Ken. Ken loves everybody who loves Janet.

   CONCLUSION: Everybody loves Janet.
   A. The facts prove the conclusion.
   B. The facts disprove the conclusion.
   C. The facts neither prove nor disprove the conclusion.

4. FACTS: Most of the Torres family lives in East Los Angeles. Many people in East Los Angeles celebrate Cinco de Mayo. Joe is a member of the Torres family.

   CONCLUSION: Joe lives in East Los Angeles.
   A. The facts prove the conclusion.
   B. The facts disprove the conclusion.
   C. The facts neither prove nor disprove the conclusion.

   4.____

5. FACTS: Five professionals each occupy one story of a five-story office building. Dr. Kane's office is above Dr. Assad's. Dr. Johnson's office is between Dr. Kane's and Dr. Conlon's. Dr. Steen's office is between Dr. Conlon's and Dr. Assad's. Dr. Johnson is on the fourth story.

   CONCLUSION: Dr. Kane occupies the top story.
   A. The facts prove the conclusion.
   B. The facts disprove the conclusion.
   C. The facts neither prove nor disprove the conclusion.

   5.____

6. FACTS: To be eligible for membership in the Yukon Society, a person must be able to either tunnel through a snowbank while wearing only a T-shirt and short, or hold his breath for two minutes under water that is 50°F. Ray can only hold his breath for a minute and a half.

   CONCLUSION: Ray can still become a member of the Yukon Society by tunneling through a snowbank while wearing a T-shirt and shorts.
   A. The facts prove the conclusion.
   B. The facts disprove the conclusion.
   C. The facts neither prove nor disprove the conclusion.

   6.____

7. FACTS: A mark is worth five plunks. You can exchange four sharps for a tinplot. It takes eight marks to buy a sharp.

   CONCLUSION: A sharp is the most valuable.
   A. The facts prove the conclusion.
   B. The facts disprove the conclusion.
   C. The facts neither prove nor disprove the conclusion.

   7.____

8. FACTS: There are gibbons, as well as lemurs, who like to play in the trees at the monkey house. All those who like to play in the trees at the monkey house are fed lettuce and bananas.

   CONCLUSION: Lemurs and gibbons are types of monkeys.
   A. The facts prove the conclusion.
   B. The facts disprove the conclusion.
   C. The facts neither prove nor disprove the conclusion.

   8.____

9. FACTS: None of the Blackfoot tribes is a Salishan Indian tribe. Salishan Indians came from the northern Pacific Coast. All Salishan Indians live each of the Continental Divide.

CONCLUSION: No Blackfoot tribes live east of the Continental Divide.
A. The facts prove the conclusion.
B. The facts disprove the conclusion.
C. The facts neither prove nor disprove the conclusion.

Questions 10-17.

DIRECTIONS: Questions 10 through 17 are based on the following reading passage. It is not your knowledge of the particular topic that is being tested, but your ability to reason based on what you have read. The passage is likely to detail several proposed courses of action and factors affecting these proposals. The reading passage is followed by a conclusion or outcome based on the facts in the passage, or a description of a decision taken regarding the situation. The conclusion is followed by a number of statements that have a possible connection to the conclusion. For each statement, you are to determine whether:
A. The statement proves the conclusion.
B. The statement supports the conclusion but does not prove it.
C. The statement disproves the conclusion.
D. The statement weakens the conclusion but does not disprove it.
E. The statement has no relevance to the conclusion.

Remember that the conclusion after the passage is to be accepted as the outcome of what actually happened, and that you are being asked to evaluate the impact each statement would have had on the conclusion.

PASSAGE:

On August 12, Beverly Willey reported that she was in the elevator late on the previous evening after leaving her office on the 16th floor of a large office building. In her report, she states that a man got on the elevator at the 11th floor, pulled her off the elevator, assaulted her, and stole her purse. Ms. Willey reported that she had seen the man in the elevators and hallways of the building before. She believes that the man works in the building. Her description of him is as follows: he is tall, unshaven, with wavy brown hair and a scar on his left cheek. He walks with a pronounced limp, often dragging his left foot behind his right.

CONCLUSION: After Beverly Willey makes her report, the police arrest a 43-year-old man, Barton Black, and charge him with her assault.

10. Barton Black is a former Marine who served in Vietnam, where he sustained shrapnel wounds to the left side of his face and suffered nerve damage in his left leg.
    A. The statement proves the conclusion.
    B. The statement supports the conclusion but does not prove it.
    C. The statement disproves the conclusion.
    D. The statement weakens the conclusion but does not disprove it.
    E. The statement has no relevance to the conclusion.

11. When they arrived at his residence to question him, detectives were greeted at the door by Barton Black, who was tall and clean-shaven.
    A. The statement proves the conclusion.
    B. The statement supports the conclusion but does not prove it.
    C. The statement disproves the conclusion.
    D. The statement weakens the conclusion but does not disprove it.
    E. The statement has no relevance to the conclusion.

12. Barton Black was booked into the county jail several days after Beverly Willey's assault.
    A. The statement proves the conclusion.
    B. The statement supports the conclusion but does not prove it.
    C. The statement disproves the conclusion.
    D. The statement weakens the conclusion but does not disprove it.
    E. The statement has no relevance to the conclusion.

13. Upon further investigation, detectives discover that Beverly Willey does not work at the office building.
    A. The statement proves the conclusion.
    B. The statement supports the conclusion but does not prove it.
    C. The statement disproves the conclusion.
    D. The statement weakens the conclusion but does not disprove it.
    E. The statement has no relevance to the conclusion.

14. Upon further investigation, detectives discover that Barton Black does not work at the office building.
    A. The statement proves the conclusion.
    B. The statement supports the conclusion but does not prove it.
    C. The statement disproves the conclusion.
    D. The statement weakens the conclusion but does not disprove it.
    E. The statement has no relevance to the conclusion.

15. In the spring of the following year, Barton Black is convicted of assaulting Beverly Willey on August 11.
    A. The statement proves the conclusion.
    B. The statement supports the conclusion but does not prove it.
    C. The statement disproves the conclusion.
    D. The statement weakens the conclusion but does not disprove it.
    E. The statement has no relevance to the conclusion.

16. During their investigation of the assault, detectives determine that Beverly Willey was assaulted on the 12th floor of the office building. 16._____
    A. The statement proves the conclusion.
    B. The statement supports the conclusion but does not prove it.
    C. The statement disproves the conclusion.
    D. The statement weakens the conclusion but does not disprove it.
    E. The statement has no relevance to the conclusion.

17. The day after Beverly Willey's assault, Barton Black fled the area and was never seen again. 17._____
    A. The statement proves the conclusion.
    B. The statement supports the conclusion but does not prove it.
    C. The statement disproves the conclusion.
    D. The statement weakens the conclusion but does not disprove it.
    E. The statement has no relevance to the conclusion.

Questions 18-25.

DIRECTIONS: Questions 18 through 25 each provide four factual statements and a conclusion based on these statements. After reading the entire question, you will decide whether:
    A. The conclusion is proved by statements I-IV;
    B. The conclusion is disproved by statements I-IV.
    C. The facts are not sufficient to prove or disprove the conclusion.

18. FACTUAL STATEMENTS: 18._____
    I. Among five spice jars on the shelf, the sage is to the right of the parsley.
    II. The pepper is to the left of the basil.
    III. The nutmeg is between the sage and the pepper.
    IV. The pepper is the second spice from the left.

    CONCLUSION: The safe is the farthest to the right.
    A. The conclusion is proved by statements I-IV;
    B. The conclusion is disproved by statements I-IV.
    C. The facts are not sufficient to prove or disprove the conclusion.

19. FACTUAL STATEMENTS: 19._____
    I. Gear X rotates in a clockwise direction if Switch C is in the OFF position.
    II. Gear X will rotate in a counter-clockwise direction is Switch C is ON.
    III. If Gear X is rotating in a clockwise direction, then Gear Y will not be rotating at all.
    IV. Switch C is ON.

    CONCLUSION: Gear X is rotating in a counter-clockwise direction.
    A. The conclusion is proved by statements I-IV;
    B. The conclusion is disproved by statements I-IV.
    C. The facts are not sufficient to prove or disprove the conclusion.

20. FACTUAL STATEMENTS:
   I. Lane will leave for the Toronto meeting today only if Terence, Rourke, and Jackson all file their marketing reports by the end of the work day.
   II. Rourke will file her report on time only if Ganz submits last quarter's data.
   III. If Terence attends the security meeting, he will attend it with Jackson, and they will not file their marketing reports by the end of the work day.

   CONCLUSION: Lane will leave for the Toronto meeting today.
   A. The conclusion is proved by statements I-IV;
   B. The conclusion is disproved by statements I-IV.
   C. The facts are not sufficient to prove or disprove the conclusion.

21. FACTUAL STATEMENTS:
   I. Bob is in second place in the Boston Marathon.
   II. Gregory is winning the Boston Marathon.
   III. There are four miles to go in the race, and Bob is gaining on Gregory at the rate of 100 yards every minute.
   IV. There are 1760 yards in a mile and Gregory's usual pace during the Boston Marathon is one mile every six minutes.

   CONCLUSION: Bob wins the Boston Marathon.
   A. The conclusion is proved by statements I-IV;
   B. The conclusion is disproved by statements I-IV.
   C. The facts are not sufficient to prove or disprove the conclusion.

22. FACTUAL STATEMENTS:
   I. Four brothers are named Earl, John, Gary, and Pete.
   II. Earl and Pete are unmarried.
   III. John is shorter than the youngest of the four.
   IV. The oldest brother is married, and is also the tallest.

   CONCLUSION: Gary is the oldest brother.
   A. The conclusion is proved by statements I-IV;
   B. The conclusion is disproved by statements I-IV.
   C. The facts are not sufficient to prove or disprove the conclusion.

23. FACTUAL STATEMENTS:
   I. Brigade X is ten miles from the demilitarized zone.
   II. If General Woundwort gives the order, Brigade X will advance to the demilitarized zone, but not quickly enough to reach the zone before the conflict begins.
   III. Brigade Y, five miles behind Brigade X, will not advance unless General Woundwort gives the order.
   IV. Brigade Y advances.

CONCLUSION: Brigade X reaches the demilitarized zone before the conflict begins.
   A. The conclusion is proved by statements I-IV;
   B. The conclusion is disproved by statements I-IV.
   C. The facts are not sufficient to prove or disprove the conclusion.

24. FACTUAL STATEMENTS:
   I. Jerry has decided to take a cab from Fullerton to Elverton.
   II. Chubby Cab charges $5 plus $3 a mile.
   III. Orange Cab charges $7.50 but gives free mileage for the first 5 miles.
   IV. After the first 5 miles, Orange Cab charges $2.50 a mile.

   CONCLUSION: Orange Cab is the cheaper fare from Fullerton to Elverton.
   A. The conclusion is proved by statements I-IV;
   B. The conclusion is disproved by statements I-IV.
   C. The facts are not sufficient to prove or disprove the conclusion.

25. FACTUAL STATEMENTS:
   I. Dan is never in class when his friend Lucy is absent.
   II. Lucy is never absent unless her mother is sick.
   III. If Lucy is in class, Sergio is in class also.
   IV. Sergio is never in class when Dalton is absent.

   CONCLUSION: If Lucy is absent, Dalton may be in class.
   A. The conclusion is proved by statements I-IV;
   B. The conclusion is disproved by statements I-IV.
   C. The facts are not sufficient to prove or disprove the conclusion.

KEY (CORRECT ANSWERS)

1.	C	11.	E
2.	B	12.	B
3.	B	13.	D
4.	C	14.	E
5.	A	15.	A
6.	A	16.	E
7.	B	17.	C
8.	C	18.	B
9.	C	19.	A
10.	B	20.	C

21. C
22. A
23. B
24. A
25. B

SOLUTIONS TO PROBLEMS

1. CORRECT ANSWER: C
   Statement 1 only tells us that some employees who work in the Testing Department are statisticians. This means that we need to allow the possibility that at least one person in this department is not a statistician. Thus, if a person works in the Testing Department, we cannot conclude whether or not this individual is a statistician.

2. CORRECT ANSWER: B
   If Hank had six coins, then the total of Gail's collection and Lawrence's collection would be four. Thus, if Gail gave all her coins to Lawrence, Lawrence would only have four coins. Thus, it would be impossible for Lawrence to have more coins than Hank.

3. CORRECT ANSWER: B
   Statement 1 tells us that nobody loves everybody. If everybody loved Janet, then Statement 3 would imply that Ken loves everybody. This would contradict statement 1. The conclusion is disproved.

4. CORRECT ANSWER: C
   Although most of the Torres family lives in East Los Angeles, we can assume that some members of this family do not live in East Los Angeles. Thus, we cannot prove or disprove that Joe, who is a member of the Torres family, lives in East Los Angeles.

5. CORRECT ANSWER: A
   Since Dr. Johnson is on the 4th floor, either (a) Dr. Kane is on the 5th floor and Dr. Conlon is on the 3rd floor, or (b) Dr. Kane is on the 3rd floor and Dr. Conlon is on the 5th floor. If option (b) were correct, then since Dr. Assad would be on the 1st floor, it would be impossible for Dr. Steen's office to be between Dr. Conlon and Dr. Assad's office. Therefore, Dr. Kane's office must be on the 5th floor. The order of the doctors' offices, from 5th floor down to the 1st floor is: Dr. Kane, Dr. Johnson, Dr. Conlon, Dr. Steen, Dr. Assad.

6. CORRECT ANSWER: A
   Ray does not satisfy the requirement of holding his breath for two minutes under water, since he can only hold is breath for one minute in that setting. But if he tunnels through a snowbank with just a T-shirt and shorts, he will satisfy the eligibility requirement. Note that the eligibility requirement contains the key word "or." So only one of the two clauses separated by "or" need to be fulfilled.

7. CORRECT ANSWER: B
   Statement 2 says that four sharps is equivalent to one tinplot. This means that a tinplot is worth more than a sharp. The conclusion is disproved. We note that the order of these items, from most valuable to least valuable are: tinplot, sharp, mark, plunk.

8. CORRECT ANSWER: C
   We can only conclude that gibbons and lemurs are fed lettuce and bananas. We can neither prove nor disprove that these animals are types of monkeys.

9. **CORRECT ANSWER: C**
We know that all Salishan Indians live east of the Continental Divide. But some non-members of this tribe of Indians may also live east of the Continental Divide. Since none of the members of the Blackfoot tribe belong to the Salishan Indian tribe, we cannot draw any conclusion about the location of the Blackfoot tribe with respect to the Continental Divide.

18. **CORRECT ANSWER: B**
Since the pepper is second from the left and the nutmeg is between the sage and the pepper, the positions 2, 3, and 4 (from the left) are pepper, nutmeg, sage. By statement II, the basil must be in position 5, which implies that the parsley is in position 1. Therefore, the basil, not the sage, is farthest to the right. The conclusion disproved.

19. **CORRECT ANSWER: A**
Statement II assures us that if switch C is ON, then Gear X is rotating in a counterclockwise direction. The conclusion is proved.

20. **CORRECT ANSWER: C**
Based on Statement IV, followed by Statement II, we conclude that Ganz and Rourke will file their reports on time. Statement III reveals that if Terence and Jackson attend the security meeting, they will fail to file their reports on time. We have no further information if Terence and Jackson attended the security meeting, so we are not able to either confirm or deny that their reports were filed on time. This implies that we cannot know for certain that Lane will leave for his meeting in Toronto.

21. **CORRECT ANSWER: C**
Although Bob is in second place behind Gregory, we cannot deduce how far behind Gregory he is running. At Gregory's current pace, he will cover four miles in 24 minutes. If Bob were only 100 yards behind Gregory, he would catch up to Gregory in one minute. But if Bob were very far behind Gregory, for example 5 miles, this is the equivalent of $(5)(1760) = 8800$ yards. Then Bob would need $8800/100 = 88$ minutes to catch up to Gregory. Thus, the given facts are not sufficient to draw a conclusion.

22. **CORRECT ANSWER: A**
Statement II tells us that neither Earl nor Pete could be the oldest; also, either John or Gary is married. Statement IV reveals that the oldest brother is both married and the tallest. By Statement III, John cannot be the tallest. Since John is not the tallest, he is not the oldest. Thus, the oldest brother must be Gary. The conclusion is proved.

23. **CORRECT ANSWER: B**
By Statements III and IV, General Woundwort must have given the order to advance. Statement II then tells us that Brigade X will advance to the demilitarized zone, but not soon enough before the conflict begins. Thus, the conclusion is disproved.

11 (#2)

24. CORRECT ANSWER: A
If the distance is 5 miles or less, then the cost for the Orange Cab is only $7.50, whereas the cost for the Chubby Cab is $5 + 3x, where x represents the number of miles traveled. For 1 to 5 miles, the cost of the Chubby Cab is between $8 and $20. This means that for a distance of 5 miles, the Orange Cab costs $7.50, whereas the Chubby Cab costs $20. After 5 miles, the cost per mile of the Chubby Cab exceeds the cost per mile of the Orange Cab. Thus, regardless of the actual distance between Fullerton and Elverton, the cost for the Orange Cab will be cheaper than that of the Chubby Cab.

25. CORRECT ANSWER: B
It looks like "Dalton" should be replaced by "Dan" in the conclusion. Then by statement I, if Lucy is absent, Dan is never in class. Thus, the conclusion is disproved.

REPORT WRITING

EXAMINATION SECTION

TEST 1

DIRECTIONS: Each question or incomplete statement is followed by several suggested answers or completions. Select the one that BEST answers the question or completes the statement. *PRINT THE LETTER OF THE CORRECT ANSWER IN THE SPACE AT THE RIGHT.*

Questions 1-4.

DIRECTIONS: Answer Questions 1 through 4 on the basis of the following report which was prepared by a supervisor for inclusion in his agency's annual report.

Line #
1   On Oct. 13, I was assigned to study the salaries paid.
2   to clerical employees in various titles by the city and by
3   private industry in the area.
4   In order to get the data I needed, I called Mr. Johnson at
5   the Bureau of the Budget and the payroll officers at X Corp.—
6   a brokerage house, Y Co. —an insurance company, and Z Inc. —
7   a publishing firm. None of them was available and I had to call
8   all of them again the next day.
9   When I finally got the information I needed, I drew up a
10 chart, which is attached. Note that not all of the companies I
11 contacted employed people at all the different levels used in the
12 city service.
13 The conclusions I draw from analyzing this information is
14 as follows: The city's entry-level salary is about average for
15 the region; middle-level salaries are generally higher in the
16 city government plan than in private industry; but salaries at the
17 highest levels in private industry are better than city em-
18 ployees' pay.

1. Which of the following criticisms about the style in which this report is written is MOST valid?
   A. It is too informal.
   B. It is too concise.
   C. It is too choppy.
   D. The syntax is too complex.

1._____

2. Judging from the statements made in the report, the method followed by this employee in performing his research was
   A. *good*; he contacted a representative sample of businesses in the area
   B. *poor*; he should have drawn more definite conclusions
   C. *good*; he was persistent in collecting information
   D. *poor*; he did not make a thorough study

2._____

43

3. One sentence in this report contains a grammatical error. This sentence begins on line number
   A. 4   B. 7   C. 10   D. 14

4. The type of information given in this report which should be presented in footnotes or in an appendix is the
   A. purpose of the study
   B. specifics about the businesses contacted
   C. reference to the chart
   D. conclusions drawn by the author

5. The use of a graph to show statistical data in a report is SUPERIOR to a table because it
   A. features approximations
   B. emphasizes facts and relationships more dramatically
   C. presents data more accurately
   D. is easily understood by the average reader

6. Of the following, the degree of formality required of a written report in tone is MOST likely to depend on the
   A. subject matter of the report
   B. frequency of its occurrence
   C. amount of time available for its preparation
   D. audience for whom the report is intended

7. Of the following, a distinguishing characteristic of a written report intended for the head of your agency as compared to a report prepared for a lower-echelon staff member is that the report for the agency head should USUALLY include
   A. considerably more detail, especially statistical data
   B. the essential details in an abbreviated form
   C. all available source material
   D. an annotated bibliography

8. Assume that you are asked to write a lengthy report for use by the administrator of your agency, the subject of which is "The Impact of Proposed New Data Processing Operation on Line Personnel" in your agency. You decide that the *most* appropriate type of report for you to prepare is an analytical report, including recommendations.
   The MAIN reason for your decision is that
   A. the subject of the report is extremely complex
   B. large sums of money are involved
   C. the report is being prepared for the administrator
   D. you intend to include charts and graphs

9. Assume that you are preparing a report based on a survey dealing with the attitudes of employees in Division X regarding proposed new changes in compensating employees for working overtime. Three percent of the respondents to the survey voluntarily offer an unfavorable opinion on the method of assigning overtime work, a question not specifically asked of the employees.
   On the basis of this information, the MOST appropriate and significant of the following comments for you to make in the report with regard to employees' attitudes on assigning overtime work is that
   A. an insignificant percentage of employees dislike the method of assigning overtime work
   B. three percent of the employees in Division X dislike the method of assigning overtime work
   C. three percent of the sample selected for the survey voiced an unfavorable opinion on the method of assigning overtime work
   D. some employees voluntarily voiced negative feelings about the method of assigning overtime work, making it impossible to determine the extent of this attitude

9._____

10. A supervisor should be able to prepare a report that is well-written and unambiguous.
    Of the following sentences that might appear in a report, select the one which communicates MOST clearly the intent of its author.
    A. When your subordinates speak to a group of people, they should be well-informed.
    B. When he asked him to leave, SanMan King told him that he would refuse the request.
    C. Because he is a good worker, Foreman Jefferson assigned Assistant Foreman D'Agostino to replace him.
    D. Each of us is responsible for the actions of our subordinates.

10._____

11. In some reports, especially longer ones, a list of the resources (books, papers, magazines, etc.) used to prepare it is included. This list is called the
    A. accreditation   B. bibliography
    C. summary   D. glossary

11._____

12. Reports are usually divided into several sections, some of which are more necessary than others.
    Of the following, the section which is ABSOLUTELY necessary to include in a report is
    A. a table of contents   B. the body
    C. an index   D. a bibliography

12._____

13. Suppose you are writing a report on an interview you have just completed with a particularly hostile applicant.
    Which of the following BEST describes what you should include in this report?
    A. What you think caused the applicant's hostile attitude during the interview
    B. Specific examples of the applicant's hostile remarks and behavior
    C. The relevant information uncovered during the interview
    D. A recommendation that the applicant's request be denied because of his hostility

14. When including recommendations in a report to your supervisor, which of the following is MOST important for you to do?
    A. Provide several alternative courses of action for each recommendation
    B. First present the supporting evidence, then the recommendations
    C. First present the recommendations, then the supporting evidence
    D. Make sure the recommendations arise logically out of the information in the report

15. It is often necessary that the writer of a report present facts and sufficient arguments to gain acceptance of the points, conclusions, or recommendations set forth in the report.
    Of the following, the LEAST advisable step to take in organizing a report, when such argumentation is the important factor, is a(n)
    A. elaborate expression of personal belief
    B. businesslike discussion of the problem as a whole
    C. orderly arrangement of convincing data
    D. reasonable explanation of the primary issues

16. In some types of reports, visual aids add interest, meaning, and support. They also provide an essential means of effectively communicating the message of the report.
    Of the following, the selection of the suitable visual aids to use with a report is LEAST dependent on the
    A. nature and scope of the report
    B. way in which the aid is to be used
    C. aid used in other reports
    D. prospective readers of the report

17. Visual aids used in a report may be placed either in the text material or in the appendix.
    Deciding where to put a chart, table, or any such aid should depend on the
    A. title of the report   B. purpose of the visual aid
    C. title of the visual aid   D. length of the report

18. A report is often revised several times before final preparation and distribution in an effort to make certain the report meets the needs of the situation for which it is designed.
    Which of the following is the BEST way for the author to be sure that a report covers the areas he intended?

A. Obtain a coworker's opinion
B. Compare it with a content checklist
C. Test it on a subordinate
D. Check his bibliography

19. In which of the following situations is an oral report preferable to a written report? When a(n)
    A. recommendation is being made for a future plan of action
    B. department head requests immediate information
    C. long-standing policy change is made
    D. analysis of complicated statistical data is involved

19.____

20. When an applicant is approved, the supervisor must fill in standard forms with certain information.
    The GREATEST advantage of using standard forms in this situation rather than having the supervisor write the report as he sees fit is that
    A. the report can be acted on quickly
    B. the report can be written without directions from a supervisor
    C. needed information is less likely to be left out of the report
    D. information that is written up this way is more likely to be verified

20.____

21. Assume that it is part of your job to prepare a monthly report for your unit head that eventually goes to the director. The report contains information on the number of applicants you have interviewed that have been approved and the number of applicants you have interviewed that have been turned down.
    Errors on such reports are serious because
    A. you are expected to be able to prove how many applicants you have interviewed each month
    B. accurate statistics are needed for effective management of the department
    C. they may not be discovered before the report is transmitted to the director
    D. they may result in loss to the applicants left out of the report

21.____

22. The frequency with which job reports are submitted should depend MAINLY on
    A. how comprehensive the report has to be
    B. the amount of information in the report
    C. the availability of an experienced man to write the report
    D. the importance of changes in the information included in the report

22.____

23. The CHIEF purpose in preparing an outline for a report is usually to insure that
    A. the report will be grammatically correct
    B. every point will be given equal emphasis
    C. principal and secondary points will be properly integrated
    D. the language of the report will be of the same level and include the same technical terms

23.____

24. The MAIN reason for requiring written job reports is to
    A. avoid the necessity of oral orders
    B. develop better methods of doing the work
    C. provide a permanent record of what was done
    D. increase the amount of work that can be done

    24.____

25. Assume you are recommending in a report to your supervisor that a radical change in a standard maintenance procedure should be adopted.
    Of the following, the MOST important information to be included in this report is
    A. a list of the reasons for making this change
    B. the names of others who favor the change
    C. a complete description of the present procedure
    D. amount of training time needed for the new procedure

    25.____

KEY (CORRECT ANSWERS)

1.	A		11.	B
2.	D		12.	B
3.	D		13.	C
4.	B		14.	D
5.	B		15.	A
6.	D		16.	C
7.	B		17.	B
8.	A		18.	B
9.	D		19.	B
10.	D		20.	C

21. B
22. D
23. C
24. C
25. A

TEST 2

DIRECTIONS: Each question or incomplete statement is followed by several suggested answers or completions. Select the one that BEST answers the question or completes the statement. *PRINT THE LETTER OF THE CORRECT ANSWER IN THE SPACE AT THE RIGHT.*

1. It is often necessary that the writer of a report present facts and sufficient arguments to gain acceptance of the points, conclusions, or recommendations set forth in the report.
   Of the following, the LEAST advisable step to take in organizing a report, when such argumentation is the important factor, is a(n)
   A. elaborate expression of personal belief
   B. businesslike discussion of the problem as a whole
   C. orderly arrangement of convincing data
   D. reasonable explanation of the primary issues

   1.____

2. Of the following, the factor which is generally considered to be LEAST characteristic of a good control report is that it
   A. stresses performance that adheres to standard rather than emphasizing the exception
   B. supplies information intended to serve as the basis for corrective action
   C. provides feedback for the planning process
   D. includes data that reflect trends as well as current status

   2.____

3. An administrative assistant has been asked by his superior to write a concise, factual report with objective conclusions and recommendations based on facts assembled by other researchers.
   Of the following factors, the administrative assistant should give LEAST consideration to
   A. the educational level of the person or persons for whom the report is being prepared
   B. the use to be made of the report
   C. the complexity of the problem
   D. his own feelings about the importance of the problem

   3.____

4. When making a written report, it is often recommended that the findings or conclusions be presented near the beginning of the report.
   Of the following, the MOST important reason for doing this is that it
   A. facilitates organizing the material clearly
   B. assures that all the topics will be covered
   C. avoids unnecessary repetition of ideas
   D. prepares the reader for the facts that will follow

   4.____

5. You have been asked to write a report on methods of hiring and training new employees. Your report is going to be about ten pages long.
   For the convenience of your readers, a brief summary of your findings should
   A. appear at the beginning of your report
   B. be appended to the report as a postscript
   C. be circulated in a separate memo
   D. be inserted in tabular form in the middle of your report

6. In preparing a report, the MAIN reason for writing an outline is usually to
   A. help organize thoughts in a logical sequence
   B. provide a guide for the typing of the report
   C. allow the ultimate user to review the report in advance
   D. ensure that the report is being prepared on schedule

7. The one of the following which is MOST appropriate as a reason for including footnotes in a report is to
   A. correct capitalization
   B. delete passages
   C. improve punctuation
   D. cite references

8. A completed formal report may contain all of the following EXCEPT
   A. a synopsis
   B. a preface
   C. marginal notes
   D. bibliographical references

9. Of the following, the MAIN use of proofreaders' marks is to
   A. explain corrections to be made
   B. indicate that a manuscript has been read and approved
   C. let the reader know who proofread the report
   D. indicate the format of the report

10. Informative, readable, and concise reports have been found to observe the following rules:
    Rule I. Keep the report short and easy to understand
    Rule II. Vary the length of sentences.
    Rule III. Vary the style of sentences so that, for example, they are not all just subject-verb, subject-verb.
    Consider this hospital laboratory report: The experiment was started in January. The apparatus was put together in six weeks. At that time, the synthesizing process was begun. The synthetic chemicals were separated. Then they were used in tests on patients.
    Which one of the following choices MOST accurately classifies the above rules into those which are violated by this report ad those which are not?
    A. II is violated, but I and III are not.
    B. III is violated, but I and II are not.
    C. II and III are violated, but I is not.
    D. I, II, and III are violated,

Questions 11-13.

DIRECTIONS: Questions 11 through 13 are based on the following example of a report. The report consists of eight numbered sentences, some of which are not consistent with the principles of good report writing.

(1) I interviewed Mrs. Loretta Crawford in Room 424 of County Hospital. (2) She had collapsed on the street and been brought into emergency. (3) She is an attractive woman with many friends judging by the cards she had received. (4) She did not know what her husband's last job had been, or what their present income was. (5) The first thing that Mrs. Crawford said was that she had never worked and that her husband was presently unemployed. (6) She did not know if they had any medical coverage or if they could pay the bill. (7) She said that her husband could not be reached by telephone but that he would be in to see her that afternoon. (8) I left word at the nursing station to be called when he arrived.

11. A good report should be arranged in logical order.
    Which of the following sentences from the report does NOT appear in its proper sequence in the report?
    A. 1   B. 4   C. 7   D. 8

12. Only material that is relevant to the main thought of a report should be included.
    Which of the following sentences from the report contains material which is LEAST relevant to this report? Sentence
    A. 3   B. 4   C. 6   D. 8

13. Reports should include all essential information.
    Of the following, the MOST important fact that is missing from this report is:
    A. Who was involved in the interview
    B. What was discovered at the interview
    C. When the interview took place
    D. Where the interview took place

Questions 14-15.

DIRECTIONS: Each of Questions 14 and 15 consists of four numbered sentences which constitute a paragraph in a report. They are not in the right order. Choose the numbered arrangement appearing after letter A, B, C, or D which is MOST logical and which BEST expresses the thought of the paragraph.

14. I.   Congress made the commitment explicit in the Housing Act of 1949, establishing as a national goal the realization of a decent home and suitable environment for every American family.
     II. The result has been that the goal of decent home and suitable environment is still as far distant as ever for the disadvantaged urban family
     III. In spite of this action by Congress, federal housing programs have continued to be fragmented and grossly under-funded.
     IV. The passage of the National Housing Act signaled a new federal commitment to provide housing for the nation's citizens.

The CORRECT answer is:
A. I, IV, III, II   B. IV, I, III, II   C. IV, I, III, II   D. II, IV, I, III

15. I. The greater expense does not necessarily involve "exploitation," but it is often perceived as exploitative and unfair by those who are aware of the price differences involved, but unaware of operating costs.
    II. Ghetto residents believe they are "exploited" by local merchants, and evidence substantiates some of these beliefs.
    III. However, stores in low-income areas were more likely to be small independents, which could not achieve the economies available to supermarket chains and were, therefore, more likely to charge higher prices, and the customers were more likely to buy smaller-sized packages which are more expensive per unit of measure.
    IV. A study conducted in one city showed that distinctly higher prices were charged for goods sold in ghetto stores than in other areas.

    The CORRECT answer is:
    A. IV, II, I, III   B. IV, I, III, II   C. II, IV, III, I   D. II, III, IV, I

16. In organizing data to be presented in a formal report, the FIRST of the following steps should be
    A. determining the conclusions to be drawn
    B. establishing the time sequence of the data
    C. sorting and arranging like data into groups
    D. evaluating how consistently the data support the recommendations

17. All reports should be prepared with at least one copy so that
    A. there is one copy for your file
    B. there is a copy for your supervisor
    C. the report can be sent to more than one person
    D. the person getting the report can forward a copy to someone else

18. Before turning in a report of an investigation he has made, a supervisor discovers some additional information he did not include in this report. Whether he rewrites this report to include this additional information should PRIMARILY depend on the
    A. importance of the report itself
    B. number of people who will eventually review this report
    C. established policy covering the subject matter of the report
    D. bearing this new information has on the conclusions of the report

KEY (CORRECT ANSWERS)

1.	A	11.	B
2.	A	12.	A
3.	D	13.	C
4.	D	14.	B
5.	A	15.	C
6.	A	16.	C
7.	D	17.	A
8.	C	18.	D
9.	A		
10.	C		

EXAMINATION SECTION
TEST 1

DIRECTIONS: Each question or incomplete statement is followed by several suggested answers or completions. Select the one that BEST answers the question or completes the statement. *PRINT THE LETTER OF THE CORRECT ANSWER IN THE SPACE AT THE RIGHT.*

1. When conducting a needs assessment for the purpose of education planning, an agency's FIRST step is to identify or provide
   A. a profile of population characteristics
   B. barriers to participation
   C. existing resources
   D. profiles of competing resources

   1.____

2. Research has demonstrated that of the following, the MOST effective medium for communicating with external publics is(are)
   A. video news releases   B. television
   C. radio   D. newspapers

   2.____

3. Basic ideas behind the effort to influence the attitudes and behaviors of a constituency include each of the following EXCEPT the idea that
   A. words, rather than actions or events, are most likely to motivate
   B. demands for action are a usual response
   C. self-interest usually figures heavily into public involvement
   D. the reliability of change programs is difficult to assess

   3.____

4. An agency representative is trying to craft a pithy message to constituents in order to encourage the use of agency program resources.
   Choosing an audience for such messages is easiest when the message
   A. is project- or behavior-based   B. is combined with other messages
   C. is abstract   D. has a broad appeal

   4.____

5. Of the following factors, the MOST important to the success of an agency's external education or communication programs is the
   A. amount of resources used to implement them
   B. public's prior experiences with the agency
   C. real value of the program to the public
   D. commitment of the internal audience

   5.____

6. A representative for a state agency is being interviewed by a reporter from a local news network. The representative is being asked to defend a program that is extremely unpopular in certain parts of the municipality.
   When a constituency is known to be opposed to a position, the MOST useful communication strategy is to present

   6.____

A. only the arguments that are consistent with constituents' views
B. only the agency's side of the issue
C. both sides of the argument as clearly as possible
D. both sides of the argument, omitting key information about the opposing position

7. The MOST significant barriers to effective agency community relations include
   I. widespread distrust of communication strategies
   II. the media's "watchdog" stance
   III. public apathy
   IV. statutory opposition

   The CORRECT answer is:
   A. I only   B. I and II   C. II and III   D. III and IV

8. In conducting an education program, many agencies use workshops and seminars in a classroom setting.
   Advantages of classroom-style teaching over other means of educating the public include each of the following, EXCEPT
   A. enabling an instructor to verify learning through testing and interaction with the target audience
   B. enabling hands-on practice and other participatory learning techniques
   C. ability to reach an unlimited number of participants in a given length of time
   D. ability to convey the latest, most up-to-date information

9. The _____ model of community relations is characterized by an attempt to persuade the public to adopt the agency's point of view.
   A. two-way symmetric   B. two-way asymmetric
   C. public information   D. press agency/publicity

10. Important elements of an internal situation analysis include the
    I. list of agency opponents   II. communication audit
    III. updated organizational almanac IV. stakeholder analysis

    The CORRECT answer is:
    A. I and II   B. I, II, and III   C. II and III   D. I, II, III and IV

11. Government agency information efforts typically involve each of the following objectives, EXCEPT to
    A. implement changes in the policies of government agencies to align with public opinion
    B. communicate the work of agencies
    C. explain agency techniques in a way that invites input from citizens
    D. provide citizen feedback to government administrators

12. Factors that are likely to influence the effectiveness of an educational campaign include the
    I. level of homogeneity among intended participants
    II. number and types of media used
    III. receptivity of the intended participants
    IV. level of specificity in the message or behavior to be taught

    The CORRECT answer is:
    A. I and II   B. I, II, and III   C. II and III   D. I, II, III, and IV

13. An agency representative is writing instructional objectives that will later help to measure the effectiveness of an educational program.
    Which of the following verbs, included in an objective, would be MOST helpful for the purpose of measuring effectiveness?
    A. Know   B. Identify   C. Learn   D. Comprehend

14. A state education agency wants to encourage participation in a program that has just received a boost through new federal legislation. The program is intended to include participants from a wide variety of socioeconomic and other demographic characteristics. The agency wants to launch a broad-based program that will inform virtually every interested party in the state about the program's new circumstances.
    In attempting to deliver this message to such a wide-ranging constituency, the agency's BEST practice would be to
    A. broadcast the same message through as many different media channels as possible
    B. focus on one discrete segment of the public at a time
    C. craft a message whose appeal is as broad as the public itself
    D. let the program's achievements speak for themselves and rely on word-of-mouth

15. Advantages associated with using the World Wide Web as an educational tool include
    I. an appeal to younger generations of the public
    II. visually-oriented, interactive learning
    III. learning that is not confined by space, time, or institutional association
    IV. a variety of methods for verifying use and learning

    The CORRECT answer is:
    A. I only   B. I and II   C. I, II, and III   D. I, II, II, and IV

16. In agencies involved in health care, community relations is a critical function because it
    A. serves as an intermediary between the agency and consumers
    B. generates a clear mission statement for agency goals and priorities
    C. ensures patient privacy while satisfying the media's right to information
    D. helps marketing professionals determine the wants and needs of agency constituents

17. After an extensive campaign to promote its newest program to constituents, an agency learns that most of the audience did not understand the intended message.
MOST likely, the agency has
    A. chosen words that were intended to inform, rather than persuade
    B. not accurately interpreted what the audience really needed to know
    C. overestimated the ability of the audience to receive and process the message
    D. compensated for noise that may have interrupted the message

17.____

18. The necessary elements that lead to conviction and motivation in the minds of participants in an educational or information program include each of the following, EXCEPT the _____ of the message.
    A. acceptability   B. intensity
    C. single-channel appeal D. pervasiveness

18.____

19. Printed materials are often at the core of educational programs provided by public agencies.
The PRIMARY disadvantage associated with print is that it
    A. does not enable comprehensive treatment of a topic
    B. is generally unreliable in term of assessing results
    C. is often the most expensive medium available
    D. is constrained by time

19.____

20. Traditional thinking on public opinion holds that there is about _____ percent of the public who are pivotal to shifting the balance and momentum of opinion—they are concerned about an issue, but not fanatical, and interested enough to pay attention to a reasoned discussion.
    A. 2   B. 10   C. 33   D. 51

20.____

21. One of the most useful guidelines for influencing attitude change among people is to
    A. invite the target audience to come to you, rather than approaching them
    B. use moral appeals as the primary approach
    C. use concrete images to enable people to see the results of behaviors or indifference
    D. offer tangible rewards to people for changes in behavior

21.____

22. An agency is attempting to evaluate the effectiveness of its educational program. For this purpose, it wants to observe several focus groups discussing the same program.
Which of the following would NOT be a guideline for the use of focus groups?
    A. Focus groups should only include those who have participated in the program.
    B. Be sure to accurately record the discussion.
    C. The same questions should be asked at each focus group meeting.
    D. It is often helpful to have a neutral, non-agency employee facilitate discussions.

22.____

23. Research consistently shows that _____ is the determinant most likely to make a newspaper editor run a news release.
    A. novelty   B. prominence   C. proximity   D. conflict

24. Which of the following is NOT one of the major variables to take into account when considering a population-needs assessment?
    A. State of program development   B. Resources available
    C. Demographics   D. Community attitudes

25. The FIRST step in any communications audit is to
    A. develop a research instrument
    B. determine how the organization currently communicates
    C. hire a contractor
    D. determine which audience to assess

KEY (CORRECT ANSWERS)

1.	A		11.	A
2.	D		12.	D
3.	A		13.	B
4.	A		14.	B
5.	D		15.	C
6.	C		16.	A
7.	D		17.	B
8.	C		18.	C
9.	B		19.	B
10.	C		20.	B

21. C
22. A
23. C
24. C
25. D

TEST 2

DIRECTIONS: Each question or incomplete statement is followed by several suggested answers or completions. Select the one that BEST answers the question or completes the statement. *PRINT THE LETTER OF THE CORRECT ANSWER IN THE SPACE AT THE RIGHT.*

1. A public relations practitioner at an agency has just composed a press release highlighting a program's recent accomplishments and success stories.
   In pitching such releases to print outlets, the practitioner should
   I. e-mail, mail, or send them by messenger
   II. address them to "editor" or "news director"
   III. have an assistant call all media contacts by telephone
   IV. ask reporters or editors how they prefer to receive them

   The CORRECT answer is:
   A. I and II   B. I and IV   C. II, III, and IV   D. III only

   1.____

2. The "output goals" of an educational program are MOST likely to include
   A. specified ratings of services by participants on a standardized scale
   B. observable effects on a given community or clientele
   C. the number of instructional hours provided
   D. the number of participants served

   2.____

3. An agency wants to evaluate satisfaction levels among program participants, and mails out questionnaires to everyone who has been enrolled in the last year.
   The PRIMARY problem associated with this method of evaluative research is that it
   A. poses a significant inconvenience for respondents
   B. is inordinately expensive
   C. does not allow for follow-up or clarification questions
   D. usually involves a low response rate

   3.____

4. A communications audit is an important tool for measuring
   A. the depth of penetration of a particular message or program
   B. the cost of the organization's information campaigns
   C. how key audiences perceive an organization
   D. the commitment of internal stakeholders

   4.____

5. The "ABCs" of written learning objectives include each of the following, EXCEPT
   A. Audience   B. Behavior   C. Conditions   D. Delineation

   5.____

6. When attempting to change the behaviors of constituents, it is important to keep in mind that
   I. most people are skeptical of communications that try to get them to change their behaviors
   II. in most cases, a person selects the media to which he exposes himself
   III. people tend to react defensively to messages or programs that rely on fear as a motivating factor
   IV. programs should aim for the broadest appeal possible in order to include as many participants as possible

   The CORRECT answer is:
   A. I and II   B. I, II and III   C. II and III   D. I, II, III, and IV

7. The "laws" of public opinion include the idea that it is
   A. useful for anticipating emergencies
   B. not sensitive to important events
   C. basically determined by self-interest
   D. sustainable through persistent appeals

8. Which of the following types of evaluations is used to measure public attitudes before and after an information/educational program?
   A. Retrieval study   B. Copy test
   C. Quota sampling   D. Benchmark study

9. The PRIMARY source for internal communications is(are) usually
   A. flow charts   B. meetings
   C. voice mail   D. printed publications

10. An agency representative is putting together informational materials—brochures and a newsletter—outlining changes in one of the state's biggest benefits programs.
    In assembling print materials as a medium for delivering information to the public, the representative should keep in mind each of the following trends:
    I. For various reasons, the reading capabilities of the public are in general decline
    II. Without tables and graphs to help illustrate the changes, it is unlikely that the message will be delivered effectively
    III. Professionals and career-oriented people are highly receptive to information written in the form of a journal article or empirical study
    IV. People tend to be put off by print materials that use itemized and bulleted (●) lists

    The CORRECT answer is:
    A. I and II   B. I, II and III   C. II and III   D. I, II, III, and IV

11. Which of the following steps in a problem-oriented information campaign would typically be implemented FIRST?
    A. Deciding on tactics
    B. Determining a communications strategy
    C. Evaluating the problem's impact
    D. Developing an organizational strategy

12. A common pitfall in conducting an educational program is to
    A. aim it at the wrong target audience
    B. overfund it
    C. leave it in the hands of people who are in the business of education, rather than those with expertise in the business of the organization
    D. ignore the possibility that some other organization is meeting the same educational need for the target audience

13. The key factors that affect the credibility of an agency's educational program include
    A. organization
    B. scope
    C. sophistication
    D. penetration

14. Research on public opinion consistently demonstrates that it is
    A. easy to move people toward a strong opinion on anything, as long as they are approached directly through their emotions
    B. easier to move people away from an opinion they currently hold than to have them form an opinion about something they have not previously cared about
    C. easy to move people toward a strong opinion on anything, as long as the message appeals to their reason and intellect
    D. difficult to move people toward a strong opinion on anything, no matter what the approach

15. In conducting an education program, many agencies use meetings and conferences to educate an audience about the organization and its programs. Advantages associated with this approach include
    I. a captive audience that is known to be interested in the topic
    II. ample opportunities for verifying learning
    III. cost-efficient meeting space
    IV. the ability to provide information on a wider variety of subjects

    The CORRECT answer is:
    A. I and II   B. I, III and IV   C. II and III   D. I, II, III and IV

16. An agency is attempting to evaluate the effectiveness of its educational programs. For this purpose, it wants to observe several focus groups discussing particular programs.
    For this purpose, a focus group should never number more than _____ participants.
    A. 5   B. 10   C. 15   D. 20

17. A _____ speech is written so that several agency members can deliver it to different audiences with only minor variations.
    A. basic B. printed C. quota D. pattern

18. Which of the following statements about public opinion is generally considered to be FALSE?
    A. Opinion is primarily reactive rather than proactive.
    B. People have more opinions about goals than about the means by which to achieve them.
    C. Facts tend to shift opinion in the accepted direction when opinion is not solidly structured.
    D. Public opinion is based more on information than desire.

19. An agency is trying to promote its educational program.
    As a general rule, the agency should NOT assume that
    A. people will only participate if they perceive an individual benefit
    B. promotions need to be aimed at small, discrete groups
    C. if the program is good, the audience will find out about it
    D. a variety of methods, including advertising, special events, and direct mail, should be considered

20. In planning a successful educational program, probably the first and most important question for an agency to ask is:
    A. What will be the content of the program?
    B. Who will be served by the program?
    C. When is the best time to schedule the program?
    D. Why is the program necessary?

21. Media kits are LEAST likely to contain
    A. fact sheets   B. memoranda
    C. photographs with captions   D. news releases

22. The use of pamphlets and booklets as media for communication with the public often involves the disadvantage that
    A. the messages contained within them are frequently nonspecific
    B. it is difficult to measure their effectiveness in delivering the message
    C. there are few opportunities for people to refer to them
    D. color reproduction is poor

23. The MOST important prerequisite of a good educational program is an
    A. abundance of resources to implement it
    B. individual staff unit formed for the purpose of program delivery
    C. accurate needs assessment
    D. uneducated constituency

24. After an education program has been delivered, an agency conducts a program evaluation to determine whether its objectives have been met.
General rules about how to conduct such an education program valuation include each of the following, EXCEPT that it
   A. must be done immediately after the program has been implemented
   B. should be simple and easy to use
   C. should be designed so that tabulation of responses can take place quickly and inexpensively
   D. should solicit mostly subjective, open-ended responses if the audience was large

25. Using electronic media such as television as means of educating the public is typically recommended ONLY for agencies that
   I. have a fairly simple message to begin with
   II. want to reach the masses, rather than a targeted audience
   III. have substantial financial resources
   IV. accept that they will not be able to measure the results of the campaign with much precision

   The CORRECT answer is:
   A. I and II   B. I, II and III   C. II and IV   D. I, II, III and IV

KEY (CORRECT ANSWERS)

1.	B		11.	C
2.	C		12.	D
3.	D		13.	A
4.	C		14.	D
5.	D		15.	B
6.	B		16.	B
7.	C		17.	D
8.	D		18.	D
9.	D		19.	C
10.	A		20.	D

21. B
22. B
23. C
24. D
25. D

EXAMINATION SECTION
TEST 1

DIRECTIONS: Each question or incomplete statement is followed by several suggested answers or completions. Select the one that BEST answers the question or completes the statement. *PRINT THE LETTER OF THE CORRECT ANSWER IN THE SPACE AT THE RIGHT.*

1. The PRIMARY purpose of program analysis as it is used in government is to
   A. replace political judgments with rational programs and policies
   B. help decision-makers to sharpen their judgments about program choices
   C. analyze the impact of past programs on the quality of public services
   D. reduce costs by eliminating waste in public programs and services

2. While there is no complete method for program analysis that is agreed to by all the experts and is relevant to all types of problems, the MOST important element in program analysis involves the
   A. development of alternatives and the definition of objectives or criteria
   B. collection of information and the construction of a mathematical model
   C. design of experiments and procedures to validate results
   D. collection of expert opinion and the combination of their views

3. Electronic data processing is a particularly valuable tool of analysis in situations where the analyst has a processing problem involving
   A. *small* input, *few* operations, and *small* output
   B. *large* input, *many* operations, and *small* output
   C. *large* input, *few* operations, and *large* output
   D. *small* input, *many* operations, and *small* output

4. In order for an analyst to use electronic data processing to solve an analytic problem, the problem must be clearly defined.
   The BEST way to prepare material for such definition in electronic data processing is to
   A. discuss the problem with computer programmers in a meeting
   B. prepare a flow diagram outlining the steps in the analysis
   C. write a memorandum with a list of the relevant program issues
   D. write a computer program using FORTRAN, BASIC, or another language

5. The "growth rate" referred to in current political and economic discussion refers to change from year to year in a country's
   A. investments
   B. population
   C. gross national product
   D. sale of goods

6. Interactive or conversational programming is important to the program analyst ESPECIALLY for
   A. preparing analyses leading to management information systems
   B. communicating among analysts in different places
   C. using canned programs in statistical analysis
   D. testing trial solutions in rapid sequence

7. Program analysts often calls for recommendation of a choice between competing program possibilities that differ in the timing of major costs. Analysts using the present value technique by setting an interest or discount rate are in effect arguing that, other things being equal,
   A. it is inadvisable to defer the start of projects because of rising costs
   B. projects should be completed within a short time period to save money
   C. expenditures should be made out of tax revenues to avoid payment of interest
   D. postponing expenditures is advantageous at some measurable rate

8. Of the following, the formula which is MOST appropriately used to estimate the net need for a given type of service is that net need equals
   A. current clients − anticipate losses + anticipated gains
   B. $\frac{\text{current supply}}{\text{standard}}$ + current clients
   C. (client population x standard) − current supply
   D. current supply − anticipated losses + anticipated gains

9. The purpose of feasibility analysis is to protect the analyst from naïve alternatives and, MOST generally, to
   A. identify and quantify technological constraints
   B. carry out a preliminary stage of analysis
   C. anticipate potential blocks to implementation
   D. line up the support of political leadership

Questions 10-11.

DIRECTIONS: Questions 10 and 11 are to be answered on the basis of the following chart. In a hypothetical problem involving four criteria and four alternatives, the following data have been assembled.

Cost Criterion	Effectiveness Criterion	Timing Criterion	Feasibility Criterion
Alternative A $500,000	50 units	3 months	probably feasible
Alternative B $300,000	100 units	6 months	probably feasible
Alternative C $400,000	50 units	12 months	probably infeasible
Alternative D $200,000	75 units	3 months	probably infeasible

10. On the basis of the above data, it appears that the one alternative which is dominated by another alternative is Alternative
    A. A   B. B   C. C   D. D

11. If the feasibility constraint is absolute and fixed, then the critical trade-off is between lower cost
    A. on the one hand and faster timing and higher effectiveness on the other
    B. and higher effectiveness on one hand and faster timing on the other
    C. and faster timing on the one hand and higher effectiveness on the other
    D. on the one hand and higher effectiveness on the other

12. A classification of an agency's activities in a program structure is MOST useful if it highlights
    A. trade-offs that might not otherwise be considered
    B. ways to improve the efficiency of each activity
    C. the true organizational structure of an agency
    D. bases for insuring that expenditures stay within limits

13. CPM, like PERT, is a useful tool for scheduling large-scale, complex processes. In CPM, the critical path is the
    A. path composed of important links
    B. path composed of uncertain links
    C. longest path through the network
    D. shortest path through the network

14. Classical evaluative research calls for the use of control groups. However, there are practical difficulties in collecting data on individuals to be used as "controls" in program evaluations.
    Researchers may attempt to overcome these difficulties by
    A. using control groups that have no choice such as prison inmates or inmates of other public institutions or facilities
    B. developing better measures of the inputs, processes, and outputs relevant to public programs and services
    C. using experimental demonstration projects with participants in the different projects serving as comparison groups for one another
    D. abandoning attempts at formal evaluation in favor of more qualitative approaches employing a journalistic style of analysis

15. During the course of an analysis of the remaining "life" of a certain city's landfill for refuse disposal, there was a great deal of debate about the impact of changing rates of garbage generation on the amount of landfill needed and about what rates of garbage generation to expect over the next decade. Faced with the need to attempt to resolve this debate, an analyst would construct a simple model of the refuse disposal system and
    A. project landfill needs without considering refuse generation in the future
    B. conduct a detailed household survey in order to estimate future garbage generation rates
    C. ask the experts to continue to debate the issue until the argument is won by one view
    D. do a sensitivity analysis to test the impact of alternative assumptions about refuse generation

16. The limitations of traditional surveys have fostered the development and use of panels.
A panel is a
    A. group of respondents that serves as a continuous source of survey information
    B. group of advisors expert in the design and implementation of surveys
    C. representative sample of respondents at a single point in time
    D. post-survey discussion group composed of former respondents

16._____

17. The difference between sensitivity analysis and risk analysis is that risk analysis
    A. is applicable only to profit and loss situations where the concept of risk is operable
    B. includes an estimate of probabilities of different values of input factors
    C. is applicable to physical problems while sensitivity analysis is applicable to social ones
    D. requires a computer simulation while sensitivity analysis does not

17._____

18. A decision tree, although initially applied to business problems, is a graphic device which is useful to public analysts in
    A. scheduling complex processes
    B. doing long-range forecasting
    C. formulating the structure of alternatives
    D. solving production-inventory problems

18._____

19. The purpose of a management information system in an agency is to
    A. structure data relevant to managerial decision-making
    B. put all of an agency's data in machine-processing form
    C. simplify the record-keeping operations in an agency
    D. keep an ongoing record of management's activities

19._____

20.

[Chart: Number of responses to alarms vs. Time, showing "total alarms" line above "false alarms" line, both slowly increasing]

Assume that an analyst is presented with the above chart for a fire department and supplied also with information indicating a stable size firefighting staff over this time.
The analyst could REASONABLY conclude regarding productivity that
    A. productivity over this time period was essentially stable for this firefighting force because the number of responses to real fires during this period was stable, as was the work force
    B. productivity was essentially increasing for this force because the number of total responses was increasing relative to a stable force

20._____

C. productivity was declining because a greater proportion of the total work effort was wasted effort in responding to false alarms
D. it is impossible to make a judgment about the productivity of the firefighting staff without a judgment about the value of a response to a false alarm

21. In the design of a productivity program for the sanitary department, the BEST measure of productivity would be
    A. tons of refuse collected annually
    B. number of collections made per week
    C. tons of refuse collected per truck shift
    D. number of trucks used per shift

21._____

22. The cohort-survival method for estimating future population has been widely employed.
    In this method,
    A. migration is assumed to be constant over time
    B. net migration within cohorts is assumed to be zero
    C. migration is included as a multiplier factor
    D. net migration within cohorts is assumed to be constant

22._____

23. Cost-effectiveness and cost-benefit analysis represent a systematic approach to balancing potential losses against potential gains as a prelude to public action.
    In addition to limitations based on difficulties of measurement and inadequacies in data that are typical of systematic program analysis, cost-benefit analysis suffers from a serious conceptual flaw in that
    A. the definition of benefit or cost does not typically distinguish to whom benefits or costs accrue
    B. a full-scale cost benefit analysis takes too long to do, is too expensive, and needs too much data
    C. it has been shown that such analyses are more suitable for defense or water resources problems
    D. such analyses are not useful in any problem involving capital and operating costs or benefits

23._____

24. If you were asked to develop a total cost estimate for one year for a program involving both a capital improvement and operating costs, the BEST way to estimate the capital cost component would be to
    A. divide the estimated cost of the capital improvement by the projected operating costs over the life of the improvement
    B. multiply the annual operating cost by the projected life of the capital improvement
    C. divide the amortized cost of the capital improvement by the projected life of the improvement
    D. multiply the portion of the capital improvement to be completed within the year by the cost of the improvement

24._____

25. In comparing the costs of two or more alternative programs, it is important to consider all relevant costs.
    The MOST important principle in defining "relevant cost" is that
    A. only marginal or incremental cost should be considered in the estimate
    B. only recurring costs should be considered for each alternative
    C. estimates should include the sunk costs for each alternative
    D. cost estimates need to be as precise as in budget preparation

25.____

26. Different techniques for projecting future costs may be suitable in different situations. Assume that it is necessary to estimate the future costs of maintaining garbage collection vehicles.
    Under which of the following conditions would it be advisable to develop a cost-estimating equation rather than to use unadjusted current data?
    A. When it is expected that more complex equipment will replace simpler equipment
    B. Whether or not it is expected that the nature of future garbage collection will change
    C. When the current unadjusted data still has to be verified
    D. When the nature of future garbage collection equipment is unknown

26.____

27. The following data has been collected on the costs of two pilot programs, each representing a different approach to the same problem.

	Total Cost	Fixed Cost	Variable Cost	Average Unit Cost	Number of Users
Program A	$45,000	$20,000	$50 per user	$90 Per User	500
Program B	$42,000	$7,000	$100 Per User	$120 Per User	350

Assume that the pilot programs are extended city-wide and other factors are constant.
Using the above data, what would a cost analysis conclude about the relative costs of the two programs?
Program
    A. B would be less costly with fewer than 300 users and Program A would be less costly with more than 300 users
    B. B would be less costly with fewer than 260 users and Program A would be less costly with more than 260 users
    C. A would be less costly without regard to the size of the program
    D. B would be less costly without regard to the size of the program

27.____

Questions 28-30.

DIRECTIONS: Questions 28 through 30 are to be answered on the basis of the following data assembled for a cost-benefit analysis.

	Cost	Benefit
No program	0	0
Alternative W	$3,000	$6,000
Alternative X	$10,000	$17,000
Alternative Y	$17,000	$25,000
Alternative Z	$30,000	$32,000

28. From the point of view of pushing public expenditure to the point where marginal benefit equals or exceeds marginal cost, the BEST alternative is Alternative   28._____
   A. W   B. X   C. Y   D. Z

29. From the point of view of selecting the alternative with the best cost-benefit ratio, the BEST alternative is Alternative   29._____
   A. W   B. X   C. Y   D. Z

30. From the point of view of selecting the alternative with the best measure of net benefit, the BEST alternative is Alternative   30._____
   A. W   B. X   C. Y   D. Z

Questions 31-35.

DIRECTIONS: The set of answers listed below applies to Questions 31 through 35. Each answer is a type of statistical test.

   A. Analysis of variance
   B. Pearson Product-Moment Correlation (r)
   C. t-test
   D. x^2 test (Chi-squared)

   Pick the test which is MOST appropriate to the situation described. An answer may be used more than once.

31. A comparison between two correlated means obtained from a small sample.   31._____
   The CORRECT answer is:
   A. A   B. B   C. C   D. D

32. A comparison of three or more means.   32._____
   The CORRECT answer is:
   A. A   B. B   C. C   D. D

33. A comparison of the divergence of observed frequencies with those expected on the hypothesis of equal probability of occurrence.   33._____
   The CORRECT answer is:
   A. A   B. B   C. C   D. D

34. A comparison of the divergence of observed frequencies with those expected on the hypothesis of a normal distribution.   34._____
   The CORRECT answer is:
   A. A   B. B   C. C   D. D

35. A comparison between two uncorrelated means obtained from small samples.   35._____
   The CORRECT answer is:
   A. A   B. B   C. C   D. D

36. There are many different models for evaluative research.
A time-series design is an example of a _____ experimental design.
   A. field   B. true   C. quasi-   D. pre-

37. In policy research, as in all kinds of research, it is important to develop research hypotheses early.
The MAIN purpose of a research hypothesis is to
   A. include the kind of statistical procedures to be used in the research
   B. provide a ready answer in case data is not available for doing research
   C. serve as a guide to the kind of data that must be collected in order to answer the research question
   D. clarify what is known and what is not known in the research problem

38. While descriptive and causal research are not completely separable, there has been a distinct effort to move in the direction of causal research.
Such an effort is epitomized by the use of
   A. predictive models and measures of deviation from predictions
   B. option and attitudinal surveys in local neighborhoods
   C. community studies and area profiles of localities
   D. individual case histories and group case studies

39. The one of the following which BEST describes a periodic report is that it
   A. provides a record of accomplishments for a given time span and a comparison with similar time spans in the past
   B. covers the progress made in a project that has been postponed
   C. integrates, summarizes, and perhaps interprets published data on technical or scientific material
   D. describes a decision, advocates a policy or action, and presents facts in support of the writer's position

40. The PRIMARY purpose of including pictorial illustrations in a formal report is usually to
   A. amplify information which has been adequately treated verbally
   B. present detail that are difficult to describe verbally
   C. provide the reader with a pleasant, momentary distraction
   D. present supplementary information incidental to the main ideas developed in the report

KEY (CORRECT ANSWERS)

1. B	11. B	21. C	31. C
2. A	12. A	22. B	32. A
3. B	13. C	23. A	33. D
4. B	14. C	24. C	34. D
5. C	15. D	25. A	35. C
6. D	16. A	26. A	36. C
7. D	17. B	27. B	37. C
8. C	18. C	28. C	38. A
9. C	19. A	29. A	39. A
10. C	20. D	30. C	40. B

TEST 2

DIRECTIONS: Each question or incomplete statement is followed by several suggested answers or completions. Select the one that BEST answers the question or completes the statement. *PRINT THE LETTER OF THE CORRECT ANSWER IN THE SPACE AT THE RIGHT.*

1. A measurement procedure is considered to be RELIABLE to the extent that
   A. independent applications under similar conditions yield consistent results
   B. independent applications under different conditions yield similar results
   C. scores reflect true differences among individuals or situations
   D. scores reflect true differences in the same individual over time

   1.____

2. Different scales of measurement are distinguished by the feasibility of various empirical operations.
   An ordinal scale of measurement
   A. is not as useful as a ratio or interval scale
   B. is useful in rank-ordering or priority setting
   C. provides the data for addition or subtraction
   D. provides the data for computation of means

   2.____

3. A widely used approach to sampling is systematic sampling, i.e., selecting every Kth element in a listing.
   Even with a random start, a DISADVANTAGE in this approach is that
   A. the listing used may contain a cyclical pattern
   B. it is too similar to a simple random sample
   C. the system does not insure a probability sample
   D. it yield an unpredictable sample size

   3.____

4. A rule of thumb sometimes used in sample size selection it to set sample size equal to five percent of the population size.
   Other things being equal, this rule
   A. tends to oversample small populations
   B. tends to oversample large populations
   C. provides an accurate rule for sampling
   D. is a relatively inexpensive basis for sampling

   4.____

5. With regard to a stratified random sample, it may be APPROPRIATE to sample the various strata in different proportions in order to
   A. approximate the characteristics of a true random sample
   B. establish classes that are internally heterogenous in each case
   C. avoid the necessity of subdividing the cases within each stratum
   D. adequately cover important strata that have small numbers of cases

   5.____

6. One possible response to the "unknown" or "no answer" category in a tabulation of survey information is to "allocate" the unknown responses, i.e., to estimate the missing data on the basis of other known information about the respondents.

   6.____

This technique is APPROPRIATE when the unknown category
- A. is very small and is randomly distributed within all subgroups of respondents
- B. is very large and is randomly distributed within all subgroups of respondents
- C. reflects an interviewing failure and a subgroup in the sample ends to produce more unknowns
- D. is a legitimate category and a subgroup in the sample tends to produce more unknowns

7. In presenting cross-tabulated data showing the relationship between two variables, it is MOST meaningful to compute percentages
    - A. in both directions in all instances
    - B. of each cell in relation to the grand total
    - C. in the direction of the smaller number of cells
    - D. in the direction of the causal factor

8. In portraying data based on a sampling operation, it is MOST meaningful and comprehensible to the reader to present
    - A. percentages for the sample and the universe
    - B. percentages by themselves
    - C. percentages and the base figures
    - D. numbers by themselves

9. A new bridge spanning a river is expected to carry 60,000 cars a day on a rainy day and 80,000 cars a day on other kinds of days.
    If there is a $5 toll and one chance in four of a rainy day, the expected value of a day's revenue is
    - A. $175,000
    - B. $375,000
    - C. $475,000
    - D. $700,000

10. The analyst who is asked to estimate the probability of a relatively rare event occurring cannot use the classical frequency measures of probability but rather should
    - A. use a random-numbers table to pick a probability
    - B. project historical data into the future
    - C. indicate that no probabilistic judgment is possible
    - D. make the best possible judgment as to the subjective probability

11. A useful source of census data for computing annual indicators is the
    - A. Public Use Sample
    - B. Continuing Population Survey
    - C. Census of Population
    - D. Census of Governments

12. An analyst presented with a set of household records showing age, ethnicity, income, and family status and wishing to study the inter-relationship of all of these variables simultaneously will probably equal
    - A. one four-way cross-tabulation
    - B. four three-way cross-tabulation
    - C. six two-way cross-tabulations
    - D. four single tabulations

13. Downward communication, from high management to lower levels in an organization, will often not be fully accepted at the lowest levels of an organization unless high-level management
    A. communicates through several levels of mid-level management, where the message can be properly modified and interpreted
    B. communicates directly with the level of the organization it wishes to reach, bypassing any intermediate levels
    C. first establishes an atmosphere in which upward communication is encouraged and listened to
    D. establishes penalties for non-compliance with its communications

14. A top-level manager sometimes has an inaccurate view of the actual lower-level operations of his agency, particularly of those operations which are not running well.
    Of the following, the MOST frequent cause of this is the
    A. general unconcern of top-level management with the way an agency actually operates
    B. tendency of the people at the lowest level in an agency to lie about their actual performance
    C. unwillingness of top-level management to deal with unfavorable information when it is presented
    D. tendency of mid-level management to edit bad news and unpleasant information from reports directed to top management

15. In the conduct of productivity analyses, work measurement is a USEFUL technique for
    A. substantiating executive decisions
    B. designing a research study
    C. developing performance yardsticks
    D. preparing a manual of procedure

16. Issue analysis is closely identified with the "fire-fighting" function of management. As such, issue analysis is a(n)
    A. systematic assessment over time of an agency's strategic options
    B. annual review of the issues that have come up during the past year
    C. basis for a set of procedures to be followed in an emergency
    D. analysis of a specific policy question often performed in a crisis environment

17. The transportation agency in a large city wishes to study the impact of fare increases on ridership in buses. Ridership data for peak hours has been assembled for the same time period for three geographic subareas (A, B, and C) with approximately the same socio-economic characteristics, residential density, and distance from the central business district (CBD). Subarea A had experienced a moderate fare increase on its bus line; Subarea B had had no fare increase; and Subarea C had experienced a major fare increase during the time period

In the design of this study, the analysis should be framed:
   A. Ridership = f (fare level)
   B. Ridership = f (fare level), distance from CBD)
   C. Fare level = f (ridership)
   D. Ridership = f (fare level, socio-economic characteristics, residential density)

18. What organizational concept is illustrated when a group is organized on an *ad hoc* basis to accomplish a specific goal?
    A. Functional Teamwork   B. Line/staff
    C. Task Force   D. Command

18.____

19. The concept of "demand" provides an appropriate theoretical basis for estimating the needs for public services or programs where the service will be on a _____ basis and _____ life-sustaining necessities.
    A. fee; involves   B. free; involves
    C. free; does not involve   D. fee; does not involve

19.____

20. Analysts should be wary of relying exclusively on traditional service standards (e.g., one acre of playground per 1,000 population).
    Such standards are often DEFICIENT because they tend to overstate
    A. the consumer view and understate behavior and values of producers
    B. the producer view and understate behavior and values of users or consumers
    C. local conditions and understate national conditions
    D. behavioral factors and understate practical effects

20.____

21. The BEST measure of the performance of a manpower program would be
    A. percentage reduction in unemployment by impacted population groups
    B. number of trainees placed in jobs at the beginning of the training program
    C. percentage of students completing a training program
    D. cost per student of the training program and the job placement effort

21.____

22. Indices are single figures that measure multi-dimensional concepts.
    The critical judgment in the construction of an index involves
    A. the trade-off between accuracy and simplicity
    B. determination of enough data to do the measurement
    C. avoidance of all possible error
    D. developing a theoretical basis for it

22.____

23. Evaluation of public programs is complicated by the reality that programs tend to reflect negotiated compromises among conflicting objectives.
    The absence of clear, unitary objectives PARTICULARLY complicates the
    A. assessment of program input or effort
    B. development of effectiveness criteria
    C. design of new programs to replace the old
    D. diagnosis of a program's processes

23.____

24. The BASIC purpose of the "Super-Agencies" is to
    A. reduce the number of departments and agencies in the city government
    B. reduce the number of high-level administrators
    C. coordinate agencies reporting to the mayor and supervise agencies in related fields
    D. supervise departments and agencies in unrelated fields

25. In most municipal budgeting systems involving capital and operating budgets, the leasing or renting of facilities is usually shown in
    A. the operating budget
    B. the capital budget
    C. a separate schedule
    D. either budget

26. New York City's budgeting procedure is unusual in that budget appropriations are considered in two parts, as follows:
    A. Capital budget and income budget
    B. Expense budget and income budget
    C. Revenue budget and expense budget
    D. Expense budget and capital budget

27. The "growth rate" referred to in current political and economic discussion refers to change from year to year in a country's
    A. gross national product
    B. population
    C. available labor force
    D. capital goods investment

Questions 28-29.

DIRECTIONS: Questions 28 and 29 are to be answered on the basis of the following illustration. Assume that the figures in the chart are cubes.

28. In the illustration above, how many times GREATER is the quantity represented by Figure III than the quantity represented by Figure II?
    A. 2   B. 4   C. 8   D. 16

29. The above illustration illustrates a progression in quantity BEST described as
    A. arithmetic   B. geometric   C. discrete   D. linear

Questions 30-35.

DIRECTIONS: Questions 30 through 35 are to be answered on the basis of the following chart.

In a national study of poverty trends, the following data have been assembled by interpretation.

Item	Persons Below Poverty, By Residence			
	Number (millions)		Percent	
	U.S.	Metropolitan Areas	U.S.	Metropolitan Areas
2010				
Total	38.8	17.0	22.0	15.3
Under 25 years	20.0	8.8	25.3	18.1
65 years & over	5.5	2.5	35.2	26.9
Black	9.9	5.0	55.1	42.8
Other	28.3	11.8	18.1	12.0
2020				
Total	24.3	12.3	12.2	9.5
Under 25 years	12.2	6.4	13.2	10.4
65 years & over	4.8	2.3	25.3	20.2
Black	7.2	3.9	32.3	24.4
Other	16.7	8.2	9.5	7.3

30. If no other source of data were available, which of the following groups would you expect to have the HIGHEST rate of poverty?
   A. Others over 65
   B. Others under 65
   C. Blacks over 65
   D. Blacks under 65

30.____

31. Between 2010 and 2020, the percentage of poor in the United States who were Black
   A. increased from 25.5% to 29.6%
   B. decreased from 55.1% to 32.3%
   C. decreased from 9.9% to 7.2%
   D. stayed the same

31.____

32. The data in the second column of the table indicate that, in the metropolitan areas, the number of poor declined by 4.7 million or 36.2% between 2010 and 2020. Yet, the fourth column shows a corresponding decline from 15.3% to 9.5%, or only 5.8%.
This apparent discrepancy reflects the fact that
   A. metropolitan areas are growing while the number of poor is contracting
   B. two columns in question are based on different sources of information
   C. difference between two percentages is not the same as the percent change in total numbers
   D. tables have inherent errors and must be carefully checked

32.____

33. The percentages in each of the last two columns of the table for 2010 and 2020 don't add up to 100%. This is for the reason that
    A. rounding off each entry to the nearest decimal place caused an error in the total such that the total is not equal to 100%
    B. these columns show the percentage of Blacks, aged, etc. who are poor rather than the percentage of poor who are Black, aged, etc.
    C. there was an error in the construction of the table which was not noticed until the table was already in print
    D. there is double counting in the entries in the table; some people ae counted more than once

34. Data such as that presented in the table on persons below poverty level are shown to a single decimal place because
    A. data in every table should always be shown to a single decimal place
    B. it is the minimal number of decimal places needed to distinguish among table entries
    C. there was no room for more decimal places in the table without crowding
    D. the more accurately a figure is shown the better it is for the user

35. In comparing the poverty of the young (under 25 years) with that of the older population (65 years and over) in 2010 and 2020, one could REASONABLY conclude that
    A. more young people than old people were poor but older people had a higher rate of poverty
    B. more older people than young people were poor but young people had a higher rate of poverty
    C. there is a greater degree of poverty among the younger population than among the older people

Questions 36-37.

DIRECTIONS: Questions 36 and 37 are to be answered ONLY on the basis of the information given in the following passage.

Two approaches are available in developing criteria for the evaluation of plans. One approach, designated Approach A, is a review and analysis of characteristics that differentiate successful plans from unsuccessful plans. These criteria are descriptive in nature and serve as a checklist against which the plan under consideration may be judged. These characteristics have been observed by many different students of planning, and there is considerable agreement concerning the characteristics necessary for a plan to be successful.
A second approach to the development of criteria for judging plans, designated Approach B is the determination of the degree to which the plan under consideration is economic. The word "economic" is used here in its broadest sense, i.e., effective in its utilization of resources. In order to determine the economic worth of a plan, it is necessary to use a technique that permits the description of any plan in economic terms and to utilize this technique to the extent that it becomes a "way of thinking" about plans.

8 #2)

36. According to <u>Approach B</u>, the MOST successful plan is generally one which   36._____
    A. costs least to implement
    B. gives most value for resources expended
    C. uses the least expensive resources
    D. utilizes the greatest number of resources

37. According to <u>Approach A</u>, a successful plan is one which is   37._____
    A. descriptive in nature
    B. lowest in cost
    C. similar to other successful plans
    D. agreed upon by many students of planning

Questions 38-40.

DIRECTIONS: Questions 38 through 40 are to be answered ONLY on the basis of the information provided in the following passage.

   The primary purpose of control reports is to supply information intended to serve as the basis for corrective action if needed. At the same time, the significance of control reports must be kept in proper perspective. Control reports are only a part of the planning-management information system. Control information includes non-financial as well as financial data that measure performance and isolate variances from standard. Control information also provides feedback so that planning information may be updated and corrected. Whenever possible, control reports should be designed so that they provide feedback for the planning process as well as provide information of immediate value to the control process.
   Since the culmination of the control process is the taking of necessary corrective action to bring performance in line with standards, it follows that control information must be directed to the person who is organizationally responsible for taking the required action. Usually the same information, though in a somewhat abbreviated form, is given to the responsible manager's superior. A district sales manager needs a complete daily record of the performance of each of his salesmen; yet, the report forwarded to the regional sales manager summarizes only the performance of each sales district in his region. In preparing reports for higher echelons of management, summary statements and recommendations for action should appear on the first page; substantiating data, usually the information presented to the person directly responsible for the operation, may be include if needed.

38. A control report serves its primary purpose as part of the process which leads   38._____
    DIRECTLY to
    A. better planning for future action
    B. increasing the performance of district salesmen
    C. the establishment of proper performance standards
    D. taking corrective action when performance is poor

39. The one of the following which would be the BEST description of a control   39._____
    report is that a control report is a form of
    A. planning   B. communication
    C. direction   D. organization

40. If control reports are to be effective, the one of the following which is LEAST essential to the effectiveness of control reporting is a system of
  A. communication
  B. standards
  C. authority
  D. work simplification

KEY (CORRECT ANSWERS)

1.	A	11.	B	21.	A	31.	B
2.	B	12.	A	22.	A	32.	C
3.	A	13.	C	23.	B	33.	B
4.	B	14.	D	24.	C	34.	D
5.	D	15.	C	25.	A	35.	A
6.	C	16.	D	26.	D	36.	B
7.	D	17.	A	27.	A	37.	C
8.	C	18.	C	28.	C	38.	D
9.	B	19.	D	29.	B	39.	B
10.	D	20.	B	30.	C	40.	D

EXAMINATION SECTION
TEST 1

DIRECTIONS: Each question or incomplete statement is followed by several suggested answers or completions. Select the one that *BEST* answers the question or completes the statement. *PRINT THE LETTER OF THE CORRECT ANSWER IN THE SPACE AT THE RIGHT.*

1. An analyst is writing a report dealing with the distribution of deaths caused by various types of cardiovascular diseases. He decides to facilitate the reader's grasp of the information presented by including in the report a device that permits comparison of parts to each other, and to the whole at the same time.
   Of the following, the *MOST* appropriate and efficient device he should use for this purpose is the

   A. graph
   B. pie diagram
   C. flow sheet
   D. line chart with one series

   1.____

2. In carrying out a cost-effectiveness analysis, the analyst should follow certain guidelines. The *MOST* important of these guidelines involves the

   A. utilization of both the fixed utility approach and the fixed budget approach
   B. proper structuring of the problem and design of the analysis
   C. necessity of building a model that is highly formal and mathematical
   D. provision for implicit treatment of uncertainty

   2.____

3. In a decision which involves fairness -- such as assigning new office equipment to workers when the agency does not receive enough new office equipment for the entire group -- the *PRIMARY* determinant of the decision's effectiveness will be the

   A. systematic or traditional approach which is emphasized in reaching the decision
   B. random nature of the assignment
   C. feedback a decisionmaker receives concerning the decision
   D. acceptance of the decision by the persons who have to execute it

   3.____

4. In order to give line personnel some insight into staff problems and vice versa it has been suggested that line and staff assignments within a particular city agency be rotated. Which of the following criticisms would be *MOST* valid for opposing such a proposal?

   A. Generally speaking, line and staff personnel have different perspectives on organizational structures which makes rotation in assignments extremely difficult.
   B. Since their educational backgrounds are often quite diverse, staff personnel are often at a disadvantage when serving in line assignments.
   C. Line personnel frequently resent having to perform the more difficult tasks that staff assignments entail.
   D. Serving in a rotating assignment may not necessarily provide the personnel with any significant degree of insight as anticipated.

   4.____

5. Which one of the following approaches to criticism of a subordinate or associate is *generally* the *MOST* appropriate and effective?
   Criticize

   A. by making a comparison with a more exemplary employee

   5.____

B. the act, not the person
C. in a humorous vein
D. in general rather than specific terms

6. Assume that two policy units have been formed to study the impact of Federal programs in the city. The two units operate in an essentially similar manner, except for their communications procedures. In unit A any member may communicate and exchange information with any other member of the unit; in unit B a member may only communicate information with the unit supervisor.
In evaluating the effect that these communications procedures have on the level of productivity, it will *generally* be found that

   A. unit A's level of productivity will be greater than unit B's level of productivity for simple problems
   B. unit B's level of productivity will be greater than unit A's level of productivity for simple problems
   C. initial levels of profuctivity are higher in unit A than unit B for complex problems
   D. initial levels of productivity are higher in unit B than in unit A for complex problems

7. In the process of communicating an idea, the following five distinct steps are generally involved:
   I. Selection of a media and transmission of the message
   II. Decoding of a message, i.e., meaning is extracted from the message
   III. Message is received
   IV. Idea is organized into a series of symbols designed to give meaning
   V. Action is taken and/or feedback is given
In what logical, sequential order should these steps be arranged for effective two-way communications to take place?

   A. V, I, II, III, IV
   B. II, I, III, IV, V
   C. IV, I, III, II, V
   D. I, III, IV, II, V

8. Informal employee groups that share certain norms and strive for member satisfaction through the achievement of group goals are known as work groups.
Which of the following statements can *generally* be considered as being *FALSE* in describing work groups in a moderate size organization?

   A. Formation of work groups is ubiquitous and inevitable.
   B. Work groups strongly influence the overall behavior and performance of their members.
   C. An organization can reap positive and negative consequences as a result of work groups.
   D. Elimination of work groups can be easily achieved by management pressure.

9. Under the management approach known as *management by objectives* which of the following criteria is *generally* used to determine whether the manager has been successful?

   A. Activities performed
   B. Results achieved
   C. Production schedules completed
   D. Financial savings accomplished

10. Of the following, the MOST accurate statement relative to job attitudes is that they

    A. cannot be influenced by only one person
    B. are always the result of work groups
    C. have no relationship to productivity
    D. are strongly influenced by work situation

11. Assume that measures to overcome a budget deficit, including attrition and a hiring freeze, have significantly decreased the work-output of a city agency. The agency administrator desires to develop a plan to restore production to its former level by increasing the work-load and responsibility of the agency's employees.
    In order to obtain *maximum* employee cooperation and *minimize* employee resistance, it would be MOST advisable for the

    A. administrator of the agency to personally describe to the employees the new work changes that they are to follow
    B. employees to decide what the optimal changes in the work load should be
    C. management representatives to consult with employee representatives on these matters
    D. immediate supervisor of the employees to decide on the work changes to be implemented

12. Eliciting the support and cooperation of others often requires a great deal of persuasion. Which one of the following persuasive techniques or practices is generally the LEAST desirable for you, an analyst, to use?

    A. Establish your expertness and authority
    B. Present your arguments without emotion
    C. In presenting your arguments, express yourself in the manner to which you are accustomed
    D. Try to find a face-saving way for your opponent to change his/her mind

13. The following illustration depicts the structure of a municipal agency.

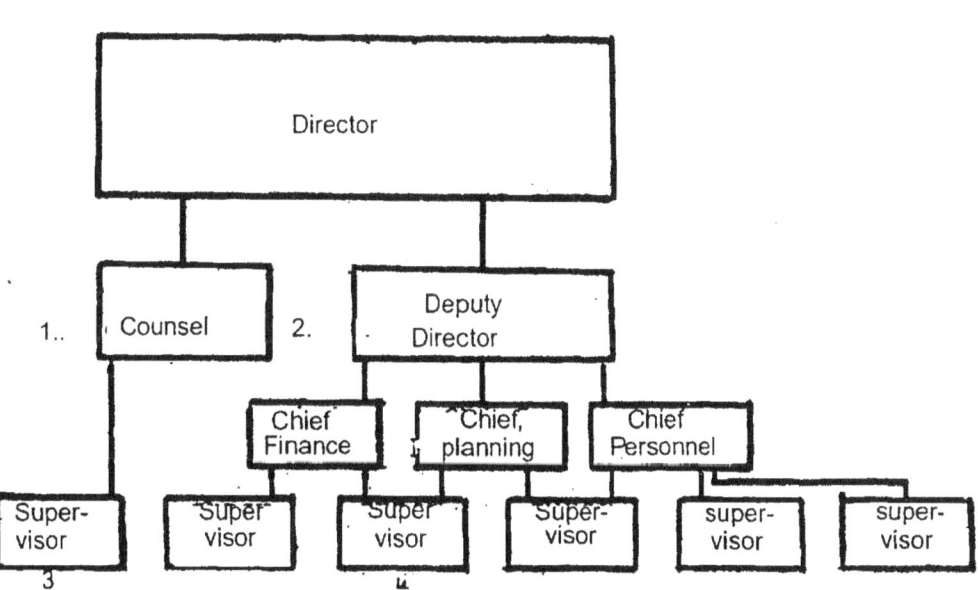

In the above illustration, which individual would generally be expected to encounter the MOST difficulty in carrying out his organizational functions?

    A. 1   B. 2   C. 3   D. 4

4 (#1)

14. An agency in which a free flow of communication exists is an agency in which no barriers or structures are erected to control or bar the flow of information and messages between and among management and staff, horizontally or vertically.
Of the following, the GREATEST disadvantage that would be most likely to occur in an agency in which such a free flow of communication exists, is that

    A. it would be difficult to determine which information is important and which is irrelevant
    B. there would be a lesser degree of staff-employee participation and cooperation in communicating
    C. more restrictive controls would be placed on managerial employees
    D. important communications would tend to be eliminated, and and trivial communications over-emphasized

14.____

15. Feedback is generally considered an essential factor in oral communication MAINLY because

    A. it enables the speaker to know whether he is understood
    B. the speed of communication is accelerated
    C. it eliminates the necessity of the speaker to use gestures and facial expressions when speaking
    D. the listener is unable to immediately respond to the speaker until the latter is finished

15.____

16. Assume that two employees are working on a joint project and they have a difference of opinion on the methodology to be used. Each employee not only listens to the other's opinion on methodology but projects him-self into the other's position.
This type of listening is *usually* considered

    A. *ineffective,* mainly because it will be impossible for the employees to reach a satisfactory agreement
    B. *effective,* mainly because each employee will then be more critical of the other's argument
    C. *ineffective,* mainly because each worker will unconsciously and unintentionally accept the other's viewpoint
    D. *effective,* mainly because each speaker can understand the other's viewpoint and can then respond intelligently to his remarks

16.____

17. The arithmetic mean is commonly used in describing data. Which one of the following statements is NOT true about the arithmetic mean?

    A. It is a measure of dispersion.
    B. The sum of the deviations around it is zero.
    C. It is easy to compute, understand and recognize.
    D. It may be treated alegebraically.

17.____

Questions 18 - 20.

DIRECTIONS: Answer Questions 18 through 20 on the basis of the following data. Assume that you are using these data in assessing the impact of Federal and State income taxes on New York City residents, and comparing it to the effect of Federal and State taxes in other areas.

EFFECT OF DEDUCTIBILITY (i.e., deductibility of taxes levied by other jurisdictions in calculating the net base of the tax in the taxing jurisdiction.)

Net income before personal exemption	Effect rate of tax				
	Federal (assuming no state tax)	State		Combined Federal and State	
		New York*	Minnesota (assuming no federal tax)	New York	Minnesota
	(1)	(2)	(3)	(4)	(5)
$20,000	25.0	4.1	6.9	27.6	27.9
50,000	42.2	5.4	9.1	44.0	43.9
100,000	56.0	5.9	9.8	57.5	57.1
200,000	69.2	6.1	10.1	69.9	69.5
1,500,000	88.0	6.3	10.5	89.3	88.9

*New York has no deductibility; the Federal government has deductibility.

18. In which of the following columns is the tax rate shown to be the LEAST progressive? 18.____

    A. 1 B. 2 C. 4 D. 5

19. Which of the following statements is TRUE about the reasons why Columns 1 and 2 do not equal Column 4 for each salary level? 19.____

    A. Personal deductions are taken into account in Column 4 but not in Columns 1 and 2.
    B. Federal deducibility of state taxes only is taken into account in Column 4 but not in Columns 1 and 2.
    C. Reciprocal deductibility is taken into account in Column 4 but not in Columns 1 and 2.
    D. State deductibility of federal taxes only is taken into account in Column 4 but not in Columns 1 and 2.

20. The EFFECT of the State's introducing deductibility, given that the Federal government maintains deductibility, is to 20.____

    A. increase Federal and State income
    B. decrease Federal and State income
    C. decrease Federal income and increase State income
    D. increase Federal income and decrease State income

21. Assume that you have been made project coordinator for a study concerning the implementation of casino gambling in the city. You have assigned each of the professional staff members simple tasks in specialized areas for the duration of the project. For you to make such job assignments would *generally* be

    A. *desirable;* the performance of simple tasks will motivate individuals to work diligently
    B. *desirable;* specialized tasks induce a sense of accomplishment to individuals
    C. *undesirable;* specialized tasks are more difficult to learn
    D. *undesirable;* specialized tasks may lead to a loss of feeling of accomplishment

22. Assume that you have been asked to submit a proposal for the reorganization of a unit that is charged with performing difficult nonroutine work. Frequently decisions must be made quickly and concurrence obtained from high-level agency heads.
    Given the above conditions, of the following it would be MOST logical to structure the organization

    A. on the basis of a relatively wide span of control
    B. on the basis of a relatively narrow span of control
    C. with many organizational levels with a wide span of control
    D. with more emphasis on line than staff units

23. Assume that a study has indicated that a recently created city *superagency* has had formal communication difficulties among various component agencies. It appears that jurisdictional overlapping among those agencies has caused frequent rerouting and unnecessary duplication of communications within the organization. Which one of the following proposals would MOST effectively deal with the communications problem encountered by this *superagency?*

    A. Create a central communications office to handle all communications for this *superagency.*
    B. Duplicate and distribute all communications to each component within this *superagency.*
    C. Reduce the overlapping areas of jurisdiction among the component agencies
    D. Decentralize the *superagency* on a *borough* basis to expedite mail delivery

24. The utilization of input-output concepts in connection with the application of the systems concept to government raises the problem of the quantification of objectives and performance (the value of the public benefit). The one of the following which is MOST easily *quantifiable* is

    A. education
    B. police service
    C. subway car maintenance
    D. the effectiveness of a welfare administrator

25. When an analyst tries to conceive of a city management problem as a *systems* problem, he is, first of all, confronted with establishing the boundaries of the system. Of the following, the city problem which can *most likely* be conceived of within a system whose boundaries are roughly equivalent to those of the city is

25.____

   A. taxation
   B. welfare
   C. fire protection
   D. transportation

KEY (CORRECT ANSWERS)

1. B	11. C
2. B	12. B
3. D	13. D
4. D	14. A
5. B	15. A
6. C	16. D
7. C	17. A
8. D	18. B
9. B	19. B
10. D	20. D

21. D
22. B
23. C
24. C
25. C

TEST 2

DIRECTIONS: Each question or incomplete statement is followed by several suggested answers or completions. Select the one that *BEST* answers the question or completes the statement. *PRINT THE LETTER OF THE CORRECT ANSWER IN THE SPACE AT THE RIGHT.*

1. When installing a new *system,* an analyst may choose among several types of installation plans - the *all-at-once type,* the *piecemeal type,* or the *parallel type* each suited to a particular problem or degree of complexity in the system.
   The one of the following situations in which the *parallel type* would be *MOST* appropriate is a situation

   A. in which a minimum installation cost is required
   B. involving a small volume of transactions
   C. in which the change is not radical or does not involve new machines
   D. involving large installation projects and intricate processing

   1.____

2. Many decision situations involve a great deal of uncertainty about the future, which is difficult to take into account in the analysis of alternatives. One technique developed for treating such uncertainty is designed to measure the possible effects on alternatives under analysis resulting from variations in uncertain elements. The analyst uses several *expected values* for uncertain parameters in an attempt to ascertain how the results vary (i.e., the relative ranking of the alternatives under consideration) in light of variations in the uncertain parameters. The analyst attempts to determine the alternative (or feasible combination of alternatives) likely to achieve a specified objective, gain or utility at the lowest cost. The one of the following which *BEST* describes the above technique is:

   A. Contingency analysis employing the fixed-budget approach
   B. Contingency analysis employing the fixed-benefits approach
   C. Sensitivity analysis employing the fixed-budget approach
   D. Sensitivity analysis employing the fixed-benefits approach

   2.____

3. In general, the analytical techniques of management science are of the *LEAST* value when

   A. the effects of a small number of controlled variables must be considered
   B. the number of relevant uncontrolled variables is small
   C. relevant causes and effects are factual in nature and can be stated and measured numerically or symbolically
   D. There are reasons to believe that past relationships will continue to hold in the future

   3.____

4. During the installation period of a new system, tight controls must be maintained over every phase of the operation. To do this, an analyst may set up a *warning system* within the system which forecasts potential bottle-necks and affords sufficient clues for correcting any problems, errors or fall-downs.
   The one of the following control devices or techniques which would be *most likely* to involve extra effort during the installation, and slow down the processing time is

   4.____

A. paper flow controls - log sheets, numerical controls, etc. (a system of logging input and output)
B. timing controls - to inform the analyst about the proper time interval between certain activities with-in the systems
C. program check points - a periodic review of processing to date at each check point
D. accounting control totals, to accumulate invoice numbers as the first and last steps in the system and compare the totals

5. Which of the following types of work measurement techniques would be MOST appropriate for obtaining details of a particular job for cost analysis purposes, such as the operating costs of various types of duplicating machines?

   A. Work sampling
   B. Predetermined time standards
   C. The time study (stop-watch timing)
   D. Historical

6. It is anticipated that a certain cancer detection program will be capable of detecting many cases at an early stage and that society will be thus enabled to cure twice as many cases as it cures currently. The benefits to society include the reduction in cost of hospitalization, etc., that would have been incurred otherwise.
Benefits such as a reduction in the cost of hospitalization are *most usually* called

   A. direct benefits
   B. secondary benefits
   C. intergenerational benefits
   D. external benefits

7. The results of departmental and agency programs can be measured in terms of *EFFECTIVENESS* or *BENEFITS*. Thus, careful budget preparation will permit the calculation of costs which can then be compared, or equated, to these results. Which one of the following statements pertaining to cost-effectiveness measurements is MOST valid?

   A. In cost-effectiveness measurements, a dollar value is assigned to the output.
   B. The measurement is expressed in terms of quality of output for a given cost.
   C. Cost effectiveness ratios express the relationship between the costs of programs
   D. A cost-effectiveness measurement will show the number of outputs which can be achieved for the expenditure of a given amount of money.

8. Assume that you have been asked to evaluate personnel programs in four city agencies The statistical test that would be MOST appropriate for testing the significance of the differences in the mean number of days absent (normality may be assumed) during the year 2004 in four different agencies is the

   A. one-way analysis of variance
   B. standard deviation
   C. regression analysis
   D. Chi-square test (x^2-test)

9. Assume that you have been asked to evaluate differences in the children just enrolled in two youth programs. In reviewing the relevant published material you find that in one particular study involving two groups, N = 9 and N = 13, there is a significant difference in the mean scores of the two groups on a characteristic which you believe to be normally distributed.
The statistical test *most likely* used in this study to determine the significance of the difference in the means of the two groups on this characteristic is the

   A. Chi-square test (x2-test)
   B. Pearson Product-Moment correlation (r)
   C. t-test
   D. two-way analysis of variance

10. In statistics, three common measures of central tendency are the mean, median and mode.
For which of the following conditions would the median generally be the *BEST* choice to use? When the

   A. distribution of scores is skewed
   B. scores are distributed symmetrically around a central point
   C. standard deviation must also be calculated
   D. most frequently occurring value is required

11. Nonparametric statistical tests are *usually* employed when

   A. large samples are used
   B. a very powerful or exact test is needed
   C. data cannot be expressed in ranks
   D. a normally distributed population cannot be assumed

12. Assume that in a report presented to you by an employee under your supervision, a coefficient of correlation of +1.73 is reported between the age at which one first smokes cigarettes and the age at which one first smokes marijuana.
You should *most reasonably* interpret this figure to mean there is a

   A. strong positive correlation
   B. weak positive correlation
   C. weak negative correlation
   D. typographical error

13. One of the major research techniques most often used in studies of organizational behavior problems is the survey. An analyst who utilizes the survey technique should be aware that its *MAJOR* drawback is

   A. the lack of depth obtained from the two major data-collection tolls used in surveys: the mailed question-naire and the personal interview
   B. its impracticality in assessing or estimating the present state of affairs with regard to a variable that changes over time for a large group of subjects
   C. the restriction of this technique to a single, or very few, units of analysis
   D. its absence of dependence upon the collection of empirical data

14. In order for an analyst to understand and interpret statistical data he/she must understand which types of data tend to approximate the normal probability curve, i.e., are normally distributed.
Which of the following types of data falls into this category?
Frequency of

   A. educational test scores for students of a given age, plotted against test score
   B. filing of income tax returns for citizens of a given age, plotted against date of filing
   C. deaths due to childhood disease plotted against age
   D. deaths due to degenerative diseases, plotted against age

14.____

15. Which of the following terms describes a line or curve formed by plotting employees salaries that increase yearly by a fixed percentage over the previous year? (In answering the question, assume that time is on the horizontal axis (abscissa) and salary is on the vertical axis (ordinate) - both axes are marked linearly.)

   A. Linear (increasing at a constant rate)
   B. Positively accelerating (increasing at an increasing rate)
   C. Negatively accelerating (increasing at a decreasing rate)
   D. Negatively decelerating (decreasing at a decreasing rate)

15.____

Questions 16 - 17

DIRECTIONS: Answer Questions 16 and 17 on the basis of the following groups, both of which depict the same information in different ways.

The x and y axes in graphs A and B are not necessarily drawn in the same scale. The points along the curves on both graphs represent corresponding points, and are the upper limits of class intervals.

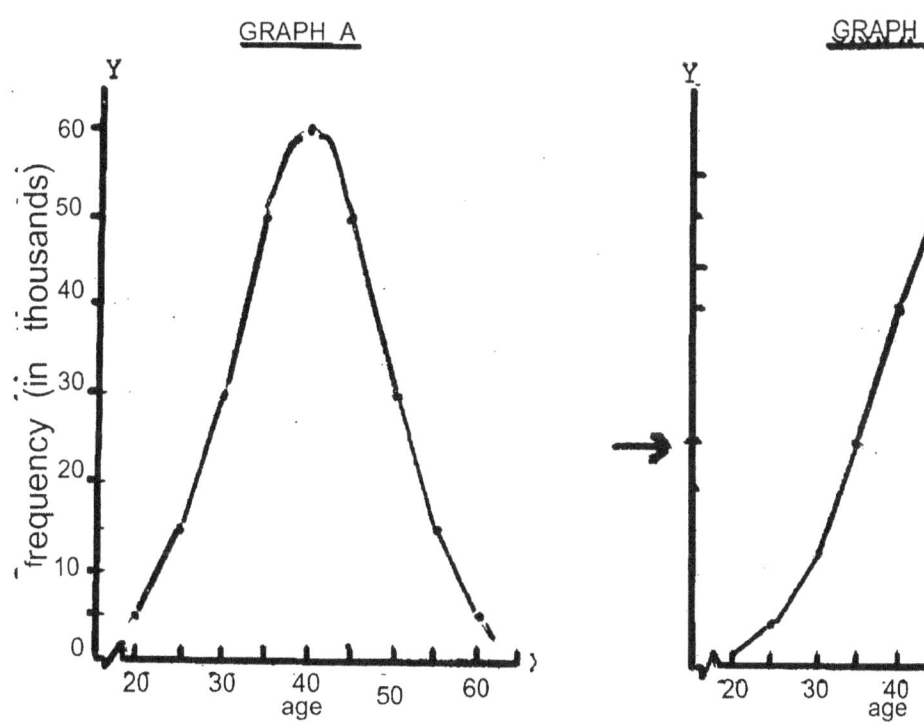
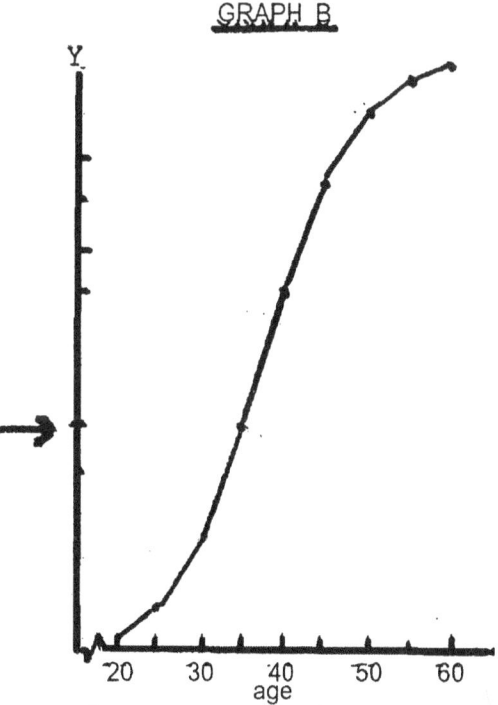

16. The ordinate (y-axis) in graph B is 16.____

    A. frequency
    B. cumulative frequency
    C. average frequency
    D. log frequency

17. The arrow on the y-axis in graph B indicates a particular number. That number is, *most nearly* 17.____

    A. 100
    B. 50,000
    C. 100,000
    D. 150,000

Questions 18 - 19

DIRECTIONS: Answer Questions 18 and 19 on the basis of the graphs that appear on the following page.

18. In Graph I, the vertical distance between lines E and T within the crosshatched area represents the 18.____

    A. savings to the city if work of less than 50 miles is performed by the city
    B. loss to the city if work of less than 50 miles is performed by the city
    C. savings to the city if work of more than 50 miles is performed by the city
    D. loss to the city if work of more than 50 miles is performed by the city

19. Graph II is identical to Graph I except that contractor costs have been eliminated. Total costs (line E) are the sum of fixed costs (line F) and variable costs. Variable costs are represented by line 19.____

    A. A
    B. B
    C. C
    D. D

ROAD REPAIR COSTS IF PERFORMED BY CITY STAFF OR AN OUTSIDE CONTRACTOR

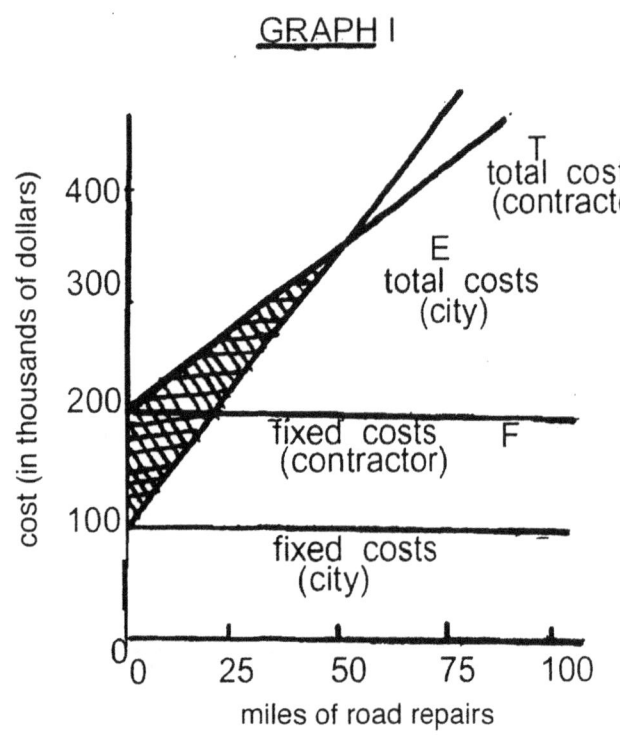
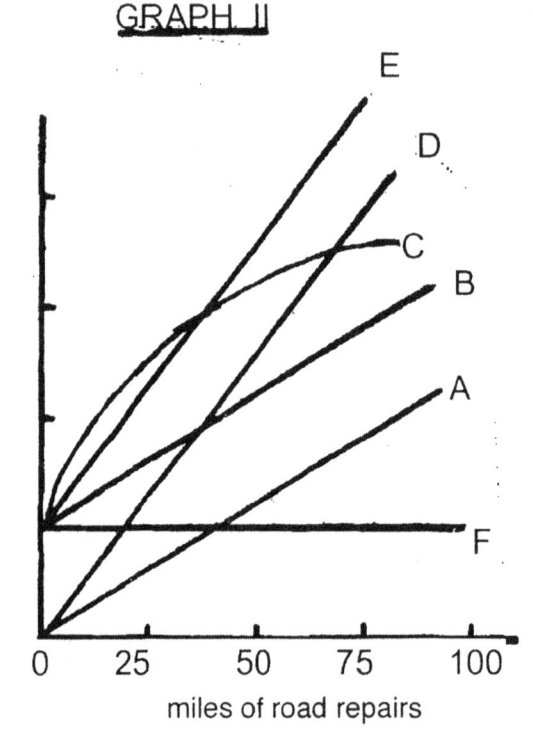

20. Fiscal experts in municipal affairs have contended that the most acute problem facing the city today seems to be the growth of the city's short-term debt.
Of the following, the LEAST likely reason for the city to engage in short-term borrowing is that the city

   A. expects money from long-term borrowing that it plans to undertake
   B. needs to be tided over until funds due from the Federal or State government arrive
   C. needs money to finance big construction outlays
   D. anticipates money from future tax collections

20.____

21. A MAJOR criticism of the *superagency* has been the

   A. additional layers of control and additional lines of command
   B. merger of departmental functions
   C. political manipulation
   D. professional incompetence in administration

21.____

22. The management of a large urban city is different in many ways from the management of other systems, particularly large business organizations.
The one of the following which does NOT exemplify these differences is:

   A. A mayor, in contrast to a manager of a large business, is often held responsible for services, etc., over which he has little authority.
   B. Top management of a large urban city must deal with a greater number of different pressures from diverse interest groups.
   C. The city government, in contrast to a large business organization, often lacks adequate management controls, and goals are often ill-defined.
   D. The multiplicity of alternatives available to city government as opposed to large businesses, are substantially greater, making decision-making haphazard.

22.____

23. The function called internal control applies to those measures taken by a government agency to protect its assets. Internal control has a role to play as an enforcer of administrative edicts as well as for purposes of asset protection.
Of the following statements relating to internal control, as described above, select the *one* usually considered to be LEAST valid.

   A. Internal control makes auditing by an external agency more difficult.
   B. The function of internal control often involves the auditing process.
   C. That people cannot be trusted to act wisely and honestly seems to be implicit in all the principles of internal control.
   D. Internal control is simply a form of self-audit by the agency itself.

23.____

24. In addition to the new effect on workers who are unskilled and undereducated, the severe effect of the high unemployment rate in the city has recently become MOST apparent among

   A. skilled craftsmen in the building trades
   B. clerical employees
   C. middle management personnel
   D. architects and engineers

24.____

25. The fact that the city has the second highest jobless rate of any major U.S. city except Detroit is considered particularly significant because, compared to Detroit, unemployment in the city

    A. is caused by city government fiscal measures rather than private business conditions
    B. exists in more than one industry
    C. results in an increase in welfare expenditures to a greater extent
    D. more seriously affects the world-wide economy

25.____

KEY (CORRECT ANSWERS)

1. D	11. D
2. D	12. D
3. A	13. A
4. A	14. A
5. C	15. B
6. A	16. B
7. D	17. C
8. A	18. A
9. C	19. D
10. A	20. C

21. A
22. D
23. A
24. A
25. B

EXAMINATION SECTION
TEST 1

DIRECTIONS: Each question or incomplete statement is followed by several suggested answers or completions. Select the one that BEST answers the question or completes the statement. *PRINT THE LETTER OF THE CORRECT ANSWER IN THE SPACE AT THE RIGHT.*

1. When a supervisor in a large office introduces a change in the regular office procedure, it is USUAL to expect
    A. immediate acceptance by office staff, unless the change is unnecessary
    B. an immediate production increase, since new procedures are more stimulating than old ones
    C. a temporary production loss, even if the change is really an overall improvement
    D. resistance to the change only if it has been put into writing

    1.____

2. A supervisor evaluates the performance of subordinates and then applies measures, where needed, which result in bringing performance up to desired standards.
Which of the following functions of management might he BEST be described as performing?
    A. Organizing   B. Controlling   C. Directing   D. Planning

    2.____

3. Assume that, as a supervisor, you have been assigned responsibility for a new and complex project which entails collection and analysis of data. You have prepared general written instructions which explain the project and procedures to be followed by several statisticians.
Which of the following procedures would be MOST advisable for you, as the supervisor, to follow?
    A. Distribute the instructions to your subordinates to come to you with any important questions
    B. Distribute the instructions and advise subordinates to come to you with any important questions
    C. Meet with subordinates as a group and explain the project using the written instructions as a handout
    D. Delegate responsibility for further explanation of the project to an immediate qualified subordinate to free you for concentration on research design

    3.____

4. Supervisors have an obligation to make careful and thorough appraisals and reports of probationary employees.
Of the following, the MOST important justification for this statement is that the probationary period
    A. should be used for positive development of the employee's understanding of the organization
    B. is the most effective period for changing a new employee's knowledges, skills, and attitudes

    4.____

C. insures that the employee will meet work standard requirements on future assignments
D. should be considered as the final step in the selection process

5. Many studies of management indicate that a principal reason for failure of supervisors lies in their ability to delegate duties effectively.
Which one of the following practices by a supervisor would NOT be a block to successful delegation?
    A. Instructing the delegate to follow a set procedure in carrying out the assignment
    B. Maintaining point-by-point control over the process delegated
    C. Transferring ultimate responsibility for the duties assigned to the delegate
    D. Requiring the delegate to keep the delegator informed of his progress

6. Crosswise communication occurs between personnel at lower or middle levels of different organizational units. It often speeds information and improves understanding, but has certain dangers.
Of the following proposed policies, which would NOT be important as a safeguard in crosswise communication?
    A. Supervisors should agree as to how crosswise communication should occur.
    B. Crosswise relationships must exist only between employees of equal status.
    C. Subordinates must keep their superiors informed about their interdepartmental communications.
    D. Subordinates must refrain from making commitments beyond their authority.

7. Systems theory has given us certain principles which are as applicable to organizational and social activities as they are to those of science.
With regard to the training of employees in an organization, which of the following is likely to be MOST consistent with the modern systems approach?
Training can be effective ONLY when it is
    A. related to the individual abilities of the employees
    B. done on all levels of the organizational hierarchy
    C. evaluated on the basis of experimental and control groups
    D. provided on the job by the immediate supervisor

8. The management of a large agency, before making a decision as to whether or not to computerize its operations, should have a feasibility study made.
Of the following, the one which is LEAST important to include in such a study is
    A. the current abilities of management and staff to use a computer
    B. projected workloads and changes in objectives of functional units in the agency
    C. the contributions expected of each organizational unit towards achievement of agency objectives
    D. the decision-making activity and informational needs of each management function

9. Managing information covers the creation, collection, processing, storage, and transmission of information that appears in a variety of forms. A supervisor responsible for a statistical unit can be considered, in many respects, an information manager.
Of the following, which would be considered the LEAST important aspect of the information manager's job?
   A. Establishing better information standards and forms
   B. Reducing the amount of unnecessary paperwork performed
   C. Producing progressively greater numbers of informational reports
   D. Developing a greater appreciation for information among management members

9._____

10. Because of the need for improvement in information systems throughout industry and government, various techniques for improving these systems have been developed.
Of these, *systems simulation* is a technique for improving systems which
   A. creates new ideas and concepts through the use of a computer
   B. deals with time controlling of interrelated systems which make up an overall project
   C. permits experimentation with various ideas to see what results might be obtained
   D. does not rely on assumptions which condition the value of the results

10._____

11. The one of the following which it is NOT advisable for a supervisor to do when dealing with individual employees is to
   A. recognize a person's outstanding service as well as his mistakes
   B. help an employee satisfy his need to excel
   C. encourage an efficient employee to seek better opportunities even if this action may cause the supervisor to lose a good worker
   D. take public notice of an employee's mistakes so that fewer errors will be made in the future

11._____

12. Suppose that you are in a department where you are given the responsibility for teaching seven new assistants a number of routine procedures that all assistants should know.
Of the following, the BEST method for you to follow in teaching these procedures is to
   A. separate the slower learners from the faster learners and adapt your presentation to their level of ability
   B. instruct all the new employees in a group without attempting to assess differences in learning rates
   C. restrict your approach to giving them detailed written instructions in order to save time
   D. avoid giving the employees written instructions in order to force them to memorize job procedures quickly

12._____

13. Suppose that you are a supervisor to whom several assistants must hand in work for review. You notice that one of the assistants gets very upset whenever you discover an error in his work, although all the assistants make mistakes from time to time.
    Of the following, it would be BEST for you to
    A. arrange discreetly for the employee's work to be reviewed by another supervisor
    B. ignore his reaction since giving attention to such behavior increases its intensity
    C. suggest that the employee seek medical help since he has such great difficulty in accepting normal criticism
    D. try to build the employee's self-confidence by emphasizing those parts of his work that are done well

14. Suppose you are a supervisor responsible for supervising a number of assistants in an agency where each assistant receives a manual of policies and procedures when he first reports for work. You have been asked to teach your subordinates a new procedure which requires knowledge of several items of policy and procedure found in the manual.
    The one of the following techniques which it would be BEST for you to employ is to
    A. give verbal instructions which include a review of the appropriate standard procedures as well as an explanation of new tasks
    B. give individual instruction restricted to the new procedure to each assistant as the need arises
    C. provide written instructions for new procedural elements and refer employees to their manuals for explanation of standard procedures
    D. ask employees to review appropriate sections of their manual and then explain those aspects of the new procedure which the manual did not cover

15. Supposes that you are a supervisor in charge of a unit in which changes in work procedures are about to be instituted.
    The one of the following which you, as the supervisor, should anticipate as being MOST likely to occur during the changeover is
    A. a temporary rise in production because of interest in the new procedures
    B. uniform acceptance of these procedures on the part of your staff
    C. varying interpretations of the new procedures by your staff
    D. general agreement among staff members that the new procedures are advantageous

16. Suppose that a supervisor and one of the assistants under his supervision are known to be friends who play golf together on weekends.
    The maintenance of such a friendship on the part of the supervisor is GENERALLY
    A. *acceptable* as long as this assistant continues to perform his duties satisfactorily
    B. *unacceptable* since the supervisor will find it difficult to treat the assistant as a subordinate

C. *acceptable* if the supervisor does not favor this assistant above other employees
D. *unacceptable* because the other assistants will resent the friendship regardless of the supervisor's behavior on the job

17. Suppose that you are a supervisor assigned to review the financial records of an agency which has recently undergone a major reorganization.
Which of the following would it be BEST for you to do FIRST?
    A. Interview the individual in charge of agency financial operations to determine whether the organizational changes affect the system of financial review
    B. Discuss the nature of the reorganization with your own supervisor to anticipate and plan a new financial review procedure
    C. Carry out the financial review as usual, and adjust your methods to any problems arising from the reorganization
    D. Request a written report from the agency head explaining the nature of the reorganization and recommending changes in the system of financial review

17.____

18. Suppose that a newly assigned supervisor finds that he must delegate some of his duties to subordinates in order to get the work done.
Which one of the following would NOT be a block to his delegating these duties effectively?
    A. Inability to give proper directions as to what he wants done
    B. Reluctance to take calculated risks
    C. Lack of trust in his subordinates
    D. Retaining ultimate responsibility for the delegated work

18.____

19. A supervisor sometimes performs the staff function of preparing and circulating reports among bureau chiefs.
Which of the following is LEAST important as an objective in designing and writing such reports?
    A. Providing relevant information on past, present, and future actions
    B. Modifying his language in order to insure goodwill among the bureau chiefs
    C. Helping the readers of the report to make appropriate decisions
    D. Summarizing important information to help readers see trends or outstanding points

19.____

20. Suppose you are a supervisor assigned to prepare a report to be read by all bureau chiefs in your agency.
The MOST important reason for avoiding highly technical accounting terminology in writing this report is to
    A. ensure the accuracy and relevancy of the text
    B. insure winning the readers' cooperation
    C. make the report more interesting to the readers
    D. make it easier for the readers to understand

20.____

21. Which of the following conditions is MOST likely to cause low morale in an office?
    A. Different standards of performance for individuals in the same title
    B. A requirement that employees perform at full capacity
    C. Standards of performance that vary with titles of employees
    D. Careful attention to the image of the division or department

22. A wise supervisor or representative of management realizes that, in the relationship between supervisor and subordinates, all power is not on the side of management, and that subordinates do sometimes react to restrictive authority in such a manner as to seriously retard management's objectives. A wise supervisor does not stimulate such reactions.
    In the subordinate's attempt to retaliate against an unusually authoritative management style, which of the following actions would generally be LEAST successful for the subordinate? He
    A. joins with other employees in organizations to deal with management
    B. obviously delays in carrying out instructions which are given in an arrogant or incisive manner
    C. performs assignments exactly as instructed even when he recognizes errors in instructions
    D. holds back the flow of feedback information to superiors

23. Which of the following is the MOST likely and costly effect of vague and indefinite instructions given to subordinates by a supervisor?
    A. Misunderstanding and ineffective work on the part of the subordinates
    B. A necessity for the supervisor to report identical instructions with each assignment
    C. A failure of the supervisor to adequately keep the attention of subordinates
    D. Inability of subordinates to assist each other in the absence of the supervisor

24. At the professional level, there is a kind of informal authority which exercises itself even though no delegation of authority has taken place from higher management. It occurs within the context of knowledge required and professional competence in a special area.
    An example of the kind of authority described in this statement is MOST clearly exemplified in the situation where a senior supervisor influences associates and subordinates by virtue of the
    A. salary level fixed for his particular set of duties
    B. amount of college training he possesses
    C. technical position he has gained and holds on the work team
    D. initiative and judgment he has demonstrated to his supervisor

25. An assistant under your supervision attempts to conceal the fact that he has made an error.
    Under this circumstance, it would be BEST for you, as the supervisor, to proceed on the assumption that

A. this evasion indicates something wrong in the fundamental relationship between you and the assistant
B. this evasion is not deliberate, if the error is subsequently corrected by the assistant
C. this evasion should be overlooked if the error is not significant
D. detection and correction of errors will come about as an automatic consequence of internal control procedures

KEY (CORRECT ANSWERS)

1. C
2. B
3. C
4. D
5. D

6. B
7. B
8. A
9. C
10. C

11. D
12. B
13. D
14. A
15. C

16. C
17. A
18. D
19. B
20. D

21. A
22. B
23. A
24. C
25. A

TEST 2

DIRECTIONS: Each question or incomplete statement is followed by several suggested answers or completions. Select the one that BEST answers the question or completes the statement. *PRINT THE LETTER OF THE CORRECT ANSWER IN THE SPACE AT THE RIGHT.*

1. The unit which you supervise has a number of attorneys, accountants, examiners, statisticians, and clerks who prepare some of the routine papers required to be filed. In order to be certain that nothing goes out of your office that is improper, you have instituted a system that requires that you review and initial all moving papers, memoranda of law and briefs that are prepared. As a result, you put in a great deal of overtime and even must take work home with you frequently.
A situation such as this is
    A. inevitable if you are to keep proper controls over the quality of the office work product
    B. indicative of the fact that the agency must provide an additional position within your office for an assistant supervisor who would do all the reviewing, leaving you free for other pressing administrative work and to handle the most difficult work in your unit
    C. the logical result of an ever-increasing caseload
    D. symptomatic of poor supervision and management

1.____

2. Your unit has been assigned a new employee who has never worked for the city.
To orient him to his job in your unit, of the following, the BEST procedure is first to
    A. assign him to another employee to whatever work that employee gives him so that he can become familiar with your work and at the same time be productive
    B. give him copies of the charter and code provisions affecting your operations plus any in-office memoranda or instructions that are available and have him read them
    C. assign him to work on a relatively simple problem and then, after he has finished it, tell him politely what he did wrong
    D. explain to him the duties of his position and the functions of the office

2.____

3. A bureau chief who supervises other supervisors makes it a practice to assign them more cases than they can possibly handle.
This approach is
    A. *right*, because it results in getting more work done than would otherwise be the case
    B. *right*, because it relieves the bureau chief making the assignments of the responsibility of getting the work done
    C. *wrong*, because it builds resistance on the part of those called upon to handle the caseload
    D. *wrong*, because superiors lose track of cases

3.____

4. Assume you are a supervisor and are expected to exercise *authority* over subordinates.
   Which of the following BEST defines *authority*? The
   A. ability to control the nature of the contribution a subordinate is desirous of making
   B. innate inability to get others to do for you what you want to get done irrespective of their own wishes
   C. legal right conferred by the agency to control the actions of others
   D. power to determine a subordinate's attitude toward his agency and his superiors

5. Paternalistic leadership stresses a paternal or fatherly influence in the relationships between the leader and the group and is manifest in a watchful care for the comfort and welfare of the followers.
   Which one of the following statements regarding paternalistic leadership is MOST accurate?
   A. Employees who work well under paternalistic leadership come to expect such leadership even when the paternal leader has left the organization.
   B. Most disputes arising out of supervisor-subordinate relationships develop because group leaders do not understand the principles of paternalistic leadership.
   C. Paternalistic leadership frequently destroys office relationships because most employees are turned into non-thinking dependent robots.
   D. Paternalistic leadership is rarely, if ever, successful because employees resent paternalistic leadership which they equate with weakness.

6. Employees who have extensive dealings with members of the public should have, as much as possible, *real acceptance* of all people and a willingness to serve everyone impartially and objectively.
   Assuming that this statement is correct, the one of the following which would be the BEST demonstration of *real acceptance* is
   A. condoning antisocial behavior
   B. giving the appearance of agreeing with everyone encountered
   C. refusing to give opinions on anyone's behavior
   D. understanding the feelings expressed through a person's behavior

7. Assume that the agency chief has requested you to help plan a public relations program because of recent complaints from citizens about the unbecoming conduct and language of various groups of city employees who have dealings with the public.
   In carrying out this assignment, the one of the following steps which should be undertaken FIRST is to
   A. study the characteristics of the public clientele dealt with by employees in your agency
   B. arrange to have employees attend several seminars on human relations
   C. develop several procedures for dealing with the public and allow the staff to choose the one which is best
   D. find out whether the employees in your agency may oppose any plan proposed by you

8. The one of the following statements which BEST expresses the relationship between the morale of government employees and the public relations aspects of their work is:
   A. There is little relationship between employee morale and public relations, chiefly because public opinion is shaped primarily by response to departmental policy formulation.
   B. Employee morale is closely related to public relations, chiefly because the employee's morale will largely determine the manner in which he deals with the public.
   C. There is little relationship between employee morale and public relations, chiefly because public relations is primarily a function of the agency's public relations department.
   D. Employee morale is closely related to public relations, chiefly because employee morale indicates the attitude of the agency's top officials toward the public.

8.____

9. As a supervisor, you are required to deal extensively with the public. The agency chief has indicated that he is considering holding a special in-service training course for employees in communications skills
   Holding this training course would be
   A. *advisable*, chiefly because government employees should receive formal training in public relations skills
   B. *inadvisable*, chiefly because the public regards such training as a *waste of the taxpayers money*
   C. *advisable*, chiefly because such training will enable the employee to aid in drafting departmental press releases
   D. *inadvisable*, chiefly because of the great difficulty involved in developing skills through formal instruction

9.____

10. Assume that you have extensive contact with the public. In dealing with the public, sensitivity to an individual's attitudes is important because these attitudes can be used to predict behavior.
    However, the MAIN reason that attitudes CANNOT successfully predict all behavior is that
    A. attitudes are highly resistant to change
    B. an individual acquires attitudes as a function of growing up in a particular cultural environment
    C. attitudes are only one of many factors which determine a person's behavior
    D. an individual's behavior is not always observable

10.____

11. Rotation of employees from assignment to assignment is sometimes advocated by management experts.
    Of the following, the MOST probable advantage to the organization of this practice is that it leads to
    A. higher specialization of duties so that excessive identification with the overall organization is reduced
    B. increased loyalty of employees to their immediate supervisors

11.____

C. greater training and development of employees
D. intensified desire of employees to obtain additional, outside formal education

12. Usually, a supervisor should attempt to standardize the work for which he is responsible.
    The one of the following which is a BASIC reason for doing this is to
    A. eliminate the need to establish priorities
    B. permit the granting of exceptions to rules and special circumstances
    C. facilitate the taking of action based on applicable standards
    D. learn the identity of outstanding employees

12._____

13. The differences between line and staff authority are often quite ambiguous.
    Of the following, the ESSENTIAL difference is that
    A. *line authority* is exercised by first-level supervisors; *staff authority* is exercised by higher-level supervisors and managerial staff
    B. *staff authority* is the right to issue directives; *line authority* is entirely consultative
    C. *line authority* is the power to make decisions regarding intra-agency matters; *staff authority* involves decisions regarding inter-agency matters
    D. *staff authority* is largely advisory; *line authority* is the right to command

13._____

14. Modern management theory stresses work-centered motivation as one way of increasing the productivity of employees.
    The one of the following which is PARTICULARLY characteristic of such motivation is that it
    A. emphasizes the crucial role of routinization of procedures
    B. stresses the satisfaction to be found in performing work
    C. features the value of wages and fringe benefits
    D. uses a firm but fair method of discipline

14._____

15. The agency's informal communications network is called the *grapevine.*
    If employees are learning about important organizational developments primarily through the grapevine, this is MOST likely an indication that
    A. official channels of communication are not functioning so efficiently as they should
    B. supervisory personnel are making effective use of the grapevine to communicate with subordinates
    C. employees already have a clear understanding of the agency's policies and procedures
    D. upward formal channels of communication within the agency are informing management of employee grievances

15._____

16. Of the following, a flow chart is BEST described as a chart which shows
    A. the places through which work moves in the course of the job process
    B. which employees perform specific functions leading to the completion of a job

16._____

C. the schedules for production and how they eliminate waiting time between jobs
D. how work units are affected by the actions of related work units

17. Evaluation of the results of training is necessary in order to assess its value. Of the following, the BEST technique for the supervisor to use in determining whether the training under consideration actually resulted in the desired modification of the behavior of the employee concerned is through
    A. inference   B. job analysis   C. observation   D. simulation

17._____

18. The usual distinction between line and staff authority is that staff authority is mainly advisory, whereas line authority is the right to command. However, a third category has been suggested-prescriptive-to distinguish those personnel whose functions may be formally defined as staff but in practice exercise considerable authority regarding decisions relating to their specialties.
The one of the following which indicates the MAJOR purpose of creating this third category is to
    A. develop the ability of each employee to perform a greater number of tasks
    B. reduce line-staff conflict
    C. prevent over-specialization of functions
    D. encourage decision-making by line personnel

18._____

19. It is sometimes considered desirable to train employees to a standard of proficiency higher than that deemed necessary for actual job performance.
The MOST likely reason for such overtraining would be to
    A. eliminate the need for standards
    B. increase the value of refresher training
    C. compensate for previous lack of training
    D. reduce forgetting or loss of skill

19._____

20. Assume that you have been directed to immediately institute various new procedures in the handling of records.
Of the following, the BEST method for you to use to insure that your subordinates know exactly what to do is to
    A. circulate a memorandum explaining the new procedure have your subordinates initial it
    B. explain the new procedures to one or two subordinates and ask them to tell the others
    C. have a meeting with your subordinates to give them copies of the procedures and discuss it with them
    D. post the new procedures where they can be referred to by all those concerned

20._____

21. A supervisor decided to hold a problem-solving conference with his entire staff and distributed an announcement and agenda one week before the meeting.
Of the following, the BEST reason for providing each participant with an agenda is that
    A. participants will feel that something will be accomplished
    B. participants may prepare for the conference
    C. controversy will be reduced
    D. the top man should state the expected conclusions

22. In attempting to motivate employees, rewards are considered preferable to punishment PRIMARILY because
    A. punishment seldom has any effect on human behavior
    B. punishment usually results in decreased production
    C. supervisors find it difficult to punish
    D. rewards are more likely to result in willing cooperation

23. In an attempt to combat the low morale in his organization, a high-level supervisor publicized an *open-door* policy to allow employees who wished to do so to come to him with their complaints.
Which of the following is LEAST likely to account for the fact that no employee came in with a complaint?
    A. Employees are generally reluctant to go over the heads of their immediate supervisors.
    B. The employees did not feel that management would help them.
    C. The low morale was not due to complaints association with the job.
    D. The employees felt that they had more to lose than to gain.

24. It is MOST desirable to use written instructions rather than oral instructions for a particular job when
    A. a mistake on the job will not be serious
    B. the job can be completed in a short time
    C. there is no need to explain the job minutely
    D. the job involves many details

25. You have been asked to prepare for public distribution a statement dealing with a controversial matter.
Of the following approaches, the one which would usually be MOST effective is to present your department's point of view
    A. as tersely as possible with no reference to any other matters
    B. developed from ideas and facts well known to most readers
    C. and show all the statistical data and techniques which were used in arriving at it
    D. in such a way that the controversial parts are omitted

KEY (CORRECT ANSWERS)

1.	D	11.	C
2.	D	12.	C
3.	C	13.	D
4.	C	14.	B
5.	A	15.	A
6.	D	16.	A
7.	A	17.	C
8.	B	18.	B
9.	A	19.	D
10.	C	20.	C

21.	B
22.	D
23.	C
24.	D
25.	B

TEST 3

DIRECTIONS: Each question or incomplete statement is followed by several suggested answers or completions. Select the one that BEST answers the question or completes the statement. *PRINT THE LETTER OF THE CORRECT ANSWER IN THE SPACE AT THE RIGHT.*

1. An administrator who supervises other supervisors makes it a practice to set deadline dates for completion of assignments.
   A NATURAL consequence of setting deadline dates is that
   A. supervisors will usually wait until the deadline date before they give projects their wholehearted attention
   B. projects are completed sooner than if no deadline dates are set
   C. such dates are ignored even though they are conspicuously posted
   D. the frequency of errors sharply increases resulting in an inability to meet deadlines

   1.____

2. Assume that you are chairing a meeting of the members of your staff. You throw out a question to the group. No one answers your question immediately, so that you find yourself faced with silence.
   In the circumstances, it would probably be BEST for you to
   A. ask the member of the group who appears to be least attentive to repeat the question
   B. change the topic quickly
   C. repeat the question carefully, pronouncing each word, and if there is still no response, repeat the question an additional time
   D. wait for an answer since someone will usually say something to break the tension

   2.____

3. Assume that you are holding a meeting with the members of your staff. John, a member of the unit, keeps sidetracking the subject of the discussion by bringing up extraneous matters. You deal with the situation by saying to him after he has raised an immaterial point, *"That's an interesting point John, but can you show me how it ties in with what we're talking about?"*
   Your approach in this situation would GENERALLY be considered
   A. *bad*; you have prevented the group from discussing not only extraneous matters but pertinent material as well
   B. *bad*; you have seriously humiliated John in front of the entire group
   C. *good*; you have pointed out how the discussion is straying from the main topic
   D. *good*; you have prevented John from presenting extraneous matters at future meetings

   3.____

4. Assume that a senior supervisor is asked to supervise a group of staff personnel. The work of one of these staff men meets minimum standards of acceptability. However, this staff man constantly looks for something at which to take offense. In any conversation with either a fellow staff man or with a superior, he views the slightest criticism as a grave insult.

   4.____

In this case, the senior supervisor should
- A. advise the staff man that the next time he refuses to accept criticism, he will be severely reprimanded
- B. ask member of the group for advice on how to deal with this staff man
- C. make it a practice to speak calmly, slowly, and deliberately to this staff man and question him frequently to make sure that there is no breakdown in communications
- D. recognize that professional help may be required and that this problem may not be conducive to a solution by a supervisor

5. Assume that you discover that one of the staff in preparing certain papers has made a serious mistake which has become obvious.
   In dealing with this situation, it would be BEST for you to begin by
   - A. asking the employee how the mistake happened
   - B. asking the employee to read through the papers to see whether he can correct the mistake
   - C. pointing out to the employee that, while an occasional error is permissible, frequent errors can prove a source of embarrassment to all concerned
   - D. pointing to the mistake and asking the employee whether he realizes the consequences of the mistake

5._____

6. You desire to develop teamwork among the members of your staff. You are assigned a case which will require that two of the staff work together if the papers are to be prepared in time. You decided to assign two employees, whom you know to be close friends, to work on these papers.
   Your action in this regard would GENERALLY be considered
   - A. *bad*; friends working together tend to do as little as they can get away with
   - B. *bad*; people who are friends socially often find that the bonds of friendship disintegrate in work situations
   - C. *good*; friends who are permitted to work together show their appreciation by utilizing every opportunity to reinforce the group leader's position of authority
   - D. *good*; the evidence suggests that more work can be done in this way

6._____

7. You notice that all of the employees, without exception, take lunch hours which in your view are excessively long. You call each of them to your desk and point out that unless this practice is brought to a stop, appropriate action will be taken.
   The way in which you handled this problem would GENERALLY be considered
   - A. *proper*, primarily because a civil servant, no matter what his professional status, owes the public a full day's work for a full day's pay
   - B. *proper*, primarily because employees need to have a clear picture of the rewards and penalties that go with public employment
   - C. *improper*, primarily because group problems require group discussion which need not be formal in character
   - D. *improper*, primarily because professional personnel resent having such matters as lunch hours brought to their attention

7._____

8. In communicating with superiors or subordinates, it is well to bear in mind a phenomenon known as the *halo effect*. An example of this *halo effect* occurs when we
   A. employ informal language in a formal setting as a means of attracting attention
   B. ignore the advice of someone we distrust without evaluating the advice
   C. ask people to speak up who have a tendency to speak softly or occasionally indistinctly
   D. react to a piece of good work by inquiring into the motivations of those who did the work

9. Which of the following dangers is MOST likely to arise when a work group becomes too tightly knit? The
   A. group may appoint an informal leader who gradually sets policies and standards for the group to the detriment of the agency
   B. group may be reluctant to accept new employees as members
   C. quantity and quality of work produced may tend to diminish sharply despite the group's best efforts
   D. group may focus too strongly on employee benefits at inappropriate times

10. The overall managerial problem has become more complex because each group of management specialists will tend to view the interests of the enterprise in terms which are compatible with the survival or the increase of its special function. That is, each group will have a trained capacity for its own function and a *trained incapacity* to see its relation to the whole.
    The *trained incapacity* to which the foregoing passage refers PROBABLY results from
    A. an imbalance in the number of specialists as compared with the number of generalists
    B. development by each specialized group of a certain dominant value or goal that shapes its entire way of doing things
    C. low morale accompanied by lackadaisical behavior by large segments of the managerial staff
    D. supervisory failure to inculcate pride in workmanship

11. Of the following, the MOST important responsibility of a supervisor in charge of a section is to
    A. establish close personal relationships with each of his subordinates in the section
    B. insure that each subordinate in the section knows the full range of his duties and responsibilities
    C. maintain friendly relations with his immediate supervisor
    D. protect his subordinates from criticism from any source

12. The BEST way to get a good work output from employees is to
    A. hold over them the threat of disciplinary action or removal
    B. maintain a steady, unrelenting pressure on them
    C. show them that you can do anything they can do faster and better
    D. win their respect and liking so they want to work for you

13. Supervisors should GENERALLY
    A. lean more toward management than toward their subordinates
    B. lean neither toward subordinates nor management
    C. lean more toward their subordinates than toward their management
    D. maintain a proper balance between management and subordinates

14. For a supervisor in charge of a section to ask occasionally the opinion of a subordinate concerning a problem is
    A. *desirable*; but it would be even better if the subordinate were consulted routinely on every problem
    B. *desirable*; subordinates may make good suggestions and will be pleased by being consulted
    C. *undesirable*; subordinates may be resentful if their advice is not followed
    D. *undesirable*; the supervisor should not attempt to shift his responsibilities to subordinates

15. The PRIMARY responsibility of a supervisor is to
    A. gain the confidence and make friends of all his subordinates
    B. get the work done properly
    C. satisfy his superior and gain his respect
    D. train the men in new methods for doing the work

16. In starting a work simplification study, the one of the following steps that should be taken FIRST is to
    A. break the work down into its elements
    B. draw up a chart of operations
    C. enlist the interest and cooperation of the personnel
    D. suggest alternative procedures

17. Of the following, the MOST important value of a manual of procedures is that it usually
    A. eliminates the need for on-the-job training
    B. decreases the span of control which can be exercised by individual supervisory personnel
    C. outlines methods of operation for ready reference
    D. provides concrete examples of work previously performed by employees

18. Reprimanding a subordinate when he has done something wrong should be done PRIMARILY in order to
    A. deter others from similar acts
    B. improve the subordinate in future performance
    C. maintain discipline
    D. uphold departmental rules

19. Most of the training of new employees in a public agency is USUALLY accomplished by
    A. formal classes   B. general orientation
    C. internship   D. on-the-job activities

20. You find that delivery of a certain item cannot possibly be made to a using agency by the date the using agency requested.
    Of the following, the MOST advisable course of action for you to take FIRST is to
    A. cancel the order and inform the using agency
    B. discuss the problem with the using agency
    C. notify the using agency to obtain the item through direct purchase
    D. schedule the delivery for the earliest possible date

21. Assume that one of your subordinates has gotten into the habit of regularly and routinely referring every small problem which arises in his work to you.
    In order to help him overcome this habit, it is generally MOST advisable for you to
    A. advise him that you do not have time to discuss each problem with him and that he should do whatever he wants
    B. ask your subordinate for his solution and approve any satisfactory approach that he suggests
    C. refuse to discuss such routine problems with him
    D. tell him that he should consider looking for another position if he does not feel competent to solve such routine problems

22. The BEST of the following reasons for developing understudies to supervisory staff is that this practice
    A. assures that capable staff will not leave their jobs since they are certain to be promoted
    B. helps to assure continued efficiency when persons in important positions leave their jobs
    C. improves morale by demonstrating to employees the opportunities for advancement
    D. provides an opportunity for giving on-the-job training

23. When a supervisor delegates some of his work to a subordinate, the
    A. supervisor retains final responsibility for the work
    B. supervisor should not check on the work until it has been completed
    C. subordinate assumes full responsibility for the successful completion of the work
    D. subordinate is likely to lose interest and get less satisfaction from the work

24. Sometimes it is necessary to give out written orders or to post written or typed information on a bulletin board rather than to merely give spoken orders. The supervisor must decide how he will do it.
    In which of the following situations would it be BETTER for him to give written rather than spoken orders?
    A. He is going to reassign a man from one unit to another under his supervision.
    B. His staff must be informed of a permanent change in a complicated operating procedure.

C. A man must be transferred from a clerical unit to an operating unit.
D. He must order a group of staff men to do a difficult and tedious inventory job to which most of them are likely to object.

25. Of the following symbolic patterns, which one is NOT representative of a normal direction in which formal organizational communications flow?

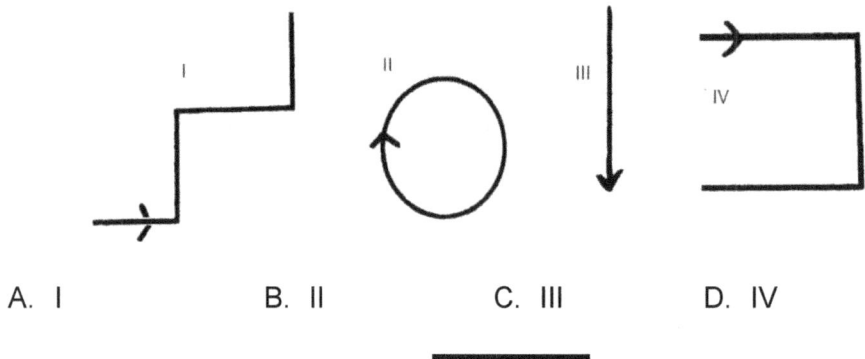

A. I   B. II   C. III   D. IV

25.____

KEY (CORRECT ANSWERS)

1. B
2. D
3. C
4. D
5. A

6. D
7. C
8. B
9. B
10. B

11. B
12. D
13. D
14. B
15. B

16. C
17. C
18. B
19. D
20. B

21. B
22. B
23. A
24. B
25. B

EXAMINATION SECTION
TEST 1

DIRECTIONS: Each question or incomplete statement is followed by several suggested answers or completions. Select the one that BEST answers the question or completes the statement. *PRINT THE LETTER OF THE CORRECT ANSWER IN THE SPACE AT THE RIGHT.*

1. The one of the following which is the CHIEF reason for the difference between the administration of justice agencies and that of other units in public administration is that
    A. correctional institutions are concerned with security
    B. some defendants are proven to be innocent after trial
    C. the administration of justice is more complicated than other aspects of public administration
    D. correctional institutions produce services their clients or customers fail to understand or ask for

    1.____

2. Of the following, the MOST important reason why employees resist change is that
    A. they have not received adequate training in preparation for the change
    B. experience has shown that when new ideas don't work, employees get blamed and not the individuals responsible for the new ideas
    C. new ideas and methods almost always represent a threat to the security of the individuals involved
    D. new ideas often are not practical and disrupt operations unnecessarily

    2.____

3. Stress situations are ideal for building up a backlog of knowledge about an employee's behavior. Not only does it inform the supervisor of many aspects of a person's behavior patterns, but it is also vitally important to have foreknowledge of how people behave under stress.
    The one of the following which is NOT implied by this passage is that
    A. a person under stress may give some indication of his unsuitability for work in an institution
    B. putting people under stress is the best means of determining their usual patterns of behavior
    C. stress situations may give important clues about performance in the service
    D. there is a need to know about a person's reaction to situations *when the chips are down*

    3.____

4. There are situations requiring a supervisor to give direct orders to subordinates assigned to work under the direct control of other supervisors.
    Under which of the following conditions would this shift of command responsibility be MOST appropriate?
    A. Emergency operations require the cooperative action of two or more organizational units.

    4.____

B. One of the other supervisors is not doing his job, thus defeating the goals of the organization.
C. The subordinates are performing their assigned tasks in the absence of their own supervisor.
D. The subordinates ask a superior officer who is not their own supervisor how to perform an assignment given them by their supervisor.

5. The one of the following which BEST differentiates staff supervision from line supervision is that
   A. staff supervision has the authority to immediately correct a line subordinate's action
   B. staff supervision is an advisory relationship
   C. line supervision goes beyond the normal boundaries of direct supervision within a command
   D. line supervision does not report findings and make recommendations

6. Decision-making is a rational process calling for a *suspended judgment* by the supervisor until all the facts have been ascertained and analyzed, and the consequences of alternative courses of action studied; then the decision maker
   A. acts as both judge and jury and selects what he believes to be the best of the alternative plans
   B. consults with those who will be most directly involved to obtain a recommendation as to the most appropriate course of action
   C. reviews the facts which he has already analyzed, reduces his thoughts to writing, and selects that course of action which can have the fewest negative consequences if his thinking contains an error
   D. stops, considers the matter for at least a 24-hour period, before referring it to a superior for evaluation

7. Decision-making can be defined as the
   A. delegation of authority and responsibility to persons capable of performing their assigned duties with moderate or little supervision
   B. imposition of a supervisor's decision upon a work group
   C. technique of selecting the course of action with the most desired consequences, and the least undesired or unexpected consequence
   D. process principally concerned with improvement of procedures

8. A supervisor who is not well-motivated and has no desire to accept basic responsibilities will
   A. compromise to the extent of permitting poor performance for lengthy periods without correction
   B. get good performance from his work group if the employees are satisfied with their pay and other working conditions
   C. not have marginal workers in his work group if the work is interesting
   D. perform adequately as long as the work of his group consists of routine operations

3 (#1)

9. A supervisor is more than a bond or connecting link between two levels of employees. He has joint responsibility which must be shared with both management and with the work group.
Of the following, the item which BEST expresses the meaning of this statement is:
   A. A supervisor works with both management and the work group and must reconcile the differences between them.
   B. In management, the supervisor is solely concerned with efforts directing the work of his subordinates.
   C. The supervisory role is basically that of a liaison man between management and the work force.
   D. What a supervisor says and does when confronted with day-to-day problems depends upon is level in the organization.

9.____

10. Operations research is the observation of operations in business or government, and it utilizes both hypotheses and controlled experiments to determine the outcome of decisions. In effect, it reproduces the future impact on the decision in a clinical environment suited to intensive study.
Operations research has
   A. been more promising than applied research in the ascertaining of knowledge for the purpose of decision-making
   B. never been amenable to fact analysis on the grand scale
   C. not been used extensively in government
   D. proven to be the only rational and logical approach to decision-making on long-range problems

10.____

11. Assume that a civilian makes a complaint regarding the behavior of a certain worker to the supervisor of the worker. The supervisor regards the complaint as unjustified and unreasonable.
In this circumstances, the supervisor
   A. must make a written note of the complaint and forward it through channels to the unit or individual responsible for complaint investigations
   B. should assure the complainant that disciplinary action will be appropriate to the seriousness of the alleged offense
   C. should immediately summon the worker if he is available so that the latter may attempt to straighten out the difficulty
   D. should inform the complainant that his complaint appears to be unjustified and unreasonable

11.____

12. Modern management usually establishes a personal history folder for an employee at the time of hiring. Disciplinary matters appear in such personal history folders. Employees do not like the idea of disciplinary actions appearing in their permanent personal folders.
Authorities believe that
   A. after a few years have passed since the commission of the infraction, disciplinary actions should be removed from folders
   B. disciplinary actions should remain in folders; it is not the records but the use of records that requires detailed study

12.____

C. most personnel have not had disciplinary action taken against them and would resent the removal of disciplinary actions for such folders
D. there is no point in removing disciplinary actions from personal history folders since employees who have been guilty of infractions should not be allowed to forget their infractions

13. While supervisors should not fear the acceptance of responsibility, they
    A. generally seek out responsibility that subordinates should exercise, particularly when the supervisors do not have sufficient work to do
    B. must be on guard against the abuse of authority that often accompanies the acceptance of total responsibility
    C. should avoid responsibility that is customarily exercised by their superiors
    D. who are anxious for promotions accept responsibility but do not exercise the authority warranted by the responsibility

14. Planning is part of the decision-making process. By planning is meant the development of details of alternative plans of action.
    The key to *effective* planning is
    A. careful research to determine whether a tentative plan has been tried at some time in the past
    B. participation by employees in planning, preferably those employees who will be involved in putting the selected plan into action
    C. speed; poor plans can be discarded after they are put into effect while good plans usually are not put into effect because of delays
    D. writing the plan up in considerable detail and then forwarding the plan, through channels, to the executive officer having final approval of the plan

15. Equating strict discipline with punitive measures and lax discipline with rehabilitation creates a false dichotomy.
    The one of the statements given below that would BEST follow from the belief expressed in this statement is that discipline
    A. is important for treatment
    B. militates against treatment programs
    C. is not an important consideration in institutions where effective rehabilitation programs prevail
    D. minimizes the need for punitive measures if it is strict

16. If training starts at the lower level of command, it is like planting a seed in tilled ground but removing the sun and rain. Seeds cannot grow unless they have help from above.
    Of the following, the MOST appropriate conclusion to be drawn from this statement is that
    A. the head of an institution may not delegate authority for the planning of an institutional training program for staff
    B. on-the-job training is better than formalized training courses
    C. regularly scheduled training courses must be planned in advance
    D. staff training is the responsibility of higher levels of comman

17. The one of the following that BEST describes the meaning of *in-service staff training* is:
    A. The training of personnel who are below average in performance
    B. The training given to each employee throughout his employment
    C. The training of staff only in their own specialized fields
    D. Classroom training where the instructor and employees develop a positive and productive relationship leading to improved efficiency on the job

18. All bureau personnel should be concerned about, and involved in, public relations.
    Of the following, the MOST important reason for this statement is that
    A. an institution is an agency of the government supported by public funds and responsible to the public
    B. institutions are places of public business and, therefore, the public is interested in them
    C. some personnel need publicity in order to advance
    D. personnel sometimes need publicity in order to ensure that their grievances are acted upon by higher authority

19. The MOST important factor in establishing a disciplinary policy in an organization is
    A. consistency of application
    B. strict supervisors
    C. strong enforcement
    D. the degree of toughness or laxity

20. The FIRST step in planning a program is to
    A. clearly define the objectives
    B. estimate the costs
    C. hire a program director
    D. solicit funds

21. The PRIMARY purpose of control in an organization is to
    A. punish those who do not do their job well
    B. get people to do what is necessary to achieve an objective
    C. develop clearly stated rules and regulations
    D. regulate expenditures

22. The UNDERLYING principle of *sound* administration is to
    A. base administration on investigation of facts
    B. have plenty of resources available
    C. hire a strong administrator
    D. establish a broad policy

23. An IMPORTANT aspect to keep in mind during the decision-making process is that
    A. all possible alternatives for attaining goals should be sought out and considered
    B. considering various alternatives only leads to confusion
    C. once a decision has been made, it cannot be retracted
    D. there is only one correct method to reach any goal

24. Implementation of accountability requires
    A. a leader who will not hesitate to take punitive action
    B. an established system of communication from the bottom to the top
    C. explicit directives from leaders
    D. too much expense to justify it

25. The CHIEF danger of a decentralized control system is that
    A. excessive reports and communications will be generated
    B. problem areas may not be detected readily
    C. the expense will become prohibitive
    D. this will result in too many *chiefs*

KEY (CORRECT ANSWERS)

1.	D		11.	D
2.	C		12.	A
3.	B		13.	B
4.	A		14.	B
5.	B		15.	A
6.	A		16.	D
7.	C		17.	B
8.	A		18.	A
9.	A		19.	A
10.	C		20.	A

21. B
22. A
23. A
24. B
25. B

TEST 2

DIRECTIONS: Each question or incomplete statement is followed by several suggested answers or completions. Select the one that BEST answers the question or completes the statement. *PRINT THE LETTER OF THE CORRECT ANSWER IN THE SPACE AT THE RIGHT.*

1. When giving orders to his subordinates, a certain supervisor often includes information as to why the work is necessary.
   This approach by the supervisor is GENERALLY
   A. *inadvisable*, since it appears that he is avoiding responsibility and wishes to blame his superiors
   B. *inadvisable*, since it creates the impression that he is trying to impress the subordinates with his importance
   C. *advisable*, since it serves to motivate the subordinates by giving them a reason for wanting to do the work
   D. *advisable*, since it shows that he is knowledgeable and is in control of his assignments

   1.____

2. Some supervisors often ask capable, professional subordinates to get some work done with questions such as: *Mary, would you try to complete that work today?*
   The use of such request orders USUALLY
   A. gets results which are as good as or better than results from direct orders
   B. shows the supervisor to be weak and lowers the respect of his subordinates
   C. provokes resentment as compared to the use of direct orders
   D. leads to confusion as to the proper procedure to follow when carrying out orders

   2.____

3. Assume that a supervisor, because of an emergency when time was essential, and in the absence of his immediate superior, went out of the chain of command to get a decision from a higher level.
   It would consequently be MOST appropriate for the immediate superior to
   A. reprimand him for his action, since the long-range consequences are far more detrimental than the immediate gain
   B. encourage him to use this method, since the chain of command is an outmoded and discredited system which inhibits productive work
   C. order him to refrain from any repetition of this action in the future
   D. support him as long as he informed the superior of the action at the earliest opportunity

   3.____

4. A supervisor gave instructions which he knew were somewhat complex to a subordinate. He then asked the subordinate to repeat the instructions to him.
   The supervisor's decision to have the subordinate repeat the instructions was
   A. *good practice*, mainly because the subordinate would realize the importance of carefully following instructions

   4.____

123

B. *poor practice*, mainly because the supervisor should have given the employee time to ponder the instructions, and then, if necessary, to ask questions
C. *good practice*, mainly because the supervisor could see whether the subordinate had any apparent problem in understanding the instructions
D. *poor practice*, mainly because the subordinate should not be expected to have the same degree of knowledge as the supervisor

5. Supervisors and subordinates must successfully communicate with each other in order to work well together.
Which of the following statements concerning communication of this type is CORRECT?
    A. When speaking to his subordinates, a supervisor should make every effort to appear knowledgeable about all aspects of their work.
    B. Written communications should be prepared by the supervisor at his own level of comprehension.
    C. The average employee tends to give meaning to communication according to his personal interpretation.
    D. The effective supervisor communicates as much information as he has available to anyone who is interested.

6. A supervisor should be aware of situations in which it is helpful to put his orders to his subordinates in writing.
Which of the following situations would MOST likely call for a written order rather than an oral order?
The order
    A. gives complicated instructions which vary from ordinary practice
    B. involves the performance of duties for which the subordinate is responsible
    C. directs subordinates to perform duties similar to those which they performed in the recent past
    D. concerns a matter that must be promptly completed or dealt with

7. Assume that a supervisor discovers that a false rumor about possible layoffs has spread among his subordinates through the grapevine.
Of the following, the BEST way for the supervisor to deal with this situation is to
    A. use the grapevine to leak accurate information
    B. call a meeting to provide information and to answer questions
    C. post a notice on the bulletin board denying the rumor
    D. institute procedures designed to eliminate the grapevine

8. Communications in an organization with many levels becomes subject to different interpretations at each level and have a tendency to become distorted. The more levels there are in an organization, the greater the likelihood that the final recipient of a communication will get the wrong message.
The one of the following statements which BEST supports the foregoing viewpoint is:
    A. Substantial communications problems exist at high management levels in organizations.

B. There is a relationship in an organization between the number of hierarchical levels and interference with communications.
C. An opportunity should be given to subordinates at all levels to communicate their views with impunity.
D. In larger organizations, there tends to be more interference with downward communications than with upward communications.

9. A subordinate comes to you, his supervisor, to ask a detailed question about a new agency directive; however, you do not know the answer.
Of the following, the MOST helpful response to give the subordinate is to
   A. point out that since your own supervisor has failed to keep you informed of this matter, it is probably unimportant
   B. give the most logical interpretation you can, based on your best judgment
   C. ask him to raise the question with other supervisors until he finds one who knows the answer, then let you know also
   D. explain that you do not know and assure him that you will get the information for him

9._____

10. The traditional view of management theory is that communication in an organization should follow the table of organization. A newer theory holds that timely communication often requires bypassing certain steps in the hierarchical chain.
However, the MAIN advantage of using formal channels of communication within an organization is that
   A. an employee is thereby restricted in his relationships to his immediate superior and his immediate subordinates
   B. information is thereby transmitted to everyone who should be informed
   C. the organization will have an appeal channel, or a mechanism by which subordinates can go over their superior's head
   D. employees are thereby encouraged to exercise individual initiative

10._____

11. It is unfair to hold subordinates responsible for the performance of duties for which they do not have the requisite authority.
When this is done, it violates the principle that
   A. responsibility cannot be greater than that implied by delegated authority
   B. responsibility should be greater than that implied by delegated authority
   C. authority cannot be greater than that implied by delegated responsibility
   D. authority should be greater than that implied by delegated responsibility

11._____

12. Assume that a supervisor wishes to delegate some tasks to a capable subordinate.
It would be MOST in keeping with the principles of delegation for the supervisor to
   A. ask another supervisor who is experienced in the delegated tasks to evaluate the subordinate's work from time to time
   B. monitor continually the subordinate's performance by carefully reviewing his work

12._____

C. request experienced employees to submit peer ratings of the work of the subordinate
D. tell the subordinates what problems are likely to be encountered and specify which problems to report on

13. There are three types of leadership: *autocratic*, in which the leader makes the decisions and seeks compliance from his subordinates; *democratic*, in which the leader consults with his subordinate and lets them help set policy; and *free rein*, in which the leader acts as an information center and exercises minimum control over his subordinates.
A supervisor can be MOST effective if he decides to
    A. use democratic leadership techniques exclusively
    B. avoid the use of autocratic leadership techniques entirely
    C. employ the three types of leadership according to the situation
    D. rely mainly on autocratic leadership techniques

13.____

14. During a busy period of work, Employee A asked his supervisor for leave in order to take an ordinary vacation. The supervisor denied the request. The following day, Employee B asked for leave during the same period because his wife had just gone to the hospital for an indeterminate stay and he had family matters to tend to.
Of the following, the BEST way for the supervisor to deal with Employee B's request is to
    A. grant the request and give the reason to the other employee
    B. suggest that the employee make his request to higher management
    C. delay the request immediately since granting it would show favoritism
    D. defer any decision until the duration of the hospital stay is determined

14.____

15. Assume that you are a supervisor and that a subordinate tells you he has a grievance.
In general, you should FIRST
    A. move the grievance forward in order to get a prompt decision
    B. discourage this type of behavior on the part of subordinates
    C. attempt to settle the grievance
    D. refer the subordinate to the personnel office

15.____

16. A supervisor may have available a large variety of rewards he can use to motivate his subordinates. However, some supervisors choose the wrong rewards.
A supervisor is MOST likely to make such a mistake if he
    A. appeals to a subordinate's desire to be well regarded by his co-workers
    B. assumes that the subordinate's goals and preferences are the same as his own
    C. conducts in-depth discussions with a subordinate in order to discover his preference
    D. limits incentives to those rewards which he is authorized to provide or to recommend

16.____

17. Employee performance appraisal is open to many kinds of errors. When a supervisor is preparing such an appraisal, he is MOST likely to commit an error if
    A. employees are indifferent to the consequences of their performance appraisals
    B. the entire period for which the evaluation is being made is taken into consideration
    C. standard measurement criteria are used as performance benchmarks
    D. personal characteristics of employees which are not job-related are given weight

17.____

18. Assume that a supervisor finds that a report prepared by an employee is unsatisfactory and should be done over.
    Which of the following should the supervisor do?
    A. Give the report to another employee who can complete it properly
    B. Have the report done over by the same employee after successfully training him
    C. Hold a meeting to train all the employees so as not to single out the employee who performed unsatisfactory
    D. Accept the report so as not to discourage the employee and then make the corrections himself

18.____

19. Employees sometimes wish to have personal advice and counseling, in confidence, about their job-related problems. These problems may include such concerns as health matters, family difficulties, alcoholism, debts, emotional disturbances, etc.
    Such assistance is BEST provided through
    A. maintenance of an exit interview program to find reasons for, and solutions to, turn-over problems
    B. arrangements for employees to discuss individual problems informally outside normal administrative channels
    C. procedures which allow employees to submit anonymous inquiries to the personnel department
    D. special hearing committees consisting of top management in addition to immediate supervisors

19.____

20. An employee is always a member of some unit of the formal organization. He may also be a member of an informal work group.
    With respect to employee productivity and job satisfaction, the informal work group can MOST accurately be said to
    A. have no influence of any kind on its members
    B. influence its members negatively only
    C. influence its members positively only
    D. influence its members negatively or positively

20.____

21. In order to encourage employees to make suggestions, many public agencies have employee suggestion programs.
    What is the MAJOR benefit of such a program to the agency as a whole?

21.____

It
- A. brings existing or future problems to management's attention
- B. reduces the number of minor accidents
- C. requires employees to share in decision-making responsibilities
- D. reveals employees who have inadequate job knowledge

22. Assume that you have been asked to interview a seemingly shy applicant for a temporary position in your department.
For you to ask the kinds of questions that begin with *What, Where, Why, When, Who, and How*, is
    - A. *good practice*; it informs the applicant that he must conform to the requirements of the department
    - B. *poor practice*; it exceeds the extent and purpose of an initial interview
    - C. *good practice*; it encourages the applicant to talk to a greater extent
    - D. *poor practice*; it encourages the applicant to dominate the discussion

23. In recent years, job enlargement or job enrichment has tended to replace job simplification.
Those who advocate job enrichment or enlargement consider it *desirable* CHIEFLY because
    - A. it allows supervisors to control closely the activities of subordinates
    - B. it produces greater job satisfaction through reduction of responsibility
    - C. most employees prefer to avoid work which is new and challenging
    - D. positions with routinized duties are unlikely to provide job satisfaction

24. Job rotation is a training method in which an employee temporarily changes places with another employee of equal rank.
What is usually the MAIN purpose of job rotation? To
    - A. politely remove the person being rotated from an unsuitable assignment
    - B. increase skills and provide broader experience
    - C. prepare the person being rotated for a permanent change
    - D. test the skills of the person being rotated

25. There are several principles that a supervisor needs to know if he is to deal adequately with his training responsibilities.
Which of the following is usually NOT a principle of training?
    - A. People should be trained according to their individual needs.
    - B. People can learn by being told or shown how to do work but best of all by doing work under guidance.
    - C. People can be easily trained even if they have no desire to learn.
    - D. Training should be planned, scheduled, executed, and evaluated systematically.

KEY (CORRECT ANSWERS)

1.	C	11.	A
2.	A	12.	D
3.	D	13.	C
4.	C	14.	A
5.	C	15.	C
6.	A	16.	B
7.	B	17.	D
8.	B	18.	B
9.	D	19.	B
10.	B	20.	D

21. A
22. C
23. D
24. B
25. C

PROGRAM EVALUATION

Table of Contents

Pages

Program Evaluation Strategy 1
    Managing for Success 1
    Types of Program Evaluation 1
    Judging vs. Coaching 1

Conducting a Program Evaluation 3
    The Need for Planning 3

Stage 1- Evaluability Assessment 3
    Performance Measurement 4
    Mission, Goals and Objectives 4
    Performance Indicators 5

Stage 2 - Designing the Evaluation 6

Stage 3 - Conducting the Study 8
    Developing Data Measurement System 8
    Determine Data Availability 9
    Collecting Data 9
    Analyzing Data 10
    Data Presentation 10
    Refining Measures 10

Stage 4 - Reporting Evaluation Findings 11

Stage 5 - Program Offices Implement Improvement Activities 12

Stage 6 - On-Going Consultation 13

PROGRAM EVALUATION

Program Evaluation Strategy

MANAGING FOR SUCCESS

An essential component of any successful organization is its ability to continually assess and evaluate its performance. To establish effective and efficient programs, managers need fundamental information regarding the position and progress of their programs, and what improvements can be made to enhance the overall quality of their operations.

In identifying this need, the PTO's Office of Planning and Evaluation (P&E) has developed an evaluation strategy for the Patent and Trademark Office. Our goal is to support PTO in planning, assessing, and improving its program activities, so that managers have the information and support they need to continually develop and advance their programs.

TYPES OF PROGRAM EVALUATION

Program evaluation is based on the fundamental idea that programs should have a demonstrable benefit.

In its simplest terms, program evaluation is defined as a systematic approach to assessing the performance of a program or service. Program evaluations are most commonly referred to as either summative or formative in nature. Summative evaluations make a judgment about a program's operations and usefulness, whereas formative evaluations describe a program's operations in order to improve the way in which it functions.

In recent years, the formative approach to evaluating has evolved into what has come to be called "evaluation research."

> Evaluation research includes:
> - Design of programs
> - Ongoing monitoring of how well programs are functioning
> - Assessment of program impact
> - Analysis of benefits relative to costs.

This approach seems to be the most productive. As internal evaluators, our goal is not only to report to managers on their program's current situation, but also assist them in developing and enhancing the resources they need for continual operational improvement.

JUDGING VS. COACHING

In conducting formative evaluations, the goal is not to judge a program's worth or usefulness, rather the goal is to provide recommendations for program improvements in addition to assessing impacts and results.

A program evaluation trainer, uses the example of a world-class figure-skating champion to differentiate the roles of a coach and judge. As a skater performs, both the judge and the coach are meticulously assessing the skaters every move; however, each has a different motive for evaluating the performance. The judge looks at the performance and impassively scores the skater against the competition, providing little, if any, feedback to the skater. The coach on the other hand, goes a step beyond assessing the performance by actually working with the skater to improve his or her performance. The judge's objective is to score the skater's single performance, whereas the coach's objective is to help the skater achieve his or her fullest potential for future performances.

The coaching perspective helps programs become as efficient and effective as possible, while reaching their fullest potential. Using the example, the coach can work with and recommend improvements to the skater, but it is the skater who is responsible for making the improvements and for eventually becoming a guide and example for others that follow. By diagnosing, consulting and informing programs on their performance, we not only help programs gain a better understanding of what works well within their organization, we also maintain PTO's strategic goal of providing our customers with the highest level of quality and service in all aspects of PTO operations.

Conducting a Program Evaluation

In order to be effective, every evaluation must be tailored to the individual program or organization.

The following are stages in conducting a program evaluation. These stages are designed to adapt to individual needs, interests and the stage of development of the organization or program being evaluated.

THE NEED FOR PLANNING

Ideally, a successful evaluation will provide the best information possible on all key issues within a given set of constraints, such as available time, staff and budget resources. This makes it important to consider at the outset that the design of the evaluation needs to be done carefully, since criticism of the findings will likely focus on the methodology used.

Given the constraints we are all under these days, you may very well ask why you should spend precious resources on planning and designing your evaluation. The answer is precisely because of those constraints. In addition to increasing credibility in the product, a careful and sound design:

- increases overall quality,
- contains costs,
- ensures timeliness of findings,
- increases the strength and specificity of findings and recommendations,
- decreases criticism of methodology,
- improves customer satisfaction, and
- results in less resources required to carry out the evaluation.

STAGE 1: EVALUABILITY ASSESSMENT

Program evaluation is essentially a process in which questions are asked about a program or activity and answers are actively sought. In order to have an effective evaluation--which will result in improved program performance--first, the right questions must be asked, and second, the evaluation team must assure that the questions can be accurately answered.

Before conducting any formal evaluation, an evaluability assessment is conducted. The purpose of the evaluability assessment is to identify the program's goals, performance indicators and data sources, which will be used to conduct the evaluation. The evaluability assessment not only answers the question of whether a program can be meaningfully evaluated, but whether the evaluation is likely to contribute to improved program performance.

During the evaluability assessment there is usually a clear indication of whether a program is ready to be evaluated. If the necessary information (goals, objectives, performance measurements, etc.) is available and is identified by the evaluators and intended users as clear, concise and realistic (given resource allocations and restrictions), the evaluation can proceed. However, if the goals, objectives and performance indicators are found to be either underdeveloped or undefined, the program office is advised to first focus on developing or redefining their performance measurements before continuing with the evaluation.

The foremost question is whether or not the program can be evaluated in a meaningful way based on what currently exists.

Program evaluations are generally concerned with whether a program or policy is achieving its intended goal or purpose. Frequently though, the goals and purposes were to attract as much support as possible for the proposed project, but may lack consistency or be too ambitious given the realities of program functions. Programs and policies that do not have clear and consistent goals can not be evaluated for their effectiveness. Thus, uncovering those goals and purposes is generally the starting point of most evaluations. This first stage of an evaluation is necessary to determine whether they can be evaluated.

Program Evaluation Criteria

- Program goals and objectives, important side effects, and priority information needs are well defined.
- Program goals and objectives are plausible.
- Relevant performance data can be obtained.
- The intended users of the evaluation results have agreed on how they will use the information.

Performance Measurement

Performance measurement is a process by which a program objectively measures how it is accomplishing its mission through the delivery of its products, services, or processes. It is a self-assessment, goal-setting, and progress monitoring tool, which provides on-going performance feedback to both management and staff. A good performance measurement system is designed to provide information which helps clarify goals and motivates performance, solves problems, and corrects deviations or alters planned directions.

Performance Measurement is crucial to the overall management of programs because of one basic principle: "What gets measured, gets done."

Mission, Goals and Objectives

The first step in performance measurement is identifying the mission, goals and objectives. The following is a brief description of each:

The mission is the purpose for which a program or organization was created. A mission answers the following questions:

- Who are we?
- What do we do?
- For whom do we do it?
- Why do we do it?

Goals are statements, usually general and abstract, about how the program expects to accomplish its mission. Goals may be quantitative ("Increase production") or qualitative ("Improve worker morale").

> ### Tips on Goal Setting
>
> - Goals may be general or specific and may encompass time spans ranging from a few months to several years.
> - Goals may be set for the entire organization, programs, and individuals.
> - Goals at the various organizational levels must be coordinated if the organization is to achieve its intended overall purpose.
> - There must be coordination of the long-term goals of the organization with the short term goals of departments and programs, and of both of these with the personal goals of workers
> - Involve both management and staff when developing goals.

Objectives are the means for accomplishing goals. They must be quantifiable containing specific statements detailing the desired accomplishments of a program's goals.

> ### Rules for Writing Objectives
>
> - Use a single issue per objective.
> - Define measurable objectives using a verb-noun structure ("Increase productivity by 15 percent by fiscal year 2015").
> - Specify an expected time for achievement.

Performance Indicators

Once goals and objectives have been established, performance indicators are developed. Performance indicators track and measure whether the goals and objectives have been reached, or how well the program is progressing toward achieving them.

In the classical sense, a performance indicator is defined as a ratio where the output of an effort is divided by the inputs (labor, energy, time, etc.) required to produce it. . For example:

$$\frac{\text{\# of customers helped}}{\text{\# of service reps}}$$

$$\frac{\text{\# of acceptable documents produced}}{\text{hours expanded for documents}}$$

> **Customer Requirements and Stakeholder Requirements** are the Building Blocks for Measurement Ratios. When designing indicators ask the question: How Do We Know We Met Customer Requirements?

Two integral components of performance indicators are effectiveness and efficiency. Effective production is defined as producing the desired results, whereas efficient production is defined as producing the desired outputs with a minimum level of input. Simply stated, effectiveness is doing the right things, and efficiency is doing things right.

Effectiveness and efficiency are both critical measures of performance and success. Organizations can temporarily survive without perfect efficiency, but would most likely die if they were ineffective. When designing performance measurements, it is essential that an organization considers both effectiveness and efficiency. Omitting either would result in performance measurements that provide inaccurate and often costly productivity information.

It bears repeating that if a program has not clearly identified its goals and objectives and set effectiveness and efficiency measures, it will be difficult to evaluate.

Four Criteria for Measurement Effectiveness and Efficiency

1. **Quality-** The measure must define and reflect quality of production or services as well as quantity. A measure that assesses only quantity outputs can lead to reduced productivity.

2. **Mission and goals-** The measure must define and assess only outputs and services that are integrated with the organizational mission and strategic goals. Measures directed to products and services that are not consistent with mission and goals threaten productivity.

3. **Rewards and Incentives-** Measures must be integrated with performance incentives, reward systems and practices. Measures that have no important contingencies will not work to improve productivity.

4. **Employee Involvement-** There must be involvement of employees and other direct stakeholders in the definition and construction of productivity measures. When lack of involvement has not resulted in commitment and buy-in, results from the measures are not likely to be received favorably or to have any impact on future productivity.

STAGE 2: DESIGNING THE EVALUATION

What's worth knowing?
How will we get it?
How will it be used?

By the time you have an idea of the evaluation capacity of your program, you may have the answers to many of the questions that lead to the design. Every question asked by an evaluation can be looked at with varying levels of intensity and thoroughness. When great precision is needed and resources are available, the most powerful of evaluations may be conducted, on the other hand when time and resources are limited and only approximate answers are needed, the level of the evaluation will differ. Given the diversity of programs, policies and projects to be evaluated, the number of questions to be answered, and the differing availability of resources, there can be no single recipe for a successful evaluation. However, these simple guidelines, once tailored, should provide a solid framework for conducting an evaluation.

In determining the design of an evaluation, the following questions are answered and an Evaluation Design Proposal is drafted.

1. Why are we doing this evaluation?

Clarify what the overall purpose of the evaluation is and what specific objectives will be accomplished. Focus not only on what the evaluation will do, but also identify what the evaluation will NOT do.

2. For whom are we doing this evaluation?

It is essential to identify who the audience is so that their needs, perspectives and constraints can be assessed. Identify both the primary audience and secondary audiences.

Who is sponsoring the evaluation? Who is authorizing the expenditure of funds and human resources? Who will be approving the report?

3. What are we evaluating?

Discuss the issues of the evaluation. Are we studying the need for a program or activity? The operations of a program or activity? The effects of a program or activity? Define the specific questions to be answered during the evaluation.

4. How are we doing this evaluation?

Make a list of the information needed to conduct the evaluation. Once the information needs are defined, identify the data collection techniques. Examples of Data Collection Techniques:

- Surveys
- Interviews
- Focus Group Sessions
- Case Studies
- Tests
- Observations
- Document Reviews
- Production Reports
- Computerized databases

5. When are we doing this evaluation?

Establish both the beginning and completion dates and interim deadlines. It may be helpful to set up a project plan to track the dates and resources.

6. Where are we doing this evaluation?

Determine the location of the evaluation. Will a special staff be pulled together? Will they need space for meetings? For working? For storage of files?

7. Who is doing this evaluation?

Assess the skills and resources needed to conduct the evaluation. Identify possible training needs and establish roles and responsibilities for each team member (Hendricks, 1994).

> **Tips on Building an Effective Study Team**
> - Keep teams small.
> - Acknowledge team members' need for high performance.
> - Reward both team leaders and team members.
> - Focus on people, not methodology.
> - Keep a skills inventory of team members.
> - Make use of project management tools to create benchmarks of success.
> - Form a policy group and a work group to involve policy makers, managers, and key staff in the evaluation.

Consider whether the skills and resources are available internally, or whether it might be more economical or beneficial to hire an external contractor to conduct the evaluation. Depending on the nature of the program or project, it may be critical that the results of the evaluation come from an outside, objective source.

One More Thing

After the design is completed, it is helpful to take an overall look at the design.

A well-designed evaluation can usually be recognized by the way it has:

1. Defined and posed questions for study.
2. Developed the methodological strategies for answering those questions.
3. Formulated a data collection plan that anticipates and addresses problems and obstacles that are likely to be encountered.
4. Provided a detailed analysis plan that will ensure that the questions posed will be answered with the appropriate data in the best possible fashion.
5. Established and maintained focus on the usefulness of the product for the intended user.

A sound design reduces downtime deciding what to do next, reduces time spent on collecting and analyzing irrelevant data and strengthens the relevance of the evaluation.

STAGE 3: CONDUCTING THE STUDY

Once the evaluation proposal is drafted and agreed upon by the evaluation team and the evaluation users, the process of collecting and analyzing the relevant data can begin.

DATA COLLECTION AND ANALYSIS

Developing A Data Measurement System

There are two methods of evaluation studies: qualitative and quantitative. Qualitative data collection systems permit the evaluator to study selected issues, cases, or events in depth and detail; data collection is not constrained by predetermined categories of analysis. Quantitative methods use standardized measures that fit diverse opinions and experiences into predetermined response categories. Considering evaluation design alternatives leads directly to consideration of the relative strengths and weaknesses of qualitative and quantitative studies, and the time and resources available for the study.

The advantage of the quantitative approach is that it measures the reactions of a great many people to a limited set of questions, thus facilitating comparison and statistical aggregation of the data. It gives a broad, generalized set of findings. Qualitative methods typically produce a wealth of detailed data about a much smaller number of people and cases. Qualitative data provide depth and detail through direct quotation and careful description of program situations, events, people, interactions, and observed behaviors.

Purposes and functions of qualitative and quantitative data are different, yet can be complementary. The statistics from standardized items make summaries, comparisons, and generalizations quite easy and precise. The narrative comments from open-ended questions are typically meant to provide a forum for elaboration, explanations, meanings, and new ideas.

It is recommended that an evaluation team engage stakeholders early because they have a different perspective, have data the evaluator needs, and can influence the evaluation positively if they are engaged, or negatively if they are ignored or threatened.

Categorizing research questions into major categories can help refine the research agenda of almost any study. Time spent in developing a detailed research design, data collection and analysis plan may improve the quality of the overall results.

Stakeholders include potential users of evaluation information and those with an investment in the organization or unit involved in the study.

Determine Data Availability

Once it has been established what to measure, it must be determined if the data for those measures is available and how to get it. If data is not available, alternative indicators must be identified.

The evaluation team should try to keep its indicators simple and use existing data whenever possible. However, do not compromise the evaluation by discarding indicators the team thinks are meaningful and important before weighing their obtainability.

    Data Availability Concerns

    1. Does the data currently exist? If not, can it be developed, and at what effort and cost?
    2. If the data exists, what will it cost to retrieve the data?
    3. What will it take to get the data converted into the established measurement values?
    4. Will a system investment be required? At what cost?
    5. Will management support this level of cost? Can a limited version be used?
    6. When will data be produced?

Collecting Data

The collection of data addresses the critical issues of making sure the correct data is identified, and a baseline is collected. The baseline data reflects the initial status of the program or process. During this phase, in addition to documenting the method of collection of the data, document any problems with the process, and work to resolve any process problems regularly. Meet with management at the end of an established trial period to evaluate results.

Analyzing Data

Once we have collected the data and before we meet with management, we must analyze the data to make sure that it will provide us with enough information and the right type of information on which to base an evaluation. We must ensure that the data fits the indicators identified to analyze. Agree to finalize the current indicators or revise them as needed, and analyze the baseline data collected for the purpose of setting goals.

DATA PRESENTATION

Once the data has been collected and analyzed, it must be decided how the data and results will be presented. Numbers by themselves are often difficult to understand, they cannot explain circumstances, and they may not easily lead to conclusions. Therefore, it is important to present the information in ways that make it easy to understand, that show relationships to other data, and that allow the information to be used to support decision-making processes. Whenever possible, use graphical tools to present data.

Measures must be shown in context. The most frequent evaluation contexts are: (1) goals compared to actual results, (2) trends in relation to previous periodic results, and (3) comparison of results to other relevant data. Using one or more of these contexts, meaningful conclusions should be drawn about the measurement result with little or no explanation.

REFINING MEASURES

Indicators may need some slight modifications or adjustment to better meet performance information needs of program or executive management. Continually check the usefulness of measurement data and adjust data collection methods if necessary.

Adjusting Measures

Are the measures working well?
What are the measures indicating?
Are additional indicators necessary?
Is data not really available (too difficult or expensive to acquire)?
Is data too difficult to use?

Balance Types Of Measures

One consideration of performance indicator development is that measures are interrelated and cannot be viewed in isolation. Timeliness, quality and cost are always in contention with each other, and the impact of improving any one or two must be weighed in relation to the expense of the third. A balance must be reached between the effectiveness and the economy and efficiency.

Consider Weighting Measures

Not all indicators are equally important. To reflect importance or priorities within measures or categories of measures, weight or index the measures. Weighting or indexing measures is an involved and advanced process and may not be necessary or appropriate for every program. However, weighting measures can provide some valuable insights into program outcomes.

Integrating with Management Process

Once performance results become available, the challenge shifts to presenting and using them effectively.

Establish Goals

Goals should be established based on: (1) policy or administrative priorities, (2) mission (3) customer feedback, (4) past history, (5) forecasted demand and (6) benchmark information.

Determine What The Measurements Say

It is extremely important to understand what the measurements say, as well as what they do not say. The measurements must be compared to performance goals, benchmarks, or past performance. Then variances or changes must be analyzed, and subsequent actions must be planned. In addition to program performance evaluation, the measurement results in the evaluation process can be used for external reporting, planning and budgeting activities and performance appraisal evaluation.

STAGE 4: REPORTING EVALUATION RESULTS

Reporting evaluation results is more of a process than a stage. Beginning on the first day of the evaluation, the evaluators should be continually reporting and discussing their findings with the evaluation users. It is not only important to keep them updated on the evaluation's progress, but also, it is important to keep them informed of any findings and recommendations that can be implemented before the full completion of the evaluation. Remember, the reason for doing an evaluation is to help an organization or program become as effective and efficient as possible. The sooner an organization can implement changes or improvements, the better.

Action-Oriented Reporting

As stated previously, the purpose of an evaluation is to improve a program or an organization's performance. The way in which evaluators do this is by providing recommendations for improvement to management and staff.

The majority of an evaluation report should be devoted to communicating the findings and specific recommendations. Reports should be action-oriented, centered mostly around the findings, but also around the recommendations and suggestions for implementation.

Action-oriented reports are often structured as a series of short reports targeted to specific audiences, rather than one all inclusive document.

Findings and recommendations should be presented clearly and concisely, in a way that meets the informational needs of the audience. In order for recommendations to be accepted by an organization, it must first understand what is being recommended and why it is relevant to their concerns. Evaluation studies are only useful if they are used.

Program Evaluation Report

Generally, an evaluation report should include:
- Executive Summary
  Purpose of Evaluation
  Program Background
  Evaluation Methodology
- Analysis of the Findings
- Recommendations

Tips for Reporting Evaluation Results

- Remember that the burden for effectively reporting results is on the evaluators, not the audience.
- Be aggressive. Instead of waiting for audiences to request information, actively look for opportunities to report results. Report regularly and frequently, appear in person if at all possible, and target multiple reports and briefings to specific audiences and /or issues.
- Simplify, simplify! Audiences are usually busy and their interest is pulled in different directions, so determine and report on the key points. If the core message creates interest, quickly follow up with more details.
- Study the audience. Learn about their backgrounds, interests, concerns, plans, pet peeves, etc.
- Focus on actions. Audiences are rarely interested in general information; they usually want guidance that will help them decide what to do next.
- Report in many different ways. Rather than using only one reporting technique or another, produce several different types of reports. Use written reports, personal briefings, screen show presentations, etc.

STAGE 5: PROGRAM OFFICES IMPLEMENT IMPROVEMENT ACTIVITIES

In this phase of the evaluation process, program office managers implement and monitor the recommendations and action plans originating from the evaluation study. The program manager facilitates the solution of problems by motivating staff and providing technical support. Particular attention must be given to customer and stakeholder requirements.

All employees should be trained in the process improvement recommendations so that they will possess the skills needed to recommend solutions to future problems. Decisions made closer to the customer and occurrence of events save time, reduce errors, and improve morale and service.

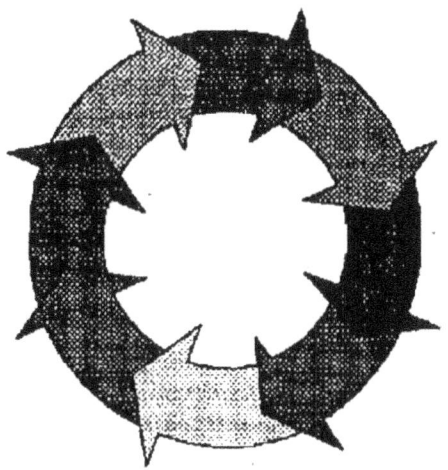

STAGE 6: ON-GOING CONSULTATION

Program evaluation is a continuous process of measuring, analyzing and refining an organization or program's performance.

A program evaluation is not an end in itself, rather it is the beginning of a continuous self-evaluation mechanism. With an effective evaluation comes additional data, refined measurements and new initiatives. In order to remain effective, organizations must continually evaluate this information to ensure the achievement of their mission, goals, and objectives.

PRINCIPLES AND PRACTICES, OF ADMINISTRATION, SUPERVISION AND MANAGEMENT

TABLE OF CONTENTS

	Page
GENERAL ADMINISTRATION	1
SEVEN BASIC FUNCTIONS OF THE SUPERVISOR	2
I. Planning	2
II. Organizing	3
III. Staffing	3
IV. Directing	3
V. Coordinating	3
VI. Reporting	3
VII. Budgeting	3
PLANNING TO MEET MANAGEMENT GOALS	4
I. What is Planning	4
II. Who Should Make Plans	4
III. What are the Results of Poor Planning	4
IV. Principles of Planning	4
MANAGEMENT PRINCIPLES	5
I. Management	5
II. Management Principles	5
III. Organization Structure	6
ORGANIZATION	8
I. Unity of Command	8
II. Span of Control	8
III. Uniformity of Assignment	9
IV. Assignment of Responsibility and Delegation of Authority	9
PRINCIPLES OF ORGANIZATION	9
I. Definition	9
II. Purpose of Organization	9
III. Basic Considerations in Organizational Planning	9
IV. Bases for Organization	10
V. Assignment of Functions	10
VI. Delegation of Authority and Responsibility	10
VII. Employee Relationships	11

DELEGATING		11
I.	WHAT IS DELEGATING:	11
II.	TO WHOM TO DELEGATE	11
REPORTS		12
I.	DEFINITION	12
II.	PURPOSE	12
III.	TYPES	12
IV.	FACTORS TO CONSIDER BEFORE WRITING REPORT	12
V.	PREPARATORY STEPS	12
VI.	OUTLINE FOR A RECOMMENDATION REPORT	12
MANAGEMENT CONTROLS		13
I.	Control	13
II.	Basis for Control	13
III.	Policy	13
IV.	Procedure	14
V.	Basis of Control	14
FRAMEWORK OF MANAGEMENT		14
I.	Elements	14
II.	Manager's Responsibility	15
III.	Control Techniques	16
IV.	Where Forecasts Fit	16
PROBLEM SOLVING		16
I.	Identify the Problem	16
II.	Gather Data	17
III.	List Possible Solutions	17
IV.	Test Possible Solutions	18
V.	Select the Best Solution	18
VI.	Put the Solution into Actual Practice	19
COMMUNICATION		19
I.	What is Communication?	19
II.	Why is Communication Needed?	19
III.	How is Communication Achieved?	20
IV.	Why Does Communication Fail?	21
V.	How to Improve Communication	21
VI.	How to Determine If You Are Getting Across	21
VII.	The Key Attitude	22
HOW ORDERS AND INSTRUCTIONS SHOULD BE GIVEN		22
I.	Characteristics of Good Orders and Instructions	22
FUNCTIONS OF A DEPARTMENT PERSONNEL OFFICE		23

SUPERVISION		23
I.	Leadership	23
	A. The Authoritarian Approach	23
	B. The Laissez-Faire Approach	24
	C. The Democratic Approach	24
II.	Nine Points of Contrast Between Boss and Leader	25
EMPLOYEE MORALE		25
I.	Some Ways to Develop and Maintain Good Employee Morale	25
II.	Some Indicators of Good Morale	26
MOTIVATION		26
EMPLOYEE PARTICIPATION		27
I.	WHAT IS PARTICIPATION	27
II.	WHY IS IT IMPORTANT?	27
III.	HOW MAY SUPERVISORS OBTAIN IT?	28
STEPS IN HANDLING A GRIEVANCE		28
DISCIPLINE		29
I.	THE DISCIPLINARY INTERVIEW	29
II.	PLANNING THE INTERVIEW	29
III.	CONDUCTING THE INTERVIEW	30

PRINCIPLES AND PRACTICES, OF
ADMINISTRATION, SUPERVISION AND MANAGEMENT

Most people are inclined to think of administration as something that only a few persons are responsible for in a large organization. Perhaps this is true if you are thinking of Administration with a capital A, but administration with a lower case *a* is a responsibility of supervisors at all levels each working day.

All of us feel we are pretty good supervisors and that we do a good job of administering the workings of our agency. By and large, this is true, but every so often it is good to check up on ourselves. Checklists appear from time to time in various publications which psychologists say tell whether or not a person will make a good wife, husband, doctor, lawyer, or supervisor.

The following questions are an excellent checklist to test yourself as a supervisor and administrator.

Remember, Administration gives direction and points the way but administration carries the ideas to fruition. Each is dependent on the other for its success. Remember, too, that no unit is too small for these departmental functions to be carried out. These statements apply equally as well to the Chief Librarian as to the Department Head with but one or two persons to supervise.

GENERAL ADMINISTRATION: General Responsibilities of Supervisors

1. Have I prepared written statements of functions, activities, and duties for my organizational unit?

2. Have I prepared procedural guides for operating activities?

3. Have I established clearly in writing, lines of authority and responsibility for my organizational unit?

4. Do I make recommendations for improvements in organization, policies, administrative and operating routines and procedures, including simplification of work and elimination of non-essential operations?

5. Have I designated and trained an understudy to function in my absence?

6. Do I supervise and train personnel within the unit to effectively perform their assignments?

7. Do I assign personnel and distribute work on such a basis as to carry out the organizational unit's assignment or mission in the most effective and efficient manner?

8. Have I established administrative controls by:

    a. Fixing responsibility and accountability on all supervisors under my direction for the proper performance of their functions and duties.

b. Preparations and submitting periodic work load and progress reports covering the operations of the unit to my immediate superior.

c. Analysis and evaluation of such reports received from subordinate units.

d. Submission of significant developments and problems arising within the organizational unit to my immediate superior.

e. Conducting conferences, inspections, etc., as to the status and efficiency of unit operations.

9. Do I maintain an adequate and competent working force?

10. Have I fostered good employee-department relations, seeing that established rules, regulations, and instructions are being carried out properly?

11. Do I collaborate and consult with other organizational units performing related functions to insure harmonious and efficient working relationships?

12. Do I maintain liaison through prescribed channels with city departments and other governmental agencies concerned with the activities of the unit?

13. Do I maintain contact with and keep abreast of the latest developments and techniques of administration (professional societies, groups, periodicals, etc.) as to their applicability to the activities of the unit?

14. Do I communicate with superiors and subordinates through prescribed organizational channels?

15. Do I notify superiors and subordinates in instances where bypassing is necessary as soon thereafter as practicable?

16. Do I keep my superior informed of significant developments and problems?

SEVEN BASIC FUNCTIONS OF THE SUPERVISOR

I. PLANNING
This means working out goals and means to obtain goals. <u>What</u> needs to be done, <u>who</u> will do it, <u>how</u>, <u>when</u>, and <u>where</u> it is to be done.

SEVEN STEPS IN PLANNING

A. Define job or problem clearly.
B. Consider priority of job.
C. Consider time-limit—starting and completing.
D. Consider minimum distraction to, or interference with, other activities.
E. Consider and provide for contingencies—possible emergencies.
F. Break job down into components.

G. Consider the 5 W's and H:
   WHY……….is it necessary to do the job? (Is the purpose clearly defined?)
   WHAT……..needs to be done to accomplish the defined purpose?
   ……….is needed to do the job? (Money, materials, etc.)
   WHO……….is needed to do the job?
   ……….will have responsibilities?
   WHERE……is the work to be done?
   WHEN……..is the job to begin and end? (Schedules, etc.)
   HOW……….is the job to bed done? (Methods, controls, records, etc.)

II. ORGANIZING

This means dividing up the work, establishing clear lines of responsibility and authority and coordinating efforts to get the job done.

III. STAFFING

The whole personnel function of bringing in and <u>training</u> staff, getting the right man and fitting him to the right job—the job to which he is best suited.

In the normal situation, the supervisor's responsibility regarding staffing normally includes providing accurate job descriptions, that is, duties of the jobs, requirements, education and experience, skills, physical, etc.; assigning the work for maximum use of skills; and proper utilization of the probationary period to weed out unsatisfactory employees.

IV. DIRECTING

Providing the necessary leadership to the group supervised. Important work gets done to the supervisor's satisfaction.

V. COORDINATING

The all-important duty of inter-relating the various parts of the work.
The supervisor is also responsible for controlling the coordinated activities. This means measuring performance according to a time schedule and setting quotas to see that the goals previously set are being reached. Reports from workers should be analyzed, evaluated, and made part of all future plans.

VI. REPORTING

This means proper and effective communication to your superiors, subordinates, and your peers (in definition of the job of the supervisor). Reports should be read and information contained therein should be used, not be filed away and forgotten. Reports should be written in such a way that the desired action recommended by the report is forthcoming.

VII. BUDGETING
This means controlling current costs and forecasting future costs. This forecast is based on past experience, future plans and programs, as well as current costs.

You will note that these seven functions can fall under three topics:

Planning   )
) Make a plan
Organizing)

Staffing   )
Directing   ) Get things done
Controlling)

Reporting)
) Watch it work
Budgeting)

PLANNING TO MEET MANAGEMENT GOALS

I. WHAT IS PLANNING?

    A. Thinking a job through before new work is done to determine the best way to do it
    B. A method of doing something
    C. Ways and means for achieving set goals
    D. A means of enabling a supervisor to deliver with a minimum of effort, all details involved in coordinating his work

II. WHO SHOULD MAKE PLANS?

Everybody!
All levels of supervision must plan work. (Top management, heads of divisions or bureaus, first line supervisors, and individual employees.) The higher the level, the more planning required.

III. WHAT ARE THE RESULTS OF POOR PLANNING?

    A. Failure to meet deadline
    B. Low employee morale
    C. Lack of job coordination
    D. Overtime is frequently necessary
    E. Excessive cost, waste of material and manhours

IV. PRINCIPLES OF PLANNING

    A. Getting a clear picture of your objectives. What exactly are you trying to accomplish?
    B. Plan the whole job, then the parts, in proper sequence.
    C. Delegate the planning of details to those responsible for executing them.
    D. Make your plan flexible.
    E. Coordinate your plan with the plans of others so that the work may be processed with a minimum of delay.
    F. Sell your plan before you execute it.
    G. Sell your plan to your superior, subordinate, in order to gain maximum participation and coordination.
    H. Your plan should take precedence. Use knowledge and skills that others have brought to a similar job.
    I. Your plan should take account of future contingencies; allow for future expansion.
    J. Plans should include minor details. Leave nothing to chance that can be anticipated.
    K. Your plan should be simple and provide standards and controls. Establish quality and quantity standards and set a standard method of doing the job. The controls will indicate whether the job is proceeding according to plan.
    L. Consider possible bottlenecks, breakdowns, or other difficulties that are likely to arise.

V. Q. WHAT ARE THE YARDSTICKS BY WHICH PLANNING SHOULD BE MEASURED?
   A. Any plan should:
   —Clearly state a definite course of action to be followed and goal to be achieved, with consideration for emergencies.
   — Be realistic and practical.
   — State what's to be done, when it's to be done, where, how, and by whom.
   — Establish the most efficient sequence of operating steps so that more is accomplished in less time, with the least effort, and with the best quality results.
   — Assure meeting deliveries without delays.
   — Establish the standard by which performance is to be judged.

   Q. WHAT KINDS OF PLANS DOES EFFECTIVE SUPERVISION REQUIRE?
   A. Plans should cover such factors as:
   — Manpower: right number of properly trained employees on the job
   — Materials: adequate supply of the right materials and supplies
   — Machines: full utilization of machines and equipment, with proper maintenance
   — Methods: most efficient handling of operations
   — Deliveries: making deliveries on time
   — Tools: sufficient well-conditioned tools
   — Layout: most effective use of space
   — Reports: maintaining proper records and reports
   — Supervision: planning work for employees and organizing supervisor's own time

MANAGEMENT PRINCIPLES

I. MANAGEMENT
   Q. What do we mean by management?
   A. Getting work done through others.

Management could also be defined as planning, directing, and controlling the operations of a bureau or division so that all factors will function properly and all persons cooperate efficiently for a common objective.

II. MANAGEMENT PRINCIPLES

   A. There should be a hierarchy—wherein authority and responsibility run upward and downward through several levels—with a broad base at the bottom and a single head at the top.

   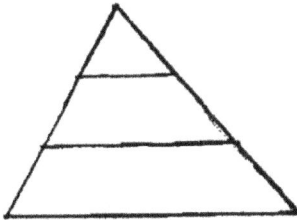

   B. Each and every unit or person in the organization should be answerable ultimately to the manager at the apex. In other words, *The buck stops here!*

C. Every necessary function involved in the bureau's objectives is assigned to a unit in that bureau.

D. Responsibilities assigned to a unit are specifically clear-cut and understood.

E. Consistent methods of organizational structure should be applied at each level of the organization.

F. Each member of the bureau from top to bottom knows: to whom he reports and who reports to him.

G. No member of one bureau reports to more than one supervisor. No dual functions.

H. Responsibility for a function is matched by authority necessary to perform that function. Weight of authority.

I. Individuals or units reporting to a supervisor do not exceed the number which can be feasibly and effectively coordinated and directed. Concept of *span of control*.

J. Channels of command (management) are not violated by staff units, although there should be staff services to facilitate and coordinate management functions.

K. Authority and responsibility should be decentralized to units and individuals who are responsible for the actual performance of operations.
Welfare – down to Welfare Centers
Hospitals – down to local hospitals

L. Management should exercise control through attention to policy problems of exceptional performance, rather than through review of routine actions of subordinates.

M. Organizations should never be permitted to grow so elaborate as to hinder work accomplishments.

III. ORGANIZATION STRUCTURE

Types of Organizations
The purest form is a leader and a few followers, such as:

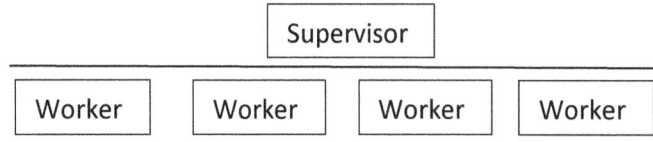

(Refer to organization chart) from supervisor to workers.

The line of authority is direct, The workers know exactly where they stand in relation to their boss, to whom they report for instructions and direction.

Unfortunately, in our present complex society, few organizations are similar to this example of a pure line organization. In this era of specialization, other people are often needed in the simplest of organizations. These specialists are known as staff. The sole purpose for their existence (staff) is to assist, advise, suggest, help or counsel line organizations. Staff has no authority to direct line people—nor do they give them direct instructions.

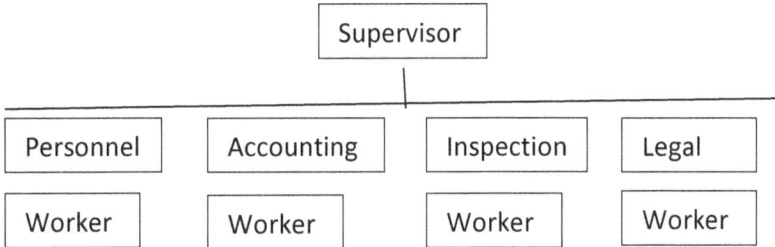

Line Functions
1. Directs
2. Orders
3. Responsibility for carrying out activities from beginning to end
4. Follows chain of command
5. Is identified with what it does
6. Decides when and how to use staff advice
7. Line executes

Staff Functions
1. Advises
2. Persuades and sells
3. Staff studies, reports, recommends but does not carry out
4. May advise across department lines
5. May find its ideas identified with others
6. Has to persuade line to want its advice
7. Staff: Conducts studies and research. Provides advice and instructions in technical matters. Serves as technical specialist to render specific services.

Types and Functions of Organization Charts
An organization chart is a picture of the arrangement and inter-relationship of the subdivisions of an organization.

A. Types of Charts:
   1. Structural: basic relationships only
   2. Functional: includes functions or duties
   3. Personnel: positions, salaries, status, etc.
   4. Process Chart: work performed
   5. Gantt Chart: actual performance against planned
   5. Flow Chart: flow and distribution of work

B. Functions of Charts:
   1. Assist in management planning and control
   2. Indicate duplication of functions
   3. Indicate incorrect stressing of functions
   4. Indicate neglect of important functions
   5. Correct unclear authority
   6. Establish proper span of control

C. Limitations of Charts:
   1. Seldom maintained on current basis
   2. Chart is oversimplified
   3. Human factors cannot adequately be charted

D. Organization Charts should be:
   1. Simple
   2. Symmetrical
   3. Indicate authority
   4. Line and staff relationship differentiated
   5. Chart should be dated and bear signature of approving officer
   6. Chart should be displayed, not hidden

ORGANIZATION

There are four basic principles of organization:
1. Unity of command
2. Span of control
3. Uniformity of assignment
4. Assignment of responsibility and delegation of authority

I. UNITY OF COMMAND

Unity of command means that each person in the organization should receive orders from one, and only one, supervisor. When a person has to take orders from two or more people, (a) the orders may be in conflict and the employee is upset because he does not know which he should obey, or (b) different orders may reach him at the same time and he does not know which he should carry out first.

Equally as bad as having two bosses is the situation where the supervisor is bypassed. Let us suppose you are a supervisor whose boss bypasses you (deals directly with people reporting to you). To the worker, it is the same as having two bosses; but to you, the supervisor, it is equally serious. Bypassing on the part of your boss will undermine your authority, and the people under you will begin looking to your boss for decisions and even for routine orders.

You can prevent bypassing by telling the people you supervise that if anyone tries to give them orders, they should direct that person to you.

II. SPAN OF CONTROL

Span of control on a given level involves:
A. The number of people being supervised
B. The distance
C The time involved in supervising the people. (One supervisor cannot supervise too many workers effectively.)

Span of control means that a supervisor has the right number (not too many and not too few) of subordinates that he can supervise well.

III. UNIFORMITY OF ASSIGNMENT

In assigning work, you as the supervisor should assign to each person jobs that are similar in nature. An employee who is assigned too many different types of jobs will waste time in going from one kind of work to another. It takes time for him to get to top production in one kind of task and, before he does so, he has to start on another.
When you assign work to people, remember that:

A. Job duties should be definite. Make it clear from the beginning what they are to do, how they are to do it, and why they are to do it. Let them know how much they are expected to do and how well they are expected to do it.
B. Check your assignments to be certain that there are no workers with too many unrelated duties, and that no two people have been given overlapping responsibilities. Your aim should be to have every task assigned to a specific person with the work fairly distributed and with each person doing his part.

IV. ASSIGNMENT OF RESPONSIBILITY AND DELEGATION OF AUTHORITY

A supervisor cannot delegate his final responsibility for the work of his department. The experienced supervisor knows that he gets his work done through people. He can't do it all himself. So he must assign the work and the responsibility for the work to his employees. Then they must be given the authority to carry out their responsibilities.

By assigning responsibility and delegating authority to carry out the responsibility, the supervisor builds in his workers initiative, resourcefulness, enthusiasm, and interest in their work. He is treating them as responsible adults. They can find satisfaction in their work, and they will respect the supervisor and be loyal to the supervisor.

PRINCIPLES OF ORGANIZATION

I. DEFINITION

Organization is the method of dividing up the work to provide the best channels for coordinated effort to get the agency's mission accomplished.

II. PURPOSE OF ORGANIZATION

A. To enable each employee within the organization to clearly know his responsibilities and relationships to his fellow employees and to organizational units
B. To avoid conflicts of authority and overlapping of jurisdiction.
C. To ensure teamwork.

III. BASIC CONSIDERATIONS IIN ORGANIZATIONAL PLANNING

A. The basic plans and objectives of the agency should be determined, and the organizational structure should be adapted to carry out effectively such plans and objectives.
B. The organization should be built around the major functions of the agency and not individuals or groups of individuals.

C. The organization should be sufficiently flexible to meet new and changing conditions which may be brought about from within or outside the department.
D. The organizational structure should be as simple as possible and the number of organizational units kept at a minimum.
E. The number of levels of authority should be kept at a minimum. Each additional management level lengthens the chain of authority and responsibility and increases the time for instructions to be distributed to operating levels and for decisions to be obtained from higher authority.
F. The form of organization should permit each executive to exercise maximum initiative within the limits of delegated authority.

IV. BASES FOR ORGANIZATION

A. Purpose (Examples: education, police, sanitation)
B. Process (Examples: accounting, legal, purchasing)
C. Clientele (Examples: welfare, parks, veteran)
D. Geographic (Examples: borough offices, precincts, libraries)

V. ASSIGNMENTS OF FUNCTIONS

A. Every function of the agency should be assigned to a specific organizational unit. Under normal circumstances, no single function should be assigned to more than one organizational unit.
B. There should be no overlapping, duplication, or conflict between organizational elements.
C. Line functions should be separated from staff functions, and proper emphasis should be placed on staff activities.
D. Functions which are closely related or similar should normally be assigned to a single organizational unit.
E. Functions should be properly distributed to promote balance, and to avoid overemphasis of less important functions and underemphasis of more essential functions.

VI. DELEGATION OF AUTHORITY AND RESPONSIBILITY

A. Responsibilities assigned to a specific individual or organizational unit should carry corresponding authority, and all statements of authority or limitations thereof should be as specific as possible.
B. Authority and responsibility for action should be decentralized to organizational units and individuals responsible for actual performance to the greatest extent possible, without relaxing necessary control over policy or the standardization of procedures. Delegation of authority will be consistent with decentralization of responsibility but such delegation will not divest an executive in higher authority of his overall responsibility.
C. The heads of organizational units should concern themselves with important matters and should delegate to the maximum extent details and routines performed in the ordinary course of business.
D. All responsibilities, authorities, and relationships should be stated in simple language to avoid misinterpretation.
E. Each individual or organizational unit charged with a specific responsibility will be held responsible for results.

VII. EMPLOYEE RELATIONSHIPS

   A. The employees reporting to one executive should not exceed the number which can be effectively directed and coordinated. The number will depend largely upon the scope and extent of the responsibilities of the subordinates.
   B. No person should report to more than one supervisor. Every supervisor should know who reports to him, and every employee should know to whom he reports. Channels of authority and responsibility should not be violated by staff units.
   C. Relationships between organizational units within the agency and with outside organizations and associations should be clearly stated and thoroughly understood to avoid misunderstanding.

DELEGATING

I. WHAT IS DELEGATING?
   Delegating is assigning a job to an employee, giving him the authority to get that job done, and giving him the responsibility for seeing to it that the job is done.

   A. What To Delegate
      1. Routine details
      2. Jobs which may be necessary and take a lot of time, but do not have to be done by the supervisor personally (preparing reports, attending meetings, etc.)
      3. Routine decision-making (making decisions which do not require the supervisor's personal attention)

   B. What Not To Delegate
      1. Job details which are *executive functions* (setting goals, organizing employees into a good team, analyzing results so as to plan for the future)
      2. Disciplinary power (handling grievances, preparing service ratings, reprimands, etc.)
      3. Decision-making which involves large numbers of employees or other bureaus and departments
      4. Final and complete responsibility for the job done by the unit being supervised

   C. Why Delegate?
      1. To strengthen the organization by developing a greater number of skilled employees
      2. To improve the employee's performance by giving him the chance to learn more about the job, handle some responsibility, and become more interested in getting the job done
      3. To improve a supervisor's performance by relieving him of routine jobs and giving him more time for *executive functions* (planning, organizing, controlling, etc.) which cannot be delegated

II. TO WHOM TO DELEGATE
   People with abilities not being used. Selection should be based on ability, not on favoritism.

REPORTS

I. **DEFINITION**
A report is an orderly presentation of factual information directed to a specific reader for a specific purpose

II. **PURPOSE**
The general purpose of a report is to bring to the reader useful and factual information about a condition or a problem. Some specific purposes of a report may be:

   A. To enable the reader to appraise the efficiency or effectiveness of a person or an operation
   B. To provide a basis for establishing standards
   C. To reflect the results of expenditures of time, effort, and money
   D. To provide a basis for developing or altering programs

III. **TYPES**

   A. Information Report: Contains facts arranged in sequence
   B. Summary (Examination) Report: Contains facts plus an analysis or discussion of the significance of the facts. Analysis may give advantages and disadvantages or give qualitative and quantitative comparisons
   C. Recommendation Report: Contains facts, analysis, and conclusion logically drawn from the facts and analysis, plus a recommendation based upon the facts, analysis, and conclusions

IV. **FACTORS TO CONSIDER BEFORE WRITING REPORT**

   A. <u>Why</u> write the report?: The purpose of the report should be clearly defined.
   B. <u>Who</u> will read the report?: What level of language should be used? Will the reader understand professional or technical language?
   C. <u>What</u> should be said?: What does the reader need or want to know about the subject?
   D. <u>How</u> should it be said?: Should the subject be presented tactfully? Convincingly? In a stimulating manner?

V. **PREPARATORY STEPS**

   A. Assemble the facts: Find out who, why, what, where, when, and how.
   B. Organize the facts: Eliminate unnecessary information
   C. Prepare an outline: Check for orderliness, logical sequence
   D. Prepare a draft: Check for correctness, clearness, completeness, conciseness, and tone
   E. Prepare it in final form: Check for grammar, punctuation, appearance

VI. **OUTLINE FOR A RECOMMENDATION REPORT**

   Is the report:
   A. Correct in information, grammar, and tone?
   B. Clear?
   C. Complete?

D. Concise?
E. Timely?
F. Worth its cost?

Will the report accomplish its purpose?

MANAGEMENT CONTROLS

I. CONTROL
What is control? What is controlled? Who controls?

The essence of control is action which adjusts operations to predetermined standards, and its basis is information in the hands of managers. Control is checking to determine whether plans are being observed and suitable progress toward stated objectives is being made, and action is taken, if necessary, to correct deviations.

We have a ready-made model for this concept of control in the automatic systems which are widely used for process control in the chemical land petroleum industries. A process control system works this way. Suppose, for example, it is desired to maintain a constant rate of flow of oil through a pipe at a predetermined or set-point value. A signal, whose strength represents the rate of flow, can be produced in a measuring device and transmitted to a control mechanism. The control mechanism, when it detects any deviation of the actual from the set-point signal, will reposition the value regulating flow rate.

II. BASIS FOR CONTROL

A process control mechanism thus acts to adjust operations to predetermined standards and does so on the basis of information it receives. In a parallel way, information reaching a manager gives him the opportunity for corrective action and is his basis for control. He cannot exercise control without such information, and he cannot do a complete job of managing without controlling.

III. POLICY

What is policy?

Policy is simply a statement of an organization's intention to act in certain ways when specified types of circumstances arise. It represents a general decision, predetermined and expressed as a principle or rule, establishing a normal pattern of conduct for dealing with given types of business events—usually recurrent. A statement is therefore useful in economizing the time of managers and in assisting them to discharge their responsibilities equitably and consistently.

Policy is not a means of control, but policy does generate the need for control.

Adherence to policies is not guaranteed nor can it be taken on faith. It has to be verified. Without verification, there is no basis for control. Policy and procedures, although closely related and interdependent to a certain extent, are not synonymous. A policy may be adopted, for example, to maintain a materials inventory not to exceed one million dollars.

A procedure for inventory control could interpret that policy and convert it into methods for keeping within that limit, with consideration, too, of possible but foreseeable expedient deviation.

IV. PROCEDURE

What is procedure?

A procedure specifically prescribes:
A. What work is to be performed by the various participants
B. Who are the respective participants
C. When and where the various steps in the different processes are to be performed
D. The sequence of operations that will insure uniform handling of recurring transactions
E. The paper that is involved, its origin, transition, and disposition

Necessary appurtenances to a procedure are:
A. Detailed organizational chart
B. Flow charts
C. Exhibits of forms, all presented in close proximity to the text of the procedure

V. BASIS OF CONTROL – INFORMATION IN THE HANDS OF MANAGERS

If the basis of control is information in the hands of managers, then reporting is elevated to a level of very considerable importance.

Types of reporting may include:
A. Special reports and routine reports
B. Written, oral, and graphic reports
C. Staff meetings
D. Conferences
E. Television screens
F. Non-receipt of information, as where management is by exception
G. Any other means whereby information is transmitted to a manager as a basis for control action

FRAMEWORK OF MANAGEMENT

I. ELEMENTS

A. Policy: It has to be verified, controlled.

B. Organization is part of the giving of an assignment. The organizational chart gives to each individual in his title, a first approximation of the nature of his assignment and orients him as being accountable to a certain individual. Organization is not in a true sense a means of control. Control is checking to ascertain whether the assignment is executed as intended and acting on the basis of that information.

C. Budgets perform three functions:
   1. They present the objectives, plans, and programs of the organization in financial terms.

2. They report the progress of actual performance against these predetermined objectives, plans, and programs.
3. Like organizational charts, delegations of authority, procedures, and job descriptions, they define the assignments which have flowed from the Chief Executive. Budgets are a means of control in the respect that they report progress of actual performance against the program. They provide information which enables managers to take action directed toward bringing actual results into conformity with the program.

D. Internal Check provides in practice for the principle that the same person should not have responsibility for all phases of a transaction. This makes it clearly an aspect of organization rather than of control. Internal Check is static, or built-in.

E. Plans, Programs, Objectives
People must know what they are trying to do. Objectives fulfill this need. Without them, people may work industriously and yet, working aimlessly, accomplish little. Plans and Programs complement Objectives, since they propose how and according to what time schedule the objectives are to be reached.

F. Delegations of Authority
Among the ways we have for supplementing the titles and lines of authority of an organizational chart are delegations of authority. Delegations of authority clarify the extent of authority of individuals and in that way serve to define assignments. That they are not means of control is apparent from the very fact that wherever there has been a delegation of authority, the need for control increases. This could hardly be expected to happen if delegations of authority were themselves means of control.

II. MANAGER'S RESPONSIBILITY

Control becomes necessary whenever a manager delegates authority to a subordinate because he cannot delegate and then simply sit back and forget4 about it. A manager's accountability to his own superior has not diminished one whit as a result of delegating part of his authority to a subordinate. The manager must exercise control over actions taken under the authority so delegated. That means checking serves as a basis for possible corrective action.

Objectives, plans, programs, organizational charts, and other elements of the managerial system are not fruitfully regarded as either controls or means of control. They are pre-established standards or models of performance to which operations are adjusted by the exercise of management control. These standards or models of performance are dynamic in character for they are constantly altered, modified, or revised. Policies, organizational set-up, procedures, delegations, etc. are constantly altered but, like objectives and plans, they remain in force until they are either abandoned or revised. All of the elements (or standards or models of performance), objectives, plans, and programs, policies, organization, etc. can be regarded as a *framework of management*.

III. CONTROL TECHNIQUES

Examples of control techniques:
A. Compare against established standards
B. Compare with a similar operation
C. Compare with past operations
D. Compare with predictions of accomplishment

IV. WHERE FORECASTS FIT

Control is after-the-fact while forecasts are before. Forecasts and projections are important for setting objectives and formulating plans.

Information for aiming and planning does not have to be before-the-fact. It may be an after-the-fact analysis proving that a certain policy has been impolitic in its effect on the relation of the company or department with customer, employee, taxpayer, or stockholder; or that a certain plan is no longer practical, or that a certain procedure is unworkable.

The prescription here certainly would not be in control (in these cases, control would simply bring operations into conformity with obsolete standards) but the establishment of new standards, a new policy, a new plan, and a new procedure to be controlled too.

Information is, of course, the basis for all communication in addition to furnishing evidence to management of the need for reconstructing the framework of management.

PROBLEM SOLVING

The accepted concept in modern management for problem solving is the utilization of the following steps:

A. Identify the problem
B. Gather data
C. List possible solutions
D. Test possible solutions
E. Select the best solution
F. Put the solution into actual practice

Occasions might arise where you would have to apply the second step of gathering data before completing the first step.

You might also find that it will be necessary to work on several steps at the same time.

I. IDENTIFY THE PROBLEM

Your first step is to define as precisely as possible the problem to be solved. While this may sound easy, it is often the most difficult part of the process.

It has been said of problem solving that you are halfway to the solution when you can write out a clear statement of the problem itself.

Our job now is to get below the surface manifestations of the trouble and pinpoint the problem. This is usually accomplished by a logical analysis, by going from the general to the particular; from the obvious to the not-so-obvious cause.

Let us say that production is behind schedule. WHY? Absenteeism is high. Now, is absenteeism the basic problem to be tackled, or is it merely a symptom of low morale among the workforce? Under these circumstances, you may decide that production is not the problem; the problem is *employee morale*.

In trying to define the problem, remember there is seldom one simple reason why production is lagging, or reports are late, etc.

Analysis usually leads to the discovery that an apparent problem is really made up of several subproblems which must be attacked separately.

Another way is to limit the problem, and thereby ease the task of finding a solution, and concentrate on the elements which are within the scope of your control.

When you have gone this far, write out a tentative statement of the problem to be solved.

II. GATHER DATA

In the second step, you must set out to collect all the information that might have a bearing on the problem. Do not settle for an assumption when reasonable fact and figures are available.

If you merely go through the motions of problem-solving, you will probably shortcut the information-gathering step. Therefore, do not stack the evidence by confining your research to your own preconceived ideas.

As you collect facts, organize them in some form that helps you make sense of them and spot possible relationships between them. For example, plotting cost per unit figures on a graph can be more meaningful than a long column of figures.

Evaluate each item as you go along. Is the source material absolutely, reliable, probably reliable, or not to be trusted.

One of the best methods for gathering data is to go out and look the situation over carefully. Talk to the people on the job who are most affected by this problem.

Always keep in mind that a primary source is usually better than a secondary source of information.

III. LIST POSSIBLE SOLUTIONS

This is the creative thinking step of problem solving. This is a good time to bring into play whatever techniques of group dynamics the agency or bureau might have developed for a joint attack on problems.

Now the important thing for you to do is: Keep an open mind. Let your imagination roam freely over the facts you have collected. Jot down every possible solution that occurs to you. Resist the temptation to evaluate various proposals as you go along. List seemingly absurd ideas along with more plausible ones. The more possibilities you list during this step, the less risk you will run of settling for merely a workable, rather than the best, solution.

Keep studying the data as long as there seems to be any chance of deriving additional ideas, solutions, explanations, or patterns from it.

IV. TEST POSSIBLE SOLUTIONS

Now you begin to evaluate the possible solutions. Take pains to be objective. Up to this point, you have suspended judgment but you might be tempted to select a solution you secretly favored all along and proclaim it as the best of the lot.

The secret of objectivity in this phase is to test the possible solutions separately, measuring each against a common yardstick. To make this yardstick try to enumerate as many specific criteria as you can think of. Criteria are best phrased as questions which you ask of each possible solution. They can be drawn from these general categories:

- Suitability – Will this solution do the job?
  Will it solve the problem completely or partially?
  Is it a permanent or a stopgap solution?

- Feasibility - Will this plan work in actual practice?
  Can we afford this approach?
  How much will it cost?

- Acceptability - Will the boss go along with the changes required in the plan?
  Are we trying to drive a tack with a sledge hammer?

V. SELECT THE BEST SOLUTION

This is the area of executive decision.

Occasionally, one clearly superior solution will stand out at the conclusion of the testing process. But often it is not that simple. You may find that no one solution has come through all the tests with flying colors.

You may also find that a proposal, which flunked miserably on one of the essential tests, racked up a very high score on others.

The best solution frequently will turn out to be a combination.

Try to arrange a marriage that will bring together the strong points of one possible solution with the particular virtues of another. The more skill and imagination that you apply, the greater is the likelihood that you will come out with a solution that is not merely adequate and workable, but is the best possible under the circumstances.

VI. PUT THE SOLUTION INTO ACTUAL PRACTICE

As every executive knows, a plan which works perfectly on paper may develop all sorts of bugs when put into actual practice.

Problem-solving does not stop with selecting the solution which looks best in theory. The next step is to put the chosen solution into action and watch the results. The results may point towards modifications.

If the problem disappears when you put your solution into effect, you know you have the right solution.

If it does not disappear, even after you have adjusted your plan to cover unforeseen difficulties that turned up in practice, work your way back through the problem-solving solutions.

> Would one of them have worked better?
> Did you overlook some vital piece of data which would have given you a different slant on the whole situation? Did you apply all necessary criteria in testing solutions? If no light dawns after this much rechecking, it is a pretty good bet that you defined the problem incorrectly in the first place.

You came up with the wrong solution because you tackled the wrong problem.

Thus, step six may become step one of a new problem-solving cycle.

COMMUNICATION

I. WHAT IS COMMUNICATION?

We communicate through writing, speaking, action, or inaction. In speaking to people face-to-face, there is opportunity to judge reactions and to adjust the message. This makes the supervisory chain one of the most, and in many instances the most, important channels of communication.

In an organization, communication means keeping employees informed about the organization's objectives, policies, problems, and progress. Communication is the free interchange of information, ideas, and desirable attitudes between and among employees and between employees and management.

II. WHY IS COMMUNICATION NEEDED?

A. People have certain social needs
B. Good communication is essential in meeting those social needs
C. While people have similar basic needs, at the same time they differ from each other
D. Communication must be adapted to these individual differences

An employee cannot do his best work unless he knows why he is doing it. If he has the feeling that he is being kept in the dark about what is going on, his enthusiasm and productivity suffer.

20

Effective communication is needed in an organization so that employees will understand what the organization is trying to accomplish; and how the work of one unit contributes to or affects the work of other units in the organization and other organizations.

III. HOW IS COMMUNICATION ACHIEVED?

Communication flows downward, upward, sideways.

A. Communication may come from top management down to employees. This is downward communication.

Some means of downward communication are:
1. Training (orientation, job instruction, supervision, public relations, etc.)
2. Conferences
3. Staff meetings
4. Policy statements
5. Bulletins
6. Newsletters
7. Memoranda
8. Circulation of important letters

In downward communication, it is important that employees be informed in advance of changes that will affect them.

B. Communications should also be developed so that the ideas, suggestions, and knowledge of employees will flow upward to top management.

Some means of upward communication are:
1. Personal discussion conferences
2. Committees
3. Memoranda
4. Employees suggestion program
5. Questionnaires to be filled in giving comments and suggestions about proposed actions that will affect field operations.

Upward communication requires that management be willing to listen, to accept, and to make changes when good ideas are present. Upward communication succeeds when there is no fear of punishment for speaking out or lack of interest at the top. Employees will share their knowledge and ideas with management when interest is shown and recognition is given.

C. The advantages of downward communication:
1. It enables the passing down of orders, policies, and plans necessary to the continued operation of the station.
2. By making information available, it diminishes the fears and suspicions which result from misinformation and misunderstanding.
3. It fosters the pride people want to have in their work when they are told of good work.
4. It improves the morale and stature of the individual to be *in the know*.

5. It helps employees to understand, accept, and cooperate with changes when they know about them in advance.

D. The advantages of upward communication:
1. It enables the passing upward of information, attitudes, and feelings.
2. It makes it easier to find out how ready people are to receive downward communication.
3. It reveals the degree to which the downward communication is understood and accepted.
4. It helps to satisfy the basic social needs.
5. It stimulates employees to participate in the operation of their organization.
6. It encourage employees to contribute ideas for improving the efficiency and economy of operations.
7. It helps to solve problem situations before they reach the explosion point.

IV. WHY DOES COMMUNICATION FAIL?

A. The technical difficulties of conveying information clearly
B. The emotional content of communication which prevents complete transmission
C. The fact that there is a difference between what management needs to say, what it wants to day, and what it does say
D. The fact that there is a difference between what employees would like to say, what they think is profitable or safe to say, and what they do say

V. HOW TO IMPROVE COMMUNICATION

As a supervisor, you are a key figure in communication. To improve as a communicator, you should:
A. Know: Knowing your subordinates will help you to recognize and work with individual differences.
B. Like: If you like those who work for you and those for whom you work, this will foster the kind of friendly, warm, work atmosphere that will facilitate communication.
C. Trust: Showing a sincere desire to communicate will help to develop the mutual trust and confidence which are essential to the free flow of communication.
D. Tell: Tell your subordinates and superiors *what's doing*. Tell your subordinates *why* as well as *how*.
E. Listen: By listening, you help others to talk and you create good listeners. Don't forget that listening implies action.
F. Stimulate: Communication has to be stimulated and encouraged. Be receptive to ideas and suggestions and motivate your people so that each member of the team identifies himself with the job at hand.
G. Consult: The most effective way of consulting is to let your people participate, insofar as possible, in developing determinations which affect them or their work.

VI. HOW TO DETERMINE WHETHER YOU ARE GETTING ACROSS

A. Check to see that communication is received and understood
B. Judge this understanding by actions rather than words
C. Adapt or vary communication, when necessary
D. Remember that good communication cannot cure all problems

VII. THE KEY ATTITUDE

Try to see things from the other person's point of view. By doing this, you help to develop the permissive atmosphere and the shared confidence and understanding which are essential to effective two-way communication.

Communication is a two-way process:
A. The basic purpose of any communication is to get action.
B. The only way to get action is through acceptance.
C. In order to get acceptance, communication must be humanly satisfying as well as technically efficient.

HOW ORDERS AND INSTRUCTIONS SHOULD BE GIVEN

I. CHARACTERISTICS OF GOOD ORDERS AND INSTRUCTIONS

A. Clear
Orders should be definite as to
—What is to be done
—Who is to do it
—When it is to be done
—Where it is to be done
—How it is to be done

B. Concise
Avoid wordiness. Orders should be brief and to the point.

C. Timely
Instructions and orders should be sent out at the proper time and not too long in advance of expected performance.

D. Possibility of Performance
Orders should be feasible:
1. Investigate before giving orders
2. Consult those who are to carry out instructions before formulating and issuing them

E. Properly Directed
Give the orders to the people concerned. Do not send orders to people who are not concerned. People who continually receive instructions that are not applicable to them get in the habit of neglecting instructions generally.

F. Reviewed Before Issuance
Orders should be reviewed before issuance:
1. Test them by putting yourself in the position of the recipient
2. If they involve new procedures, have the persons who are to do the work review them for suggestions.

G. Reviewed After Issuance
Persons who receive orders should be allowed to raise questions and to point out unforeseen consequences of orders.

H. Coordinated
Orders should be coordinated so that work runs smoothly.

I. Courteous
Make a request rather than a demand. There is no need to continually call attention to the fact that you are the boss.

J. Recognizable as an Order
Be sure that the order is recognizable as such.

K. Complete
Be sure recipient has knowledge and experience sufficient to carry out order. Give illustrations and examples.

A DEPARTMENTAL PERSONNEL OFFICE IS RESPONSIBLE FOR THE FOLLOWING FUNCTIONS

1. Policy
2. Personnel Programs
3. Recruitment and Placement
4. Position Classification
5. Salary and Wage Administration
6. Employee performance Standards and Evaluation
7. Employee Relations
8. Disciplinary Actions and Separations
9. Health and Safety
10. Staff Training and Development
11. Personnel Records, Procedures, and Reports
12. Employee Services
13. Personnel Research

SUPERVISION

I. LEADERSHIP

All leadership is based essentially on authority. This comes from two sources: It is received from higher management or it is earned by the supervisor through his methods of supervision. Although effective leadership has always depended upon the leader's using his authority in such a way as to appeal successfully to the motives of the people supervised, the conditions for making this appeal are continually changing. The key to today's problem of leadership is flexibility and resourcefulness on the part of the leader in meeting changes in conditions as they occur.

Three basic approaches to leadership are generally recognized:

A. The Authoritarian Approach
   1. The methods and techniques used in this approach emphasize the *I* in leadership and depend primarily on the formal authority of the leader. This authority is sometimes exercised in a hardboiled manner and sometimes in a benevolent

manner, but in either case the dominating role of the leader is reflected in the thinking, planning, and decisions of the group.
2. Group results are to a large degree dependent on close supervision by the leader. Usually, the individuals in the group will not show a high degree of initiative or acceptance of responsibility and their capacity to grow and develop probably will not be fully utilized. The group may react with resentment or submission, depending upon the manner and skill of the leader in using his authority.
3. This approach develops as a natural outgrowth of the authority that goes with the leader's job and his feeling of sole responsibility for getting the job done. It is relatively easy to use and does not require must resourcefulness.
4. The use of this approach is effective in times of emergencies, in meeting close deadline as a final resort, in settling some issues, in disciplinary matters, and with dependent individuals and groups.

B. The Laissez-Faire or Let 'em Alone Approach
1. This approach generally is characterized by an avoidance of leadership responsibility by the leader. The activities of the group depend largely on the choice of its members rather than the leader.
2. Group results probably will be poor. Generally, there will be disagreements over petty things, bickering, and confusion. Except for a few aggressive people, individuals will not show much initiative and growth and development will be retarded. There may be a tendency for informal leaders to take over leadership of the group.
3. This approach frequently results from the leader's dislike of responsibility, from his lack of confidence, from failure of other methods to work, from disappointment or criticism. It is usually the easiest of the three to use and requires both understanding and resourcefulness on the part of the leader.
4. This approach is occasionally useful and effective, particularly in forcing dependent individuals or groups to rely on themselves, to give someone a chance to save face by clearing his own difficulties, or when action should be delayed temporarily for good cause.

C. The Democratic Approach
1. The methods and techniques used in this approach emphasize the *we* in leadership and build up the responsibility of the group to attain its objectives. Reliance is placed largely on the earned authority of the leader.
2. Group results are likely to be good because most of the job motives of the people will be satisfied. Cooperation and teamwork, initiative, acceptance of responsibility, and the individual's capacity for growth probably will show a high degree of development.
3. This approach grows out of a desire or necessity of the leader to find ways to appeal effectively to the motivation of his group. It is the best approach to build up inside the person a strong desire to cooperate and apply himself to the job. It is the most difficult to develop, and requires both understanding and resourcefulness on the part of the leader.
4. The value of this approach increases over a long period where sustained efficiency and development of people are important. It may not be fully effective in all situations, however, particularly when there is not sufficient time to use it properly or where quick decisions must be made.

All three approaches are used by most leaders and have a place in supervising people. The extent of their use varies with individual leaders, with some using one approach predominantly. The leader who uses these three approaches, and varies their use with time and circumstance, is probably the most effective. Leadership which is used predominantly with a democratic approach requires more resourcefulness on the part of the leader but offers the greatest possibilities in terms of teamwork and cooperation.

The one best way of developing democratic leadership is to provide a real sense of participation on the part of the group, since this satisfies most of the chief job motives. Although there are many ways of providing participation, consulting as frequently as possible with individuals and groups on things that affect them seems to offer the most in building cooperation and responsibility. Consultation takes different forms, but it is most constructive when people feel they are actually helping in finding the answers to the problems on the job.

There are some requirements of leaders in respect to human relations which should be considered in their selection and development. Generally, the leader should be interested in working with other people, emotionally stable, self-confident, and sensitive to the reactions of others. In addition, his viewpoint should be one of getting the job done through people who work cooperatively in response to his leadership. He should have a knowledge of individual and group behavior, but, most important of all, he should work to combine all of these requirements into a definite, practical skill in leadership.

II. NINE POINTS OF CONTRAST BETWEEN *BOSS* AND *LEADER*

   A. The boss drives his men; the leader coaches them.
   B. The boss depends on authority; the leader on good will.
   C. The boss inspires fear; the leader inspires enthusiasm.
   D. The boss says I; the leader says *We*.
   E. The boss says *Get here on time*; the leader gets there ahead of time.
   F. The boss fixes the blame for the breakdown; the leader fixes the breakdown.
   G. The boss knows how it is done; the leader shows how.
   H. The boss makes work a drudgery; the leader makes work a game.
   I. The boss says *Go*; the leader says *Let's go*.

EMPLOYEE MORALE

Employee morale is the way employees feel about each other, the organization or unit in which they work, and the work they perform.

I. SOME WAYS TO DEVELOP AND MAINTAIN GOOD EMPLYEE MORALE

   A. Give adequate credit and praise when due.
   B. Recognize importance of all jobs and equalize load with proper assignments, always giving consideration to personality differences and abilities.
   C. Welcome suggestions and do not have an *all-wise* attitude. Request employees' assistance in solving problems and use assistants when conducting group meetings on certain subjects.
   D. Properly assign responsibilities and give adequate authority for fulfillment of such assignments.

E. Keep employees informed about matters that affect them.
F. Criticize and reprimand employees privately.
G. Be accessible and willing to listen.
H. Be fair.
I. Be alert to detect training possibilities so that you will not miss an opportunity to help each employee do a better job, and if possible with less effort on his part.
J. Set a good example.
K. Apply the golden rule.

II. SOME INDICATIONS OF GOOD MORALE

A. Good quality of work
B. Good quantity
C. Good attitude of employees
D. Good discipline
E. Teamwork
F. Good attendance
G. Employee participation

MOTIVATION

DRIVES

A drive, stated simply, is a desire or force which causes a person to do or say certain things. These are some of the most usual drives and some of their identifying characteristics recognizable in people motivated by such drives:

A. Security (desire to provide for the future)
Always on time for work
Works for the same employer for many years
Never takes unnecessary chances
Seldom resists doing what he is told

B. Recognition (desire to be rewarded for accomplishment)
Likes to be asked for his opinion
Becomes very disturbed when he makes a mistake
Does things to attract attention
Likes to see his name in print

C. Position (desire to hold certain status in relation to others)
Boasts about important people he knows
Wants to be known as a key man
Likes titles
Demands respect
Belongs to clubs, for prestige

D. Accomplishment (desire to get things done)
    Complains when things are held up
    Likes to do things that have tangible results
    Never lies down on the job
    Is proud of turning out good work

E. Companionship (desire to associate with other people)
    Likes to work with others
    Tells stories and jokes
    Indulges in horseplay
    Finds excuses to talk to others on the job

F. Possession (desire to collect and hoard objects)
    Likes to collect things
    Puts his name on things belonging to him
    Insists on the same location

Supervisors may find that identifying the drives of employees is a helpful step toward motivating them to self-improvement and better job performance. For example: An employee's job performance is below average. His supervisor, having previously determined that the employee is motivated by a drive for security, suggests that taking training courses will help the employee to improve, advance, and earn more money. Since earning more money can be a step toward greater security, the employee's drive for security would motivate him to take the training suggested by the supervisor. In essence, this is the process of charting an employee's future course by using his motivating drives to positive advantage.

EMPLOYEE PARTICIPATION

I. WHAT IS PARTICIPATION

Employee participation is the employee's giving freely of his time, skill, and knowledge to an extent which cannot be obtained by demand.

II. WHY IS IT IMPORTANT?

The supervisor's responsibility is to get the job done through people. A good supervisor gets the job done through people who work willingly and well. The participation of employees is important because:

A. Employees develop a greater sense of responsibility when they share in working out operating plans and goals.
B. Participation provides greater opportunity and stimulation for employees to learn, and to develop their ability.
C. Participation sometimes provides better solutions to problems because such solutions may combine the experience and knowledge of interested employees who want the solutions to work.
D. An employee or group may offer a solution which the supervisor might hesitate to make for fear of demanding too much.

E. Since the group wants to make the solution work, they exert pressure in a constructive way on each other.
F. Participation usually results in reducing the need for close supervision.

II. HOW MAY SUPERVISORS OBTAIN IT?

Participation is encouraged when employees feel that they share some responsibility for the work and that their ideas are sincerely wanted and valued. Some ways of obtaining employee participation are:

A. Conduct orientation programs for new employees to inform them about the organization and their rights and responsibilities as employees.
B. Explain the aims and objectives of the agency. On a continuing basis, be sure that the employees know what these aims and objectives are.
C. Share job successes and responsibilities and give credit for success.
D. Consult with employees, both as individuals and in groups, about things that affect them.
E. Encourage suggestions for job improvements. Help employees to develop good suggestions. The suggestions can bring them recognition. The city's suggestion program offers additional encouragement through cash awards.

The supervisor who encourages employee participation is not surrendering his authority. He must still make decisions and initiate action, and he must continue to be ultimately responsible for the work of those he supervises. But, through employee participation, he is helping his group to develop greater ability and a sense of responsibility while getting the job done faster and better.

STEPS IN HANDLING A GRIEVANCE

1. Get the Facts
    a. Listen sympathetically
    b. Let him talk himself out
    c. Get his story straight
    d. Get his point of view
    e. Don't argue with him
    f. Give him plenty of time
    g. Conduct the interview privately
    h. Don't try to shift the blame or pass the buck

2. Consider the Facts
    a. Consider the employee's viewpoint
    b. How will the decision affect similar cases
    c. Consider each decision as a possible precedent
    d. Avoid snap judgments—don't jump to conclusions

3. Make or Get a Decision
    a. Frame an effective counter-proposal
    b. Make sure it is fair to all
    c. Have confidence in your judgment
    d. Be sure you can substantiate your decision

4. Notify the Employee of Your Decision
   Be sure he is told; try to convince him that the decision is fair and just.

5. Take Action When Needed and If Within Your Authority
   Otherwise, tell employee that the matter will be called to the attention of the proper person or that nothing can be done, and why it cannot.

6. Follow through to see that the desired result is achieved.

7. Record key facts concerning the complaint and the action taken.

8. Leave the way open to him to appeal your decision to a higher authority.

9. Report all grievances to your superior, whether they are appealed or not.

DISCIPLINE

Discipline is training that develops self-control, orderly conduct, and efficiency.

To discipline does not necessarily mean to punish.

To discipline does mean to train, to regulate, and to govern conduct.

I. THE DISCIPLINARY INTERVIEW

Most employees sincerely want to do what is expected of them. In other words, they are self-disciplined. Some employees, however, fail to observe established rules and standards, and disciplinary action by the supervisor is required.

The primary purpose of disciplinary action is to improve conduct without creating dissatisfaction, bitterness, or resentment in the process.

Constructive disciplinary action is more concerned with causes and explanations of breaches of conduct than with punishment. The disciplinary interview is held to get at the causes of apparent misbehavior and to motivate better performance in the future.

It is important that the interview be kept on an impersonal a basis as possible. If the supervisor lets the interview descend to the plane of an argument, it loses its effectiveness.

II. PLANNING THE INTERVIEW

Get all pertinent facts concerning the situation so that you can talk in specific terms to the employee.

Review the employee's record, appraisal ratings, etc.

Consider what you know about the temperament of the employee. Consider your attitude toward the employee. Remember that the primary requisite of disciplinary action is fairness.

Don't enter upon the interview when angry.

Schedule the interview for a place which is private and out of hearing of others.

III. CONDUCTING THE INTERVIEW

A. Make an effort to establish accord.
B. Question the employee about the apparent breach of discipline. Be sure that the question is not so worded as to be itself an accusation.
C. Give the employee a chance to tell his side of the story. Give him ample opportunity to talk.
D. Use understanding—listening except where it is necessary to ask a question or to point out some details of which the employee may not be aware. If the employee misrepresents facts, make a plain, accurate statement of the facts, but don't argue and don't engage in personal controversy.
E. Listen and try to understand the reasons for the employee's (mis)conduct. First of all, don't assume that there has been a breach of discipline. Evaluate the employee's reasons for his conduct in the light of his opinions and feelings concerning the consistency and reasonableness of the standards which he was expected to follow. Has the supervisor done his part in explaining the reasons for the rule? Was the employee's behavior unintentional or deliberate? Does he think he had real reasons for his actions? What new facts is he telling? Do the facts justify his actions? What causes, other than those mentioned, could have stimulated the behavior?
F. After listening to the employee's version of the situation, and if censure of his actions is warranted, the supervisor should proceed with whatever criticism is justified. Emphasis should be placed on future improvement rather than exclusively on the employee's failure to measure up to expected standards of job conduct.
G. Fit the criticism to the individual. With one employee, a word of correction may be all that is required.
H. Attempt to distinguish between unintentional error and deliberate misbehavior. An error due to ignorance requires training and not censure.
I. Administer criticism in a controlled, even tone of voice, never in anger. Make it clear that you are acting as an agent of the department. In general, criticism should refer to the job or the employee's actions and not to the person. Criticism of the employee's work is not an attack on the individual.
J. Be sure the interview does not destroy the employee's self-confidence. Mention his good qualities and assure him that you feel confident that he can improve his performance.
K. Wherever possible, before the employee leaves the interview, satisfy him that the incident is closed, that nothing more will be said on the subject unless the offense is repeated.

TECHNIQUES OF DECISION MAKING

CONTENTS

INSTRUCTIONAL OBJECTIVES	1
CONTENT	1
Introduction	1

1. What is Decision Making?

2. A Formula for Decision Making 2

   A. Isolate the Problem 3
      What Is the Real Problem?
      What Are the Problems?
      What Are the Symptoms?

   B. Analyze the Facts 5
      How Many Facts Should be Gathered?
      Where Are the Needed Facts Obtained?

   C. Organizing the Facts 7
      Grouping the Facts
         Cost
         Time
         Past Precedent
         Procedure
         Leadership
         Quality
         Productivity

   D. Stating the Real Problem 9
      Is There a Real Problem or Just Symptoms?
      What Objective Is To Be Achieved?

   E. Developing Alternative Solutions 10
      Present All Alternatives for Consideration
      List the Alternatives

   F. Selecting the Best Alternative Solution 11
      List the Consequences of the Decision
      Be a Devil's Advocate
      Scrutinize the Final Alternatives Thoroughly
      Involve Your Superiors

   G. Implement the Decision 13

3. Summation 13

STUDENT LEARNING ACTIVITIES	14
TEACHER MANAGEMENT ACTIVITIES	15
EVALUATION QUESTIONS	17

TECHNIQUES OF DECISION MAKING

INSTRUCTIONAL OBJECTIVES
1. Ability to define decision making.
2. Ability to learn the decision-making formula.
3. Ability to learn how to state problems simply and accurately.
4. Ability to determine the difference between a symptom and a cause.
5. Ability to determine which facts are most important to a decision.
6. Ability to be able to qualify information according to importance and subject classification.
7. Ability to learn to identify two or more alternative solutions for a problem.
8. Ability to develop an openness to creative ideas.
9. Ability to learn to weigh the consequences of alternative decisions.
10. Ability to select and justify the most appropriate decision.

CONTENT

INTRODUCTION

Every person, each day, is faced by numerous situations which require the making of many decisions throughout the course of the day. It is necessary to answer such questions as: *When do I get up in the morning? What clothes will I wear? What will I have for breakfast? Which route will I take to school?*

Working in the field of public service, an individual is constantly faced with a series of situations which require him to take some particular course of action. Many such actions may not require special decision making on his part, because his particular organization has provided ways for him to make these decisions rather automatically. For example, there are department policies, and standard ways of performing certain jobs. A person also has his own past experiences of success which enable him to easily make certain decisions for such things as: the hours he should work, his rate of pay, and the required forms which must be completed for certain kinds of activities. All of these things are handled rather automatically on the job, because people have methods of handling certain things in certain ways. These become habit. They fit within a regular pattern.

There are many situations faced by a decision maker where the consequences of his action are so minor that it doesn't really matter which way he decides to solve a given problem as long as it is resolved: for example, what pencil to choose; the color of the paper on a final report; the diverting of automobiles during a traffic jam.

However, there are also other situations where the way a manager or supervisor solves a problem has great impact on an organization. Sometimes a person doesn't have a chance to actually know what is right and what is wrong. Judgment might have no well established basis. The opportunity to select between two alternatives of equal value does not exist. The situation is not clearcut. It requires thought and careful judgment; it has far-reaching consequences on the organization-affecting the quality of service, costs, schedules, the relationships between people in a working unit. Appropriate action must be taken in such assorted areas as overtime, employee dismissal, grievances, types of equipment to purchase, ways to reduce waste. The effectiveness and efficiency of the decision-making process of one individual can have far-reaching impact on a public-service organization.

Good decisions allow individuals to control and monitor their operations. Bad ones can cause worse problems and hinder the effectiveness of an organization. Things just don't happen by chance. They are made to happen. They are arranged. They can quite often be developed over a period of time which has been required by the nature of the problem or activity.

1. <u>WHAT IS DECISION MAKING?</u>

Decision making involves a conscious choice or selection of one behavior alternative from a group of two or more behavior alternatives.

Thus, there are two basic elements in a decision-making process: one, the matter of conscious choice, and the other of alternatives. *To decide, then, really means to cut off, to come to a conclusion, to end.*

2. *<u>A FORMULA FOR DECISION MAKING</u>*

Decision-making is a skill that can be developed. One way in which it can be developed is through a formula, a procedure which provides a formal process or system involving the basic rules of decision-making. There are no born decision makers, but some people appear to act very efficiently on the basis of hunches. These people may never be seen with charts and graphs, or performing a lot of analytical tasks. However, they've probably developed their own way of sifting facts and of solving problems. Good decision makers usually know their personnel; have prior experience; they can put together difficult possibilities quickly. They have their own personal *formulas* of decision making.

An effective technique to help make decisions is through the aid of a formula – a kind of check-off list to help find answers to difficult situations, to resolve problems, to handle unique situations. Such a formula enables one to take advantage of his past experiences, to see the whole picture, and to utilize all the facts he can find which are applicable to the solution.

A decision-making formula worthy of our consideration has six steps:

- *Isolate* - State the apparent problem or situation with which you plan to deal.

- *Analyze* - Gather the facts.

- *Diagnose* - Organize and interpret the facts.

- *Prescribe procedures* - State the <u>real</u> problem or situation.

- *Implement procedures -* Develop alternative solutions.

- *Evaluate* - Select the most appropriate alternative. <u>Decide.</u>

We will consider each of these steps separately. However, it should be kept in mind that these separate steps are really all related and part of the whole process of decision making.

A. *Isolate the Problem*. A problem can be a situation, question, matter, or person that is perplexing or difficult, that obstructs the way to achieving a goal or objective.

Almost everyone has problems: students have study problems when they don't know answers to test questions; people have money problems when they can't pay all of their bills. Individuals have problems with people who are unfriendly; problems with their girlfriends or boyfriends; growth problems; health problems; psychological problems.

There are professionals and specialists to whom people can go with their problems. A person takes his malfunctioning car to a mechanic, he calls on the plumber to fix leaky pipes, contacts the doctor when he doesn't feel well. These specialists are skilled problem solvers in a particular area. They have had special training and experience. They may even have had to pass examinations to obtain certificates or licenses.

In decision making, one must recognize problems as well as symptoms of problems. It is particularly important to be able to separate symptoms from causes.

What is the Real Problem? Problems are often presented in very broad terms: "Gee, John, they've really fouled up in accounting. Go straighten them out." "Boy, do we have a morale problem." "We have to introduce that new system right away." "Those two managers just don't get along."

Consider the question of morale, for example. Is morale really the problem, or is it more accurately the symptom of another problem? Chances are that it is a symptom of a problem rather than the real problem itself. The problem situation might be poor organizational structure, bad working conditions, an unfriendly supervisor, unfair treatment, or a number of other difficulties.

To help in determining what is a symptom and what is a cause, several questions must be asked:

- *"How else might the problem be stated?"* The placement of accountants in one isolated department, without the opportunity to discuss actual income and outgo with supervisors, has given us unrealistic budget figures.

    The lack of adding machines, a broken calculator, dim light, uncomfortable room temperatures, and individual working spaces has caused a greater number of absences.

    The accounting manager has openly criticized senior staff members in front of their fellow workers.

    The department secretaries were all forced to work overtime for staying five minutes past their lunch hours.

- *"What else is involved?"*

    If there are no communications between accountants and supervisors, neither group will know the reasons behind the requests or needs of the others.

    There has been talk about a computer eliminating some of the accounting jobs.

    The senior accountants have been slow to pick up the new accounting procedures.

    This is the tenth time this month that the financial unit has been unable to take care of the people in line because the secretaries were not here.

- *"Are there similar problems in other departments?"*

    The people in supplies have been ordering the wrong equipment.

    There have been layoffs in several departments.

    Several department managers are competing for the job of assistant director of our organization.

    None of the other departments have problems with secretaries.

- *"Is this a problem or a symptom?"*

    The real problem is that the accountants have not been properly informed of the organizational structure, and thus have very poor understanding of the departments which comprise the organization.

    Another organization nearby has announced opportunities for accountants at higher pay, and in new offices.

    The accounting manager and his senior staff do not plan departmental modifications together.

    Only one of the secretaries has a watch and it is five minutes slow. They play bridge at lunch time several days each month.

- *"How do others perceive the problem?"*

    Talk to all the accountants and managers individually.

    Talk to personnel about accounting re-classification.

    Interview the senior staff.

Visit with the secretaries.

<u>What are the Problems? What are the Symptoms?</u> If your automobile won't start, it might not be because it's old, the engine is dirty, or your windshield wipers don't work the car may be out of gas. It might, however, be time to give it some other attention, too. If you can recognize the symptoms, you can avoid a lot of problems.

B. <u>Analyze the Facts.</u> When the problem is recognized, then all the facts required for a successful decision can, and should be accumulated. Too often, people think they have all the facts, but they don't. It's like trying to put together a jigsaw puzzle, and recognizing, after many frustrating hours, that six pieces are missing.

Frequently, the decision maker feels that because he is in a particular situation, he knows it better than anyone else can know it. The issue may, therefore, be somewhat clouded. This cloudiness may prevent him from seeing what is actually there.

How many times have individuals had to make a decision and found that they didn't have the right facts or sufficient quantities of facts to insure a good decision? Both the quality and effectiveness of most decisions can be seriously reduced without good facts.

When gathering facts, one should write them down, and gather them into one comprehensive list. The decision maker can then visualize them all at the same time, and is much less likely to overlook or forget any of them. In dealing with large amounts of information, he can grade sub-topics and keep track of them in a systematic way.

How many facts should be gathered? The number usually depends on the nature and complexity of the situation.

Basically it means that the amount of information accumulated depends upon such factors as:

- The amount of time available.

- Is it an emergency situation or not?

- The seriousness of the situation.

- The availability of information, etc.

Where are the Needed Facts Obtained?

- First, he might turn to available records. He usually has financial records, personal records, records of transactions, and records of activities.

- Second, he may have references: newspapers, journals, old letters, the like.

- Third, and very importantly, he has other people, or he has a staff. There is a great deal of expertise within most public-service organizations: specialists in economics, human relations, law, health, safety, and other areas; all responsive to the request of the decision-maker. An outside expert, or consultant, may be required in difficult situations.

- Finally, look at other organizational units which have been confronted with similar problems. Quite often, through investigation, the decision-maker finds that precedents have been set which he may have to follow. In law, for example, he may have to base a decis.ion on the verdict of a case held on the same issue, long ago in a distant place.

Sources of information are unlimited. It takes a great deal of initiative to uncover them.

How should the facts be obtained? Here again, there are questions we must ask ourselves:

- What kinds of facts are available?

- What information is available?

- Is there enough?

- Is help needed, and where can it be obtained?

- Who else might have the information needed?

Going back to the morale problem, which was found to be the result of a basic lack of communication between accountants and departmental managers, how might the decision-maker proceed?

In gathering the facts, he would have to obtain both the accountant's records and the manager's records. The decision-maker might call upon organizations of similar size and activity, to see how they handle difficulties of this nature. He might talk to one or more senior accountants in a large public accounting firm or contact the governmental auditors. He might even write letters to colleagues seeking their advice.

The decision-maker might hold a meeting of selected members of his staff, or assign a task force of accountants and managers to look into the matter.

As he begins to gather his facts, the decision-maker will discover that other information is required. Additionally, he will uncover sources of other facts. The quality of the facts he gathers ultimately affects the quality of his decisions. The better the data, the better the opportunity to make a good decision.

C. Organizing the Facts. Once the facts have been collected, it becomes very important that they be organized to help the decision-maker interpret what they really mean. To do this, it's helpful to set them up in categories -- to pull like items together.

This procedure helps people to know whether certain facts are more important than others, and thus deserve special consideration.

Grouping the Facts. There are several categories into which information can be grouped, such as: cost, time, past precedent, procedures, leadership, quality, and productivity:

Cost. In cost considerations, one must look at unit costs, personnel costs, material costs, equipment costs, mailing costs, etc. If, for example, an individual is attempting to determine the cost of mailing out new contracts to several hundred vendors with whom the agency deals, the following costs may have to be considered, among others:

- *Duplication costs per duplicated copy.*

- *Salary costs of writing new contract.*

- *Salary costs of typing contracts.*

- *Costs of new contract forms.*

- *Costs of envelopes.*

- *Costs of writing departmental letters.*

Time.   Time is usually calculated in terms of the personnel costs or salaries paid. The basic periods of time hours, days, weeks, months, years are quite often combined in terms of man-hours, man-weeks, man-years, etc., to enable the numbers of hour units to be multiplied by salary allocations. Equipment time, particularly in this age of computers, can be quite expensive.

Past Precedent.   This is a category relating together data on similar situations in the past, and to consider the decisions arrived at in those situations for their bearing on the decision to be made in the present.

Procedures.   These are also important. Most public-service organizations have certain ways of accomplishing functions or providing services. They have been proven over a period of time to be most appropriate to particular situations. Here, too, is where organizational policy making may be involved and possibly changed and modified.

Leadership. This would include the directions and decisions which brought about a particular situation, and permit review of the factors which were present when prior decisions were made.

Quality. The quality of facts is important. There must be an assurance that the right data, and the most applicable figures and information, are available.

Productivity. This category would enable a comparison between various activities which would bring about particular results. It would provide an opportunity to look at the output of a department or project team.

In pulling together like items, one can see trends, certain facts which may be more important than others, and areas where there are gaps in the information.

In organizing facts, the following questions should be asked:

- Which facts are related to each other?

- Are these facts related to any not listed?

- What is the extent of their relationship?

- Are they relevant to this situation?

- What is the level of reliability of the facts?

- Can the problem be more clearly defined with the information listed?

- How can it be done?

- How much time is there for further organization?

- Are these facts recurring or one time events?

D. <u>Stating the Real Problem</u>. Having examined the data, the decision-maker is now in a position to state the *real* problem or situation with which he has to deal. He now knows whether he has a problem, or just a misunderstanding. Was the original statement just a symptom, or was it a real situation? It might be that there are several problems. Whatever the situation, it must be stated in clear and simple terms. It should be written down.

A problem is a situation which deviates from an expected standard, or norm of desired performance. In decision making, one starts with an *apparent* problem. The decision maker gathers more information in order to more accurately identify the situation with which he is going to deal.

<u>*Is there a real problem? or just symptoms?*</u> The data have been gathered and organized. Now it is necessary to zero in on the actual situation, and to see whether there is a real problem. Was the initial identification a symptom of a problem, or was it a real cause? Is there one problem, or several?

If the decision-maker neglected to gather the facts, and then to organize, analyze, and categorize them, he might find himself working on the wrong situation. He could spend a great deal of time and effort on symptoms, and could actually be working on the wrong problem. Certainly, he could overlook a number of relevant factors.

If a medical doctor spent all of his time studying symptoms, he might be too late to address an actual problem and his patient could die. Similarly, in a public-service organization, *if too much time and energy is spent in chasing symptoms instead of causes, problems can become crises.*

<u>*What objective is to be achieved?*</u> Remember, one must still think about decision making in terms of fulfilling objectives.

When it is known what kind of performance should be achieved, and what kind of performance has been received, the necessary effort is simple merely to measure the difference between those two points. The decision-maker must identify the deviation and its extent. He will also have to specifically state the standard, or *norm,* toward which he is trying to return.

In other words, not only does he have to state the problem to which he is going to address himself, but he must specifically state the objective he wants to achieve.

In the previous illustration of the public-service organization and the communication problems between the accountants and managers, the objectives could, perhaps, be restated in this manner: *it is necessary to design a realistic and accurate budget for costs.*

This stage would complete the problem identification part of the decision-making process. Now, he can get on with decision-making itself.

E. <u>Developing Alternative Solutions</u>. With the *real* problem determined and stated, the decision-maker is now in a position to begin the development of alternative solutions. Notice that there is an "s" on the end of "solution." Decision-makers should be interested in as many solutions to a problem as can be developed.

This particular phase of the decision making process should be very free-wheeling. It should produce a number of ideas. The decision-maker should keep his mind open. He should not be too judgmental, but should avoid premature criticism. *Criticism given too early can destroy new ideas that could be beneficial.*

Picture a staff meeting, where the assistant director of the agency presents an entirely new approach to providing recreational opportunities for senior citizens. He is interrupted by his superior, the director, who tells him that his idea is ridiculous. It is unlikely that he would ever bring up the subject again unless he were extremely persistent and unafraid of the director. *Creative thinking can be squelched by a superior who criticizes without having much of a basis for criticism.*

The number of alternatives that can be developed at any one point in time is a function of how much time is spent in developing these alternatives. It's always helpful to stop and ask: "If I didn't have any rules to follow in this organization, would I handle the situation any differently?" Or, "What else could I do?" Perhaps it is desirable to modify several previously stated alternatives to produce one better alternative.

<u>Present all alternatives for consideration.</u> By considering all ideas as initially feasible, they can be brought out into the open. Such occasions are often called brain storming sessions. Regardless of how silly an idea might seem at first, perhaps when it is considered in the light of other possibilities it may turn out to be a fairly useable solution; or maybe a portion of that idea might be able to be combined with another idea and thereby produce the ultimate solution.

What, for example, would have happened if someone stifled the idea of the paper clip? "Isn't that stupid, who'd want to hold pieces of paper together with bent up wire?" Evidently, people laughed at Columbus, and his idea of a round world; they laughed at John Fulton and his steamship; and even at a young man named Fosbury, who high-jumped backwards. Regardless of ridicule, however, each of these men, in his solution to the problem at hand, succeeded in his particular project.

How many people have been shot-down in creative projects, by comments such as these: "We've tried it and it didn't work," "That's against policy," "It would cost too much," "He hasn't got the experience," "He"'s too young."

List the Alternatives. Looking at the positive side of the argument, there should be positive consideration of all methods, objects, and persons available, to satisfy the needs of decision-making. Once again, write down all of the alternatives, so that they can be comprehensively considered.

To do this, one can list all of the alternatives across the top of a chart and then systematically consider all the factors under each alternative. This chart, or *matrix*, as it is called, can then be used to evaluate the best solution.

As an example, let us assume legislation is passed in each state to award home and business loans and educational benefits to veterans of the Vietnam war. Then a matrix somewhat like this can be made:

	ALTERNATIVES				
	#1	#2	#3	#4	#5
Staff involved					
Labor costs					
Material costs					
Equipment costs					
Services included					
Services excluded					
facilities needed					
Number of veterans processed per day					
Publicity requirements					
Applicable policy					
New policies needed, etc.					

The list can be long, but it is well worth it. If, for example, one is considering attending a community college or university, but can't make up his mind. He can develop a chart with all of the things that are important to him on the side of the chart, and the schools under consideration acros the top. Then a five-point scale can *be* applied to each item, with five being the highest mark and zero the lowest. The school with the most points might be the most likely alternative under all the prevailing circumstances. Still, one cannot be completely definite on this basis alone, so it is necessary to move to the next step in the decision-making process, that of selection.

F. Selecting the Best Alternative Solution. The most important part of the decision-making process is the selection of the most appropriate alternative: *deciding.* This is the stage during which criticism is appropriate. Judgment must be made on all facets of the problem and the alternative solutions. The effectiveness of each of the solutions must be evaluated in terms of the objectives towards which the decision-maker is oriented. He must look carefully at, and criticize severely, such items as cost, timeliness, workability, acceptability, and implementation.

- Can the solution be made to work?
- Will the staff cooperate?
- Will those who are served make the necessary adjustments?
- Are there the skills in the organization to carry out the program?

List the Consequences of the Decision. As these and other items are considered, it is desirable to write down <u>all</u> of the consequences of <u>each</u> of the decisions. List the pro's and con's. It is not enough to add them together and make a decision on that basis, such as in the selection of a college, in the previous section. Not only does one use some type of scale, but he assigns different weights to different items. Using the previous college selection chart, the decision-maker might have to weight costs higher than the availability of co-educational dormitories, or the scholastic reputation of the school over the strength of its football team.

Be a Devil's Advocate. The more desirable alternatives should be scrutinized in a negative way. Take the opposite position, that is, play the *devil's advocate.* Mentally implement the plan and consider the adverse consequences.

Take one of the most favorable-looking alternatives. Ask:

- "Will it affect other departments?"
- "What could go wrong?"
- "What are the potential sources of breakdown?"
- "What new problem might it create?"
- "Where would the resistance be?"

Consider the extent to which these consequences will probably come about and the degree of seriousness of each one. Select second and even third choices in order to plan for contingencies.

Scrutinize the Final Alternative Thoroughly. Once the alternatives have been narrowed to only one, which appears to fill the need, then this one alternative should be subjected to one final round of positive questions:

- Will this decision fulfill the original goal?
- Can the agency live with the decision permanently?
- Is the timing of the decision right?
- Does the decision bring about the greatest benefit for the greatest number?

Involve Your Superiors. It is often necessary and desirable to go to the superiors with the decision. Ordinarily, the problem would be presented, with the attendant factors affecting it, and the alternative solutions which could resolve it. Then the decision-maker would indicate his reasons, with their consequences, for selection of the particular alternative.

G. Implement the Decision. After a decision is made, it must be implemented. The necessary steps must be initiated to carry it out. The whole management cycle of planning, organizing, and controlling must be brought into action, as well as other available management tools.

3. SUMMATION

No phase of the management cycle or any other organizational function could be carried out if decisions were not made. Planning, organizing, controlling, as well as motivating, communicating, and setting standards; these all require endless strings of decisions or choices. This is why the final process of decision making is so important.

Good decisions are the result of understanding responsibilities, involving others, knowing the organization, understanding one's own strengths and weaknesses, and being accountable for decisions made.

In understanding the responsibilities involved, one must know where to get information and be cognizant of the extent to which people can take action.

Through involving others, they gain a sense of ownership in the decision, and become more committed. They remove their defense mechanisms.

Knowing an organization requires an awareness of its organizational history and objectives, where the power centers lie, the limits of one's authority, and the way in which work is actually accomplished.

One's understanding of himself and his own shortcomings insures that he will seek out expertise he does not possess himself, and will develop ways to improve his own skills.

The individual should have this motto: *Remember, when you get right down to it, one person may have to decide – YOU!*

STUDENT LEARNING ACTIVITIES

- Prepare a definition of *decision making,*

- Write a brief paper on the decision-making formula.

- Participate in a class discussion about decision making in a selected public-service agency. Try to identify top, middle, and low-level decisions.

- Prepare a definition of the term *problem*.

- Interview a public-service official to identify a problem within his organization. Follow with a class discussion.

- Prepare a brief paper describing three examples of symptoms and their causes.

- Participate in a problem-solving case study.

- Write a brief paper on why facts must be gathered to aid in the decision-making process.

- Identify the kinds of facts and resources you must use to prepare for making decisions about a teacher-assigned topic.

- Participate in a discussion about fact finding.

- Develop with the class, and have at least 20 students complete, a survey questionnaire with open-ended questions on ways in which your school can be improved. Organize responses according to subject and year ranking of importance.

- Participate in a class discussion on the results of the questionnaire survey.

- After the class has decided on one or more ways in which the school can be improved, prepare a report on one of the objectives including:

    statement of an objective,

    facts needed and how obtained,

    categorizing the facts.

- Deliver an oral version of your report. Respond to questions and comments from the class,

- Choose five articles from the newspaper on five different topics: sports, politics, crime, etc. State the actual problem being addressed.

- Participate in a class discussion about problem identification, and problem statements. Sharpen your problem statements if necessary.

- Participate in a class discussion about problems identified and possible alternative solutions.

- Using the example of the State legislature passing a bill awarding home and business loans and educational benefits to veterans of the Gulf War, develop a set of alternative plans as to how the legislation may be carried out.

TEACHER MANAGEMENT ACTIVITIES

- Have students define *decision making*.

- Assign students a paper on the decision-making formula.

- Conduct a class discussion about decision-making in a selected public service agency.

- Have students prepare their own definitions of the term *problem*.

- Assign students interviews with public-service officials to identify selected organizational problems.

- Conduct a class discussion on problems in public-service organizations.

- Have students develop and discuss reports and three examples of symptoms and their causes.

- Select and assign a case study to the class in problem solving.

- Assign a paper on why facts must be gathered to aid in the decision-making process.

- Prepare a list of considerations in several public-service agencies. Have each student select one consideration around which he will gather essential facts to make a decision.

- Conduct a discussion on fact finding.

- Assign the class a survey project, entitled "How Can Our School be Improved?" Have students develop their own questionnaire and administer it to at least 20 students. Ask them to organize their results according to subject and rank of importance.

- Organize a class discussion on the results of the surveys.

- Once one or more items of possible school improvement have been agreed upon, assign the students a report to contain the following:

16

        statement of an objective,

        facts needed and how obtained,

        categorizing of facts.

- Organize oral presentations of student reports.

- Assign students the reading of five articles from a newspaper on five different topics: sports, polttfcs, crime, etc. Have them state the actual problem being discussed.

- Conduct a class discussion on problem identification and problem statements.

- Assign a brief paper on the symptoms of five problems and the causes in a public service agency selected by each student.

- Conduct a class discussion on the problems and solutions identified.

- Using the example of the new bill for veterans of the Gulf War, have students develop a set of alternatives.

- Insure that the students are open to new and abstract suggestions.

- Direct oral presentations of students in which they review their original problems, the sources and categories of facts, the alternatives available for solution, their respective consequences, and their ultimate decisions. Have students challenge one another's decisions.

17

Evaluation Questions
Techniques of Decision Making

Read the problem carefully, and answer each of the following questions.

You are a library assistant. Mrs. Smith, the librarian, has two high school aides, Susan and Mary. Mrs. Smith has told you that she may fire Susan if her attitude does not improve. She complained about Susan's laziness and stated that Susan's work was never finished. Mrs. Smith asked you to talk to Susan about improving her attitude. When you tried to talk to Susan about this, she got upset and went home.

After observing the aides' workload for a few days, you notice that Susan has much more work than Mary.

1. What is the problem? _____

2. Name one solution. _____

3. What are the consequences of this solution? _____

4. List another solution. _____

5. What are the consequences of this solution? _____

6. Which do you think is the best solution? _____

Read the problem carefully, and answer each of the following questions.

You are in charge of the recreation program at the community center. Your job is to keep activities running smoothly. On the daily schedule, one-half hour has been set aside for basketball. While you have stepped out for a moment, ten of the Green Hornets and ten of the Purple Dragons arrived to play basketball. As each group has two teams set up, neither group would give in. Unfortunately, a fight began. The fight ended just as you returned. Each group plans to play tomorrow. You must make a decision.

1. What is the problem? _____
   _____
   _____
   _____

2. Name one solution. _____
   _____
   _____
   _____

3. What are the consequences of this solution? _____
   _____
   _____
   _____

4. List another solution. _____
   _____
   _____
   _____

5. What are the consequences of this solution? _____
   _____
   _____
   _____

6. Which do you think is the best solution? _____
   _____
   _____
   _____

Answer Key

Answers will vary on this test. The instructor may wish to have a discussion after the test, with students justifying their selections. Students may be evaluated on the soundness of their judgement.